Stanislaus
The Struggle for a River

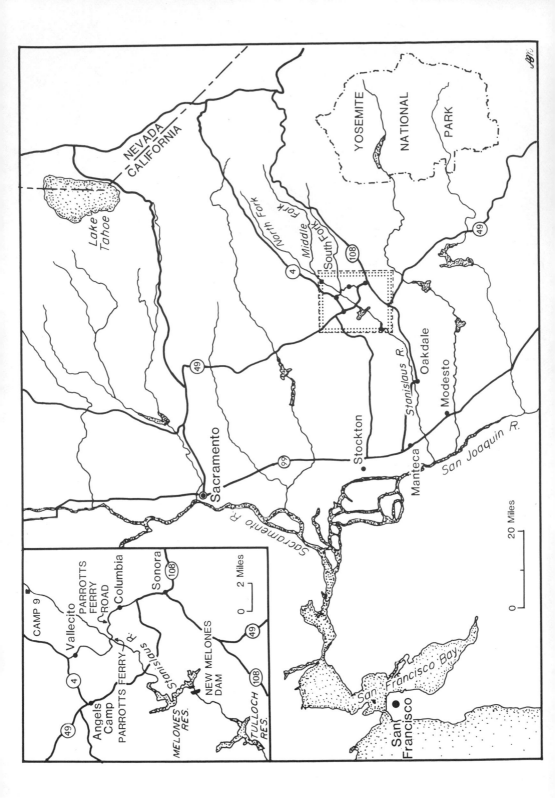

Tim Palmer

Stanislaus
The Struggle for a River

UNIVERSITY OF CALIFORNIA PRESS / BERKELEY / LOS ANGELES / LONDON

University of California Press
Berkeley and Los Angeles, California

University of California Press, Ltd.
London, England

©1982 by
The Regents of the University of California

**Library of Congress Cataloging in
Publication Data**

Palmer, Tim.
   Stanislaus, the struggle for a river.

Bibliography: p.
Includes index.
1. Stream conservation—California—
Stanislaus River. 2. Wild and scenic rivers—
California—Stanislaus River. 3. Stanislaus
River (Calif.) I. Title.
QH76.5.C2P34   333.91'6216'0979457   81-43692
ISBN 0-520-04605-6   AACR2

Printed in the United States of America
1 2 3 4 5 6 7 8 9

Except as indicated, all photos are by
the author.

Contents

Cast of
Characters

Milton Kramer	campaign professional
Cliff Humphrey	dam supporter
Al Sorrenti	farmer, water district leader
Thorne Gray	newsman

Government people, state

Huey Johnson	resources secretary
Guy Phillips	assistant resources secretary, economist
Richard Hammond	deputy resources secretary
Jim Burns	assistant resources secretary
Ron Robie	director, department of water resources

Government people, federal

Cecil Andrus	secretary of the interior
Joe Nagel	special assistant to the secretary of the interior
Guy Martin	assistant secretary of the interior
Robert Herbst	assistant secretary of the interior
Colonel Donald O'Shei	district engineer, Army Corps of Engineers
Joe Countryman	planning chief, Army Corps of Engineers

Politicians

Jerry Brown	governor
Peter Behr	state senator
Jimmy Carter	presidential candidate and president
Phillip Burton	congressman
Don Edwards	congressman
John McFall	congressman
Bizz Johnson	congressman
Don Clausen	congressman
Tony Coelho	congressman
Norman Shumway	congressman
Mike Gage	state assemblyman
Norman Waters	state assemblyman
John Garamendi	state senator

Chronology
Major Events in the New Melones Dam Controversy

1944 First authorization of the dam
1962 Final authorization of the dam
1964 Christmas Day flood
1965 First appropriation of construction money
1966 Beginning of construction
1968 Jerry Meral canoes the Stanislaus and begins the dam fight
1973 Environmental Defense Fund court case
1973 Decision 1422 of the State Water Resources Control Board
1974 Friends of the River formed to campaign for Proposition 17
1974 Proposition 17 loses
1974 Dam construction 20 percent complete
1975 FOR re-forms as a statewide river protection group
1975 FOR lobbies Governor Brown to save the river
1976 Senator Behr's bill introduced to put the Stanislaus in the state scenic rivers system
1976 FOR successful in stopping dams on the North Fork Stanislaus
1977 Administrative actions to delay New Melones, including Camp Nine bridge delay
1978 Dam completed
1979 Mark Dubois chains himself to the river to stop the flooding of Parrotts Ferry
1979 National wild river bill introduced and FOR wild river study completed
1980 Parrotts Ferry temporarily flooded
1980 National wild river bill considered, loses in congressional committee
1981 New Melones Reservoir temporarily extended above Parrotts Ferry
1981 Second initiative campaign launched

List of
State & Federal
Agencies

Office of Audit and Investigation
Water Resources Council (independent agency chaired by Dept.
  of Int. Sec.)
U.S. General Accounting Office (GAO)

Council of Economic Advisors
Council on Environmental Quality
U.S. Office of Management and Budget

National Water Commission (9/68—9/73)

Acknowledgments

Many people offered time, information, and inspiration to me while I wrote this book. A few deserve special mention.

Jim Barr, a newswriter, read the manuscript and supplied hundreds of helpful suggestions. Perhaps a dozen people read the draft, but the first, and one of the most helpful, was André Pessis. Lisa Van Dusen, Melinda Wright, and Sharon Negri penciled suggestions on the draft. For the Valley chapter, Tom Hershenow provided reactions with the understanding that only a Valley native can have. The American Rivers Conservation Council's Howard Brown, perhaps the most knowledgeable person on river protection nationwide, reviewed sections dealing with non-California rivers and water policy issues.

Reports and articles by other writers helped me immensely. I am particularly grateful to Stephen Mikesell of the University of California at Davis for New Melones Dam history, especially before 1969. Marc Reisner has written excellent articles about western water and California irrigation. Newspaper articles by Thorne Gray, Tom Harris, and Harold Gilliam were helpful, as were interviews with Gray and Harris. Betty Andrews and Dick Roos-Collins yielded a seemingly inexhaustible reservoir of government reports and data.

Information was supplied by dozens of government employees, many of whom shared their knowledge freely. I would especially like to thank Guy Phillips, Jerry Meral, and Jonas Minton of the Resources Agency of California, Joe Countryman of the Army Corps of Engineers, Guy Martin of the United States Department of the Interior, and staff members from the Bureau of Reclamation, Bureau of Land Management, Heritage, Conservation and Recreation Service, Forest Service, and Park Service. Stanford Young of the Park Service, while not involved in the Stanislaus in particular, was generous in his encouragement and his insight regarding river protection.

Congressional staff, especially Bob Wiekowski, provided information available only from them.

Most of the Stanislaus story came from dozens of people who were directly involved in the New Melones controversy. Interviews and quotations throughout the book show who these people are. The cooperation and candor of Mark Dubois and John Hertle were essential.

Ronnie James contributed many suggestions to the draft, spent many evenings typing the manuscript, and supplied constant encouragement. Mark Anderman printed the photographs, Ed Grady furnished copies at a price I could afford, and Ann Snyder helped with typing.

Ernest Callenbach of the University of California Press encouraged me from the beginning, offered excellent advice when asked, and supported the book throughout its development. Peter Dreyer contributed many improvements to the text.

Most of all, I want to thank friends whose enthusiasm for this story kept me going.

Tim Palmer

CHAPTER ONE

The Canyon

July 1979

It seems an impossible load: black waterproof duffels piled waist high, metal coolers that require two people to heft, army surplus ammunition cans for watches and cameras, the essential bailing bucket, an air pump in case our raft springs a leak, oars stacked like slabwood. The makings of a river trip.

Catherine Fox is not dismayed by the task. She loves it. This is her weekend away from the office of the Friends of the River Foundation and on the river itself, too rare an event. She is pleased to leave the fog of San Francisco for the heat of the Sierra foothills here at Camp Nine, the put-in for Stanislaus River trips. She is about five foot six, slender and svelte, but strong, and has no trouble swinging gear into place on the frame of the seventeen-foot rubber raft. With a good sense of leverage and a grunt, she relocates a cooler to its place in the puzzle of a load under construction. It goes amidships so that the guide's feet can alternately press against it or against the footbrace of the rowing frame as she pulls on the long ash oars, fending off rocks at Devil's Staircase, Mother Rapid, and Rock Garden. Catherine turns to look up with a smile that is characteristic of her during her time on this river. The first wrinkles of age show around her eyes and at her high cheekbones; her teeth are slightly misaligned. She is more attractive for her imperfections. Her hair is long and tied back, the color of dry sand on a Stanislaus beach. Uniform of the day is a bathing suit or shorts; Catherine wears both. I hand her the black bags that protect twelve people's clothes and sleeping bags.

It is an unimaginative name, Camp Nine, the ninth road construction camp for a Pacific Gas and Electric hydro plant. The old bridge connects the contorted one-lane access road from Vallecito to the power plant and to a dirt road on the south side.

The upper limits of the put-in are the bridge and a dam, about ten feet high, that evens out the surge of water from the hydroelectric plant, half a mile farther up. Put-in Rapid marks the lower reach of the access area with a radical left turn and a big rock lurking head-on, one that has now stuck a raft. From here to Parrotts Ferry is nine miles.

We are only one scene in the frenzy of activity at Camp Nine. Incongruously for the entrance to an American wilderness, the place hums high with human energy. Our group, Friends of the River (FOR) and guests, will fill four boats. Another thirty are being loaded for one- or two-day canyon tours. The colors alone are dazzling. Kayaks shine. People are brightly dressed. Most are young adults, with a few children and a fair share of middle-aged clients. Fourteen outfitting companies guide these passengers down the river, $40 for one day, $90 for a first-class overnight expedition. Orange is predominant in the piles of life jackets and the outfitters' old school buses disgorging guests from the Bay Area, Los Angeles, Sacramento, and as far away as San Diego. For a quarter mile, the shoreline is a kaleidoscope of movement. Escape. Run the river. Challenge the rapids. Get soaked to the skin. See the canyon while it lasts.

It may not last much longer. New Melones Dam would bury the canyon all the way to Camp Nine. The dam has been built, but its reservoir is not yet filled. On this river trip, we shall see what is at stake.

The guides—bearded men and long-haired women—are bronze from the sun. They wear gym shorts, thongs, usually a visor hat, and knives in leather cases attached to waist cords of nylon. They are busy pumping up rafts, or loading like Catherine. Tourists pass gear from their bus to the river. Four men in black wetsuits are readying for a descent on surf-mats. They will clutch four-foot ethafoam boards in their contact sport with the rapids, and risk hitting their heads on rocks or getting their feet wedged between underwater boulders. Other people are loading "kamikaze kits"—tiny yellow rafts of shiny plastic that would hiss if given a swift kick. These folks load beer especially, and their rafts are easily overloaded. Somehow, even with toy oars that come from K-Mart, most will be okay now that the water-level is low.

The air is full of anticipation—in the smiles, the mix of people, the hustle, the preparation, the view downriver. Downriver is the Stanislaus Canyon, the only free-flowing, undammed reach of this waterway's main fork above the Central Valley. A glance reveals whitewater, but it is distant and seems innocuous, like a beginner's riffle, from here. Above are steep wilderness hillsides. The canyon is a wonder: you can still board Catherine's raft, powered by gravity and her, and enter an ancient, natural world. Travelers will be dependent on their own skills, hardiness, and equipment.

To leave this put-in beach, linked by road to what we call the civilized world, is an act of faith. Once in the canyon, you go to the end. There is no exit road. That excites people. I am very excited. Since 1977, when I met Alexander Gaguine, another of the FOR people, I've wanted to see this river. I sense that it is different from the other rivers I've been on—that it is special, like these people.

Catherine seems indigenous, but she grew up in Ohio, then migrated west to college at Santa Clara. She worked for a service agency helping blind people to live on their own. That brought her in contact with a group called etcetera or etc—Environmental Traveling Companions—who sponsor wilderness outings for the blind, the disabled, center-city children, and other people in special need. Catherine found the Stanislaus through social work. For four years she labored on the FOR staff; now she fund-raises for the FOR Foundation (FORF).

Cole Wilbur was invited by Catherine. Like me, he awaits his first Stanislaus trip. The director of a San Francisco-based foundation, he is fifty or so; tall and bald, but not desk-moribund. For a warm-up, he swims across the river and back like Johnny Weissmuller. Returning, he helps Gracielle Rossi load her raft.

Gracielle is a California native, tanned dark, unlike the red-brown of most Anglo river guides. Her hair is black, long and loose, curled all over, full of air spaces that make you want to squeeze it. Gracielle is a leader, a central one, of etcetera, and four handicapped people will be on this trip.

Mark Dubois stands over us all, greeting people with his bear hug, smiling from his height of six foot eight. He is the leader of FOR; not through election or choice, he simply is. Most people call it charisma, and I can see why. He meets Wally and Bonnie Nackleg and smiles a welcome. Now he has an arm on each, and they are already a part of the group. His size alone draws attention. Because of his height, he seems thin, but that is an illusion. If his length were compressed to mine, he would be broad and chunky with muscles. Without showing effort, he can lift a deflated raft, or most any person you can name. Now, as almost always, he is barefoot. Shoes are not the only thing he does without. Dubois owns almost no material goods. No car, few clothes. He does not own a razor either. His beard is brown: not long, but probably trimmed a month ago. He believes in living simply. Very simply; yet this river has complicated his life. I know nobody whose lifestyle is so basic, but whose job and dedication lead to such complexity, to such a feverish pace.

Today is different. Today the pace of our group is slow. Under Gracielle's subtle direction, people fix lunch. Don Briggs is a long-time river guide and an FOR supporter; Larry Wagner, an etcetera leader, is responsible for the safety of the disabled—Kit Chin Lau, Jim Brunotte, Curtis Wilson, and Mary Regan. The other people in the group are Jerri Brunotte, Jim's wife; Tom Burton, an FOR researcher; Tom's friend

Lynn Fretz; Carol Nelson from the FOR staff; and Megan Eymann, a brand-new staff member, who is taking a semester off from college.

In another hour, it is time to go. We are a dozen people in four rafts and Mark's kayak. Catherine, Mary Regan, and I launch first. Multiple sclerosis has crippled Mary's legs. Mark and I had to lift her into the front of the raft, where she now sits next to me, her feet propped on an upside-down bailing bucket. Camp Nine's anticipation is in crescendo, increasing as it approaches the real thing.

First we drift slowly, breaking away from the security of the rocky shoreline. The unknown comes at the river's pace, not ours. As a passenger, I'm free to look around, take photographs, be unresponsible. The guide is mediator between us and the river. I watch Catherine as she controls our future by more or less directing the raft. She directs it more as we enter Put-in Rapid. Oars squeak on their pins, she pulls to the left, and we splash through.

The water is fairly low and Rock Garden looms ahead—a goulash of boulders, a maze of chutes and backcurrent eddies. Catherine directs the raft less. There is no choice; we will hit some rocks as we pinball downhill. We collide with a flat boulder and are followed by a crew of inner-tubers. One of them bounces against us, pushing us farther onto the rock. Another tuber whisks near, missing the boat, but pinning his small raft-load of beer against us. Catherine is battling her best with poor odds and unequal leverage against the current. In the middle of this river that is the epitome of motion, we go nowhere. I get out of the raft, balance myself on a butter-slick rock, and try to heave the lighter end of the rubber boat. Catherine wrenches the oars as I lift, and we burst free. Seeing I am going to be left behind, I make a dive and sprawl onto the floor of the raft. Mary laughs; she is an old hand at this. Sometimes she rows.

There is no warm-up to this river: the most demanding rapids hit you in the first three miles. Bailey Falls is the biggest. Moulding this rapid, a tributary called Stoney Creek has brought acre-feet of rocks from the foothills during floods and dumped them at the river's edge. The Stanislaus glances off the delta and funnels down hard right to a channel that for thousands of years has tried to move a cliff. The water is at least half air, white as a Bret Harte blizzard in the Sierra Nevada. Catherine lets me out and waits at Stoney Creek so that I can walk downriver and take pictures of the other rafts when Bailey swallows them. The upstream view is one of the most scenic on the river: a foreground of bubbles, a background of cliffs, and a tall ponderosa pine among boulders. The sound is that of Niagara.

Gracielle and her passengers pass without incident. Next is a paddle boat—instead of one guide rowing, everyone paddles. Experienced Don Briggs is in the back, yanking his end away from the cliff where 60

percent of the river smashes. He yells for everybody to backpaddle.
Some do and some don't, and the boat collides head-on with a jagged
fragment of the foothills. The speed of the boat hits zero, but that of
Megan Eymann does not. She tumbles over the right tube and into the
drink, disappearing for an instant between the raft and the cliff. Then
her long, braided hair and orange life jacket pop into view behind the
boat. She floats low in the foam, quenching her thirst and then some.
For safety, Megan tries to keep her feet pointed downstream and high,
so that they don't snag a rock, but she has little say in the matter. She
is powerless, finally grounding at the whitewater's end, cold
but unharmed.

Catherine leads us into Bailey. We miss the cliff, but get plastered
with water as we smack a wall of it. I look sideways, and Mary Regan is
a blur through a wave that passes between us. There should be fish on
our floor, and I bail an ocean back into the river.

Rose Creek is ahead. On the left, we beach against a cluster of great
bedrock ledges, metamorphosed schist or chert. Lower Rose Creek,
more than any other site, illustrates the geology of this region. The
Calaveras complex of formations—critical to interpretation of the
Sierra geology—is seen clearly here. Geologists say that several
mountain ranges in turn reared high and eroded; then lava filled the
river valleys. The high volcanic formations of Table Mountain, seen
from the Camp Nine road, are remains of the ancient riverine lava
flow. New rivers cut through the bedrock as the Sierra Nevada range
was pushed up, perhaps far beyond its modern height. For nine
million years, the Stanislaus wore into the mountains, moving them
downward a particle at a time. The United States is lowered one foot
every 10,000 years, hydrologists say, but here the rate has been faster.
Earth that filled this canyon now blankets the Central Valley as
fertile soil.

Geologist Terry Wright of Sonoma State University says that the
canyon, and the mouth of Rose Creek in particular, are a significant
Sierra Nevada study area. Maybe the best. Hundreds of students from
dozens of schools use this site for field work in geology, and also in
botany, archaeology, nature study, recreation management, and
outdoor skills. Not to mention a more personal training where we
learn about the peace and excitement of the natural world. Here every
person can overcome a hardship. Here, each faces danger at Bailey
Falls and each overcomes it.

After tying up the rafts, we wander off in small groups for a Rose
Creek hike. A lot of other people, probably a hundred, have the same
idea. Rafts are pinned at the creek's mouth tube-to-tube, like a
Safeway supermarket on Friday. We clamber along rocky ledges to
a spot where bedrock outlines a bowl whose inlet is an eight-foot

waterfall. It plunges into a pool full of swimmers, and I can't help thinking of pictures of Hawaii. People are everywhere: in the falls, sliding from slick limestone into the pool, lying on the rocks, splashing, diving together, hugging each other, jumping off a ten-foot cliff. It is a composite of all the good times I have had along streams. There are children in wading pools, old people watching and smiling. A girl dives at the foot of the falls, and underwater her image ripples surrealistically.

We walk a mile to a jumping rock, thirty feet high. There are thirty people there, twenty-seven strangers to me, but we all sit on the smooth stone and cheer as each one jumps. "This place brings people together," Catherine says. Three of us hold hands at the edge of the cliff, then leap together.

We hike back to the Stanislaus, and Don Briggs tells me that Rose Creek, alone, was enough to draw him into the New Melones dam fight. A full reservoir would drown this place up to its treetops.

After an hour or two, we return to the river, and by the names on the rafts—OARS, ARTA, ECHO, Mother Lode, Zephyr—I can tell that commercial trips have stopped here. Though it's the perfect lunch stop, nobody is eating. We're not allowed—"BLM regulation," Briggs says. "Rose Creek gets crowded enough as it is."

BLM is the Bureau of Land Management of the U.S. Department of the Interior, the department that includes the National Park Service, which preserves rivers, and the Bureau of Reclamation, which dams them and will operate New Melones Dam. Though the Park Service and Forest Service (in the Department of Agriculture) administer the best-known recreation areas of the country, BLM oversees more government land—mostly sage brush, desert, and tundra—than any other agency. The Stanislaus, seen by some river cognoscenti as one of the most scenic rivers on the West Coast, is BLM's crown jewel. And, being an agency that deals more with beef cattle than with recreation, they have their hands full. If you had sat yourself down on a big rock at Parrotts Ferry for three months in 1978, you could have counted 90,000 people. BLM registered 34,683 rafters and paddlers. The Youghiogheny of Pennsylvania, the South Fork of the American above Sacramento, and the Snake below Grand Teton Park are the only whitewater rivers in America that see more use. BLM manages the canyon in ways that will protect the river and its users. For example, no commercial lunches at Rose Creek.

Resource managers require each outfitter to have a permit allowing one trip per day, with a maximum of twenty-five people. Companies are assigned campsites to avoid crowding and squabbling late in the day. All waste is packed out. This includes human waste, in airtight army ammunition cans. Everybody must wear a life jacket, and a ranger is at Camp Nine or patrolling the river to check. By and large, the outfitters accept and welcome the BLM rules; they see the need for them. In fact, the outfitters originally invited BLM to develop a management program to limit the size of rafting groups. This is in stark contrast to some other areas: for example, the Boundary Waters of Minnesota, where guides hustle for all the permits they can get; or the Rogue in Oregon, where there seems to be an annual debate over maximum use. The Stanislaus guides couldn't believe it when I told them that permits on the Youghiogheny allow eighty people per trip. That seemed unmanageable to them, far too many for the flavor of wilderness.

Afternoon is wearing on. Time for us to drift down to our campsite. We are not a commercial rafting company, so our site is wherever we find it. As they say of water in the West, first in time, first in right.

The deepness of the canyon is striking after Rose Creek. Side slopes accelerate in steepness, and the limestone is almost white, pocked with caves and crevices. The walls are awesome above Wool Hollow. The limestone rises 800 feet, and erosion has left a nearly sheer drop to the Stanislaus on one side and Wool Hollow on the other. From this downstream angle, the wall looks like the prow of a ship. Right here, it is easy to believe this is the deepest limestone canyon on the West Coast. At the base of Wool Hollow churns Mother Rapid, one of the big ones, and the cliffs make it the most spectacular. Just below the rapid, we land at a small beach on the left, our campsite.

Warm sand feels good under everyone's feet, soaked from the unbailable two inches of water on the floors of the rafts. People stretch and relax, while the last sunlight gleams from the cliffs above Wool Hollow and Grapevine Gulch. Everybody helps unload. Personal gear ends up everywhere. Gracielle adds discipline to the portage of food and cooking gear, which is piled near a makeshift fireplace. Each of the guides tends first to the emptying of his own boat. I carry gear away as Catherine unties it. Mark, arriving by kayak, has no raft duties, so he sets up the ammo-can john in the woods below the campsite. Along rivers, winds usually blow downstream at night as cool air drops off the mountains.

Having occupied the beach, we graduate to new jobs. Tom, Megan, Cole, and I gather dead sticks for firewood. On the side of a rock, we find a cluster of long-legged spiders, a hundred or more, packed together so tight that their legs look like fur. None of us have ever seen the like before. The corners, side hollows, and crannies of the canyon could keep you searching and discovering for a lifetime.

Briggs and Brunotte build a fireplace; that is, they set stones in a circle and prop the grill on top. Other people are already claiming sleeping sites with their groundcloths. I never did see Dubois pick a site. Who knows, maybe he slept on the river. A guide for OARS (Outdoor Adventure River Specialists), Scott Stevens, does just that. He takes a floating raft that is tied to a tree, turns the boat upside-down, and sleeps on the bottom—a canyon waterbed.

After a few trips up the hill and back, we have sticks piled like a beaver lodge for Jim and Jerri Brunotte to break. It is a good job for Jim, who can do anything not requiring the use of his legs, which were lost in Vietnam. Brunotte can also do things that usually require legs, like breaking wild horses at his ranch for disabled people near San Luis Obispo.

I see carrots, peppers, celery, onions, and a knife, so I start slicing on top of a cooler. Mark joins me. "Bet you've camped here before," I say.

Mark smiles. "Oh, I guess so." We each start with a whole carrot and race through the slicing. He is winning, but lets me catch up.

Dubois has camped at most of the Stanislaus sites many times. He has probably stayed at some of them twenty nights or more. He has spent time on this river. It was not rapids that first brought him to foothill country, but the black of caves. With his brother, Gar, Mark explored many of the caverns that honeycomb the canyon. They would rappel down cliffs to reach inaccessible openings, spending full days inside the canyon walls. A few years later, Mark led etcetera trips with blind people and others into the caves. Deep inside, he would switch off the light and allow the blind people to lead the way out; they were no more handicapped than anybody else in the grotto dark. In fact, they were the experts. "What we found was that we learned a lot from blind people," Mark says. "It was exciting."

A high school friend of Mark's in caving was Ron Coldwell, who became a guide for the American River Touring Association (ARTA), with headquarters six miles from the Stanislaus near Vallecito. Ron encouraged Mark to join the guide staff, then helped train him. Dubois flipped and soaked his first raftload of passengers in high water in 1968. But he caught on. He became a proficient boatman, a faultless reader of whitewater. For the entire second day of our trip, he kayaked without a paddle, using only his hands and the shift of his body weight to guide himself through Class II and III rapids. For Dubois, the fewer tools the better.

While we are slicing vegetables, pounds of them, for dinner, a group camps a quarter of a mile below us at Grapevine Gulch, and another settles just above, both on the other shore. From either of those sites, you would be slightly aware of another party, just beyond. So it goes, Camp Nine to Parrotts Ferry. "It's amazing," Mark says, "that so many people can be touched by this canyon at once."

Dubois is clutched fast to this place. Since 1972 it has been his life: caving, guiding, campaigning for sympathetic politicians, analyzing

Stanislaus above Parrotts Ferry

Catherine Fox

Suspension Bridge Rapid

Chicken Falls

Megan Eymann above campsite

Dubois rowing

Catherine Fox

Rafts tied at Rose Creek

One mile above the Stanislaus on South Fork

Miwok grinding hole

Kit Chin Lau "sees" a frog

Black tail deer

Stanislaus below South Fork

Jumping rock below
Mother Rapid

the plans of the Army Corps of Engineers and the Bureau of
Reclamation, lobbying, helping to collect 500,000 signatures for a
statewide initiative, meeting with senators, rowing government
officials and singer Jackson Browne down the river, staging a float
trip from here to San Francisco, flying to Washington, debating
with farmers on TV, promoting water conservation, raising funds,
trying to keep FOR operating in places where his stubbornness
and independence, spawned in dedication, can make for trouble.

Environmentalists often talk of their cause without talking about
people. Not Dubois. He seems to be in love with them. "All these
people. Every night there's just a lot of energy resting in this place.
People come out refreshed," he says.

There are wild lands where I want to go alone, to not see a soul. Not
a plume of campfire smoke. Not a footprint in the sand. There, I am
unsociable. But this river is different. People below, people above,
eleven friends elbow to elbow. This is a people's river, a people's
wilderness, if that is not a hopeless contradiction.

There may be another river that fits the role as well, but it is not the Youghiogheny, most floated whitewater on the continent. You aren't allowed to camp along the Yough. It is not the South Fork of the American, another popular Sierra foothills river—many of its shores are private land with owners who don't want to see so much as a flag of ripstop nylon. The Tuolumne is too difficult and demanding; it is a boatman's river. The Delaware is a people's river—lots of visitors spending good times—but nothing to approach the Stanislaus's intensity. What of the Russian or lower American, the two most used rivers of California? More people, yes. Wild river, no. The Russian is the backyard escape of San Francisco, the American is an urban greenway of Sacramento, but the Stanislaus is where fairy tales could be filmed. It is the stock image of California applied to a river: sandy beaches, good swimming, laughter from campsites, a friendly place in the sun. It lacks the mosquitos, the rain, and the cold of rivers in Alaska, Minnesota, or Maine. You can drink the water.

One night in 1972, camping along the river, Dubois and friends built a riverside sauna by heating rocks and then pouring water over them inside a small tepee. Heated up by the steam, Mark ran from the beach and dove into a cold pool—he thought. He knew the river well, but Pacific Gas and Electric had added a new dimension. They had cut the flow from the dam above Camp Nine, and the water level had fallen two feet. His friends helped Mark out, and discovered that he had a broken neck. They braced it, and floated him out in a raft the next day. "First they were worried," Dubois says. "Then when the doctor saw I had to be moving around, he said I'd be okay." In five weeks, with a cast, Dubois was hiking Northern California's Trinity County. In three months, he was rowing rivers again.

With Fred Dennis, Dubois started etcetera, which they ran for almost nothing. Junk rafts were dug out of an army surplus dump in Vallejo. Food was brought by guests or donated. The guides—Dubois and Fred Dennis—came free, and center-city kids from San Francisco had the time of their lives. Dennis Fantin and Bob Metts are graduates of the program. Dennis is blind; he rows. Bob has had polio. With one good arm and one good leg, he sits behind and directs Dennis. They began on the Stanislaus and have since explored North America, running the Rogue, the Salmon, and other waters. Now they hold workshops to help other people with combinations of disabilities. Who says they are handicapped?

When supper is ready, we all work our way toward the fire. We settle down on the still-warm sand, facing everybody else. After we eat, people do their own dishes. With Mary Regan, I scrub the black pots. Then, with darkness closing in, a few of us take tin cups of white wine and sit in a circle near the river.

Tom Burton has worked with FOR for more than two years. He was a student, active in an ecology center at the University of Southern California, researching California water policy. "These people hit the office for a few days—guitars, jeans, flannel shirts, dressed kind of shabby. I thought they must be from Northern California. We talked and I found they were working on the same thing I was, and they were doing something. So when I graduated I went to Sacramento as an intern, then stayed at the FOR house for $2,000 a year as researcher," he explains. This was a big change for Burton, who grew up the son of a Los Angeles attorney and businessman. At FOR they leave the plug in the bathroom shower, collecting water, which is then dipped by bucket to flush the commode, saving four gallons. "I had to do some adjusting," Burton reflects. Other people adjusted to Tom as well. His normal schedule was to sleep in until noon, start work at two, then labor into the night. He developed a reputation as a California water expert—one of the most knowledgeable in the state. "We were one or two people up against a swarm of specialists, but we could compete because we cared. The bureaucrats mostly mess around; it takes them forever to do something that we'd get right into."

Now, Burton is ready to leave FOR. It is a bad time to go. He knows that there is a lot breaking on the Stanislaus, so he hangs on, but he is drained. Tired. He has fought and studied, red-eyed, and he is worn thin on this question of New Melones Dam. He needs a change, "Maybe a job like making sandwiches in a delicatessen," he says. Tom Burton is burned out and will return to college for a master's degree.

Catherine and Don both understand. "You sacrifice an awful lot," Catherine says. "I know this river sure has affected my personal life, and some of it is real difficult. It isn't for the money. There really isn't any. Sometimes we don't get paid at all. And winning isn't too much the reward either—maybe on the other rivers, but not here. You invest so much, and then . . ." She doesn't finish, because nobody is saying that Friends of the River might lose this fight for the Stanislaus. No one talks about that, but I suppose everybody thinks about it. "The only way to give up is to die, in a sense. This part of you would die."

She recalls when she, like Burton, felt stretched thin on saving rivers. It was when the FOR San Francisco office was in her apartment, and she had no relief. "Independence Day," she still says in a tone of celebration, "November 1, 1978. The day FOR opened a real office, complete with hold buttons on telephones, the day my telephone quit ringing every two minutes and at 1:00 A.M."

Briggs, too, has given up a lot for the river. His chief job is rowing rafts in the Grand Canyon. For most of this summer, he has worked with FOR, hustling nationwide publicity on the dam issue. Don was active in the state initiative in 1974, and since then he has come and gone from the Stanislaus fight. He will leave again in a few weeks to guide a National Geographic river trip in Yemen.

We are all pretty slow now, dulled by the multiple effects of a long day, exercise, sunshine, a good meal, and another cup of wine, please. Mark comes over, upbeat as usual, acting as though he were ready to paddle the kayak to Parrotts Ferry and back again. Maybe to dismantle New Melones Dam. He asks if we've seen what's coming. It is the moon, glowing white from behind Table Mountain, getting ready to shine silver over the Stanislaus.

I look around, and most of our group has settled in for the night. We eventually do, too, finding places that are level near the trees on sand brought down by a flooding river. The Stanislaus hisses against our sandy beach and rumbles from the rapids that bound this quarter-mile length of canyon.

It is almost dawn. The sky is that deep navy blue that comes before the light. I have slept well, interrupted only by a skunk waddling through camp in the middle of the night. I cannot sleep any more, so I get up, raid the cooler for an orange, and organize my camera gear. Megan sits up, waves at me across a line of bodies, and squirms out of her sleeping bag. I suggest that we walk down the river to the mouth of a small, unnamed stream and hike up the shoulder that separates the canyon of the Stanislaus from the canyon of the creek. This will take us high above Razorback Cliff to the rim, or so I think.

The riverfront is packed tight with vines, boulders, fallen logs, rotting driftwood, and alder trees—a green jungle brought by the river to the dry hills of oak and chaparral. Birds sing: I spot the Bullock's oriole and Lincoln's sparrow. Deer and raccoon left tracks last night. I watch for signs of the gray fox, sometimes seen near the river. We jump the remains of the creek, mostly dry, slick with algae where it is damp. An orange newt squats on a stone. Following no trail, we plunge again into the riverine forest. Animal trails crisscross beneath us, this watery edge being their favorite among the five kinds of Stanislaus Canyon habitat—riverine, grassland, chaparral, oak, and ponderosa pine. We will see all of them up where we are going.

Bulling through, we make it to the parched open slopes. Grasses are golden yellow, seedy with needlesharp carriers that stab the nylon of my running shoes, seeds that work through your clothes with one-way barbs to itch against your skin. The dry, hard stems of the grasses are slick. You could ski down the slopes, but our path is filled with rocks and poison oak, which we detour, stretching and bending like slow-motion slalom racers avoiding gate-poles. The ridge rises above us in the early sun. Irregular through weathering, the limestone is studded with ledges, boulders, steep ascents, and stoop landings. I shoot a picture that shows Megan on a peninsula of limestone at the edge of the world, the Stanislaus curling below. The sun fires our horizon. At the river's edge, our neighbors' rafts are tied, squashed doughnuts from up here. All is silent, but for my heart and lungs and the distant whitewater. From the scale of the digger pines in a cool pocket on the other slope, I guess our height to be 200 feet above the river. If filled, New Melones Reservoir would lap against the cliff below us.

Now the going is tough. I climb left around a two-story rock that is perched to run us over. Wrong way. Nothing but a ledge verdant with poison oak. We go right, clinging to a slope that is steep, but conveniently roughened—like when you take the flat of a butter knife and pat the creamy icing of a cake, drawing up sharp, diminutive waves. Our route levels off again. I can see that we are now as high as Razorback Cliff, which is downstream, separated from our ridge by a steep, 300-yard grassy swatch.

Megan and I have reached the limit. The rocks go straight up. We can see the crackly tangle of chaparral that covers the higher slopes. Stands of six-foot-tall chamise are impenetrable with switching stems, yellow flowers, and leaves like shredded wheat. A family of valley oaks are burly on a beach in the tributary canyon. Ponderosa and Colter pine begin in a buckshot pattern on the cooler northern slope. Perhaps we would forget caution if breakfast were sizzling on top of the next giant's staircase, but it is far below where smoke curls through the cover of oaks.

After breakfast, people cram their black bags full of sleeping bags and clothes. Kit, a blind etcetera guest, stands near the river where Gracielle is loading her raft. "Ever been in a kayak?" Mark asks, putting a gentle hand on Kit's shoulder, which is not too far above his waist. "Oh, never," the young Chinese woman giggles. Steadying the otherwise skittish boat, Dubois helps her in, after her hand has toured the kayak's shape. Stuffing the bottom of her long red dress around her knees, Kit negotiates the seat opening. Try it blindfolded sometime. Mark clutches the boat and speaks quietly. Kit experiments for stability, leaning first one way, then another. Then, as Mark coaches, she shifts her weight inside the boat rather than leaning with her shoulders. He explains the concept of a feathered paddle—one blade angled differently from the other. Kit feels the difference and, slowly, carefully, excitedly, she moves the kayak forward. Mark wades along, but the water gets deep, even for him. He jumps onto a raft, grabs a paddle, and trails Kit around the big pool. She is destined for a collision. Wally yells, "You're paddling ashore," and she answers by singing "Michael Row the Boat Ashore." Bumping the bank, she steers back toward the current, scribing a rainbow arc toward a party of OARS, Inc., rafters drifting by. It is an unusual sight, but the guide recognizes Mark and needs no explanation. Kit's natural pull to the left brings her home.

By now, everybody is done packing, so we climb on our rafts, shoot a rapid, then stop at the Razorback rope swing. Almost everybody gets out to climb the willow tree and sail from the end of an elephant rope to crash into the river. Kit is scared this time, but Catherine helps her up the trunk of the tree. It seems that Catherine has helped many blind people. Kit has some reasonable questions: "How high am I? When do I let go of the rope?" When she is at the point of giving up, Curtis, his voice strained by the effects of cerebral palsy, yells from the raft, "Come on, Kit; you can do it, Kit!" and she flies. Dress and hair streaming behind, her tiny form arcs into space, then disappears with a sneakers-first smack into the water. She dog-paddles back toward cheers, just a little bit confused by another group of drifting rafters, who caught the performance and also cheer.

We, enjoying this river because it is in our spirits, fill only an instant of Stanislaus history. People of the river go back long before rubber boats and fiberglass kayaks. We know little of the ancient tribes who lived here thousands of years ago, but the more recent Miwok left many signs. We stop near Chinese Camp at rocks larger than a raft. On the rocks are bowllike depressions, two or three clustered together, six inches across, four to eight inches deep. They look drilled, but they weren't . . .

Beginning hundreds of years ago, ending with the Gold Rush, this place was the home of the Miwok. They lived in the canyon through winter. In summer, groups migrated into the Sierra—Miwok vacationland—where the air was cool and the game plentiful. A gentle people, they dwelt in the open, or in small huts, on the flood plains and sandbars where gulches join the river. Salmon, a staple in the natives' diet, migrated from the ocean each summer or fall. But acorns were the main thing, gathered by the thousand and ground into a soft meal, mortar-and-pestle fashion, against the rocks where we stand. Generations of grinding made bowllike depressions in the stone. Archaeologists find some Miwok skeletons with worn-down teeth, abraded by the grit from the grinding hole that we, including Kit, are now feeling with our hands. Dubois can talk for hours about the Miwok—where they lived, what they ate. He can tell you what most of their food tastes like: acorn meal, buckeye meal, cattail shoots, fiddlenecks, ants seasoning a salad of wild greens. "Anthropologists say the Miwok probably spent about eighteen hours a week gathering food. Now we spend forty hours; but then, we buy extra." Mark yanks on my camera strap. "We put more emphasis on material goods; they didn't."

A Spanish explorer, Gabriel Moraga, gave the first European account of this river, calling it El Rio de Nuestra Señora de Guadalupe (the river of Our Lady of Guadalupe). Jedediah Smith, the first United States explorer to cross the Sierra, visited the Stanislaus in 1827. In May of that year, 300 or 400 Indians escaped from the mission at San Jose. They were probably families going on a clover harvest to evangelize neighboring tribes, but somewhere along the line they decided to bolt. The Indians were led by Estanislao, named by the Spanish missionaries after the Polish Saint, Stanislaus, known as a great early humanist. Since Jed Smith was in the Valley at the time, Padre Duran of San Jose blamed the famous fur trapper–scout for the natives' escape, and authorized an expedition, which found Smith's men, but no Jedediah and no Indians.

Two years after the escape, in May 1829, about forty Mexican soldiers were sent to resubjugate the Indians, who presumably had raided Mexican rancheros. They found Estanislao's band entrenched in a mile-square tangle of riparian jungle, most likely along the lower Stanislaus. The Mexicans aligned their cannon for a fusillade into the viney thicket that obscured the native Californians, but it blew up with the first shot. Next, it seems, they tried to rout the Indians, but got nowhere and incurred two casualties. So ended the first expedition against Estanislao.

The next was led by Vallejo. He meant business, firing the thicket where the Indians hid, then killing and capturing them as they retreated to a fortified village. It was stone age weaponry versus nineteenth-century firearms, but the Miwok didn't give up. Vallejo offered an ultimatum. Reportedly, the Indians' answer was that they would live free or die. Estanislao escaped, then returned to the mission to give himself up. No one knows why, but the results are fairly clear: raids on the river Indians were ended, Estanislao was pardoned, and Padre Duran wrote letters demanding the court-martial of Vallejo. In glass cases at the Mission San Jose museum are three articles about Estanislao. One says he died in battle, one says he died of smallpox in 1836, and one says he escaped to freedom. Folk legend has him living along the Stanislaus almost until the Gold Rush.

When John C. Frémont later mapped the area for the United States government, he titled the river "Stanislaus." Signs of white man's history are all around us today. While the land looks mostly natural, the gold miners in particular left their mark. The 1848 discovery of nuggets at Sutter's mill on the American River triggered the stampede to the Mother Lode—a foothill zone of gold deposits running 120 miles north-south, crossing the grain of the Sierra rivers. We're in the Mother Lode now. Forty-niners worked the Stanislaus from Camp Nine down, first panning on the bars, then shoveling gravel into sluice boxes where water would wash rocks and sand away and leave the weightier nuggets behind. Thousands of money-seekers from the East,

England, Wales, Australia, and elsewhere worked elbow-to-elbow along this river, staking and squabbling over claims to the placer (water transported) deposits of gold. After the streambed and shoreline were dredged and sluiced, the miners turned to the deltas where tributaries joined the Stanislaus and the higher benches of the flood plains, like this one at Chinese Camp.

Chinese men, shipped like slaves to America to labor on the railroads, turned to the gold fields after the transcontinental tracks were laid. It was an age of brutal exploitation: the peaceful Miwok were annihilated, land was stripped and soil washed out to sea, and laws forbade the Chinese from mining any land that had not already been worked twice. The Chinese had to be tough and resourceful. They didn't just dig and sluice. They piled rocks in rows, leaving soil and gravel that could be sluiced more completely than the white miners had done. The Chinese walls of jagged rock remain, winding like Vermont stonerows or Civil War battlements through the regrown oak and manzanita. Up and down the river, we saw other remnants of mining: a rusty steam donkey—an engine for winching stone—above Mother Rapid; remains of a flume that diverted water from Rose Creek, another from Grapevine Gulch; piles of tailings and cast iron machinery at the South Fork.

Mark's heritage reaches to this era. His Irish grandmother was born on the east side of the Sierra during the silver-mining days described by Mark Twain in *Roughing It*. His grandfather was a German who worked for the Yuba Dredge Company, and Mark's mother, Connie, was born in Sacramento. On his father's side, Mark's great-grandfather was a tailor in Alsace-Lorraine, France. He left that country, troubled by war with Germany. He was a draft-dodger, so to speak. Dubois sailed around Cape Horn to alluring San Francisco. There Mark's grandfather was born, practiced pharmacy, and raised Mark's father, Noel Dubois. Few people have roots in California as deep as this friend of the river.

During the Gold Rush, ferryboats carried people, equipment, and supplies across the Stanislaus at Camp Nine, Parrotts Ferry, and Abbeys Ferry (below the South Fork). Albert and Victoria, two elephants in a traveling circus, crossed at Abbeys, but not easily. Victoria panicked, fell into the rapids, and became a raft without oars through Sierra Club Rapid, where she was badly injured.

Over six hundred archaeological and historical sites, covering 3,000 years of settlement, have been found between Camp Nine and Melones, all to be flooded by New Melones Dam. The federal Heritage, Conservation and Recreation Service declared the entire canyon eligible for the National Register of Historic Places—status protecting historic resources from federal development and encouraging

preservation. But the canyon was never formally included on
the register.

We leave the Miwok grinding-holes and Chinese walls. Destination:
Coral Cave. People in kayaks stop to talk to Mark. Everybody on the
river seems to know him. They always ask about the fight against New
Melones. "The support is growing. I've never felt stronger or better
about it than now," Mark says. He's said that during some pretty
rough times. That is what Dubois almost always says.

Being close to the water, Coral Cave is one of the best for river
travelers to visit. In single file, we scramble up a rocky, yellow-dust
trail to the entrance. We enter a black mouth to a golden vestibule,
where Dubois tells us how the cave got here—how runoff dissolves
the limestone; how eerie formations sprout with the timeless work of
water; how the Indians who predated the Miwok sometimes buried
their dead in Stanislaus caves; how Mark and Ron Coldwell discovered
a treasure of gold miners' hardware in a cave. Like people at the
movies, we sit on an angled rock slab, all facing downhill. But there
is no movie. We make our own pictures from what Dubois says. He
finishes, "Anyway, we can go on in, real slow, all at your own speed."

We are too many to be swallowed at once. The first shift disappears
from the yellow light while eight of us rest on the cool limestone. I
would guess the temperature to be in the high fifties, and it feels good.
After fifteen minutes, the first group shuffles out and we shuffle in.
Tom Burton blazes trail with a flashlight; Megan carries another as we
duck-walk a tight threshold, careful not to touch or smudge the walls,
which are shades of green-gray that I have never seen before. After a
few bends and some split-levels, we discover a room where we can all
stand. Stalactites and stalagmites encircle us. Burton shines the light
on cave coral—one of many Stanislaus varieties of speleothen, or
calcium carbonate designs. They are leafy, very fragile. Some are
twisted like corkscrews, bizarre. The Bureau of Land Management sees
the need for a program to protect the caves. Their job will be easier if
New Melones is filled. Thirty caves would be accessible only to skin
divers. This one would be at high tide, flooded when the impoundment
is brimfull.

Tom and Megan turn out the lights, and it is pitchy, obsidian black,
totally silent except for someone's breathing. The silence is too much.
Somebody starts talking about lunchtime. They decide to leave, but
Megan, Wally, and I wait to grope through the darkness. Just to get the
feel of it. With short steps, my hands ahead of me, I inch outward. We
talk a lot, the sweet sound of security. Where the channel splits, Wally
and I go one way, Megan the other; but we can hear her. We hit dead
ends, and backtrack, regroup, and follow the far right conduit. It rises

too high, but shows a glimmer of light. We retreat again, then crawl into the exit route and outward to greet high noon.

Back at the beach, the other people are ready to go. We drop through a few rapids and stop for lunch at the South Fork. It tumbles into the Stanislaus over a bar, the extension of a great delta. Miners dug thirty feet deep in some of the bars. Later in the summer, after the water level goes down, river travelers hike a mile upstream to small falls and deep crystalline pools, where they swim and lie like lizards on the warm ledges. Beyond these pools, the South Fork trail is only a thread, though it used to be a gold miner's thoroughfare to Pine Log Crossing, where a bustling town of tents and shacks stood in 1850. Except for modern-day recreational mining at Italian Bar, the South Fork remains wild for twenty miles upstream, almost to Lyons Reservoir. Forty miles up is the recreational complex of Pinecrest, and beyond that the stream is a gem of the Sierra, twisting from elevations of 10,000 feet across alabaster granite, dropping through hundreds of potholes and cauldrons where you can swim or sit.

The final leg of our river trip runs for three and a half miles below the South Fork confluence. Just past the confluence lies one of the largest limestone cliffs. Part of it is travertine—calcium carbonate deposits from the dripping of water—looking like a shark's mouth.

Sierra Club Rapid and then Chinese Dogleg plunge toward Parrotts Ferry. With Mother Rapid and Bailey Falls, the Dogleg is one of the most beautiful drops of the river, carving an S-bend at low water level. Catherine pulls hard to the left to miss boulders, then to the right as the current slices back and boils into a silent pool. Mark steers his kayak with body english and cupped palms. We pass fishermen casting for rainbow and brown trout, and inner-tubers, who hike up the trails from Parrotts Ferry, then spin down laughing in the white and green current. A family jumps in right now—two kids, mom, dad, and Labrador retriever. We pass sandy beaches on the left, great slabs of bedrock on the right, people camping all over. Even though it is early evening, we are still suffused by the foothills heat. Catherine takes a five-gallon bailing bucket, dips it into the river, and dumps it over her head, the flash of Stanislaus water splashing from her like jewels in the low, golden light of the sun.

CHAPTER TWO

The Valley

The Sierra foothills drop to the west and fade to a billiard-table flatness where only a surveyor or an irrigator would see a slope. Farther west, the Coastal Range runs north-south. They are sandbox hills compared to the Sierra, but they rise suddenly and form the western edge of the flatlands. To the north, we can wander a long way with the gradual climb of the Sacramento River, which yields one-third of the water in California. From Stockton we go past the state capital to Marysville, Oroville, and Chico, to Redding—two hundred miles or so. Due south, we can climb the unhurried gradient of the San Joaquin River from Stockton to Modesto and Fresno. Bakerfield lies farther south, 250 miles from Stockton.

This is the Central Valley of California. Above all else, it is flat, fertile, and dry. Long ago the Valley soaked as an inland sea. Now it is a sea of soil. For eons the flatlands have been a sink for alluvium from the Sierra Nevada, dumped here by the rivers. In summer the Valley bakes at 105 degrees for days on end. Tule fogs, soupy and gray, shroud the land during mild winters that allow twelve months of farming.

You don't often see uninterrupted horizons of cropland or an unbroken range of corn and wheat, as in the Midwest. Most of the Valley is far more settled than that. Roads checker the flatness, peppered with tidy bungalow homes, rambling ranch houses, shacks, dusty farming towns, and sprawling suburban cities.

The Valley is 450 miles long, 30 to 60 miles wide. From a satellite, it would look cigar-shaped, but the entire Sacramento–San Joaquin basin might look like the wing of a bird gliding west. The front of the wing is the Valley; the feathers streaming back are Sierra rivers. The American, Yuba, and Feather surge into the Sacramento from 400-inch snowpacks. The Cosumnes, Mokelumne, Stanislaus, Tuolumne, and

Merced meld into the San Joaquin. The Kings, Kaweah, and Kern
Rivers are at the edge of this basin, but are channeled south by canal.
The Sacramento and the San Joaquin collide head-on, heaping a
Mississippi load of silt into a mazy delta of sloughs, islands, and
brackish tidewater: 690,000 acres of land, 50,000 of water, our
country's largest inland delta outside Alaska. It is the beginning of
San Francisco Bay.

In 1840 pronghorn antelope and tule elk grazed the Valley in herds.
Fat edges of green accented the waterways with oak, willow, and
cottonwood, shading 775,000 acres where runoff was plentiful in
winter and spring. Swamps weltered in low places; the Valley had 5
million acres of wetlands. Golden beaver, otter, and mink swam here,
and the Miwok Indians settled on the riverbanks and ate salmon,
sturgeon, and perch. King salmon and steelhead trout spawned in
most foothill streams. All of this would change; most would be lost.

With the Gold Rush of the 1850s, hydraulic miners flushed silt into
the streams, plastering over the gravel beds needed for fish eggs to
hatch. On the Stanislaus and other rivers, dams were built in the
1920s, impassable barriers to the seagoing, or anadromous, fish.
Diversions for irrigation killed more fish, and the survivors faced hot,
polluted water from the fields. After cutting the trees, farmers
cultivated the fertile flood plain to the river's edge.

By 1950 only 3 percent of the riparian forest remained. The Delta and
San Francisco Bay lost 60 percent of their wetlands to the silt generated
by gold miners and farmers. Only 4 percent of the Valley wetlands
survived. The pronghorn's range had long since been lost to the
Hereford, and the gravel beds of the steelhead to catfish bottoms of
mud. On the Stanislaus, a king salmon run of 150,000 a year was
reduced to 6,000 in the 1960s; 2,000 in the 70s. The yellow-billed
cuckoos, vireos, and warblers of the riverside were mostly replaced
by the cowbird.

Early Valley settlers were dryland farmers. Not that they had a
choice—the lower San Joaquin gets only six inches of rain a year. In
the upper reaches of the Central Valley, it rains twenty inches a year.
Rainfall gives one-tenth to one-third of the water that most crops need,
and it falls at the wrong time—December through March. So it was
dryland farming: beef, sheep, wheat, barley. This was an era
graphically described in *The Octopus,* a classic American novel by
Frank Norris, published in 1901. More people came, and within a few
years single-cropping exhausted the soil. The grain yields shrank.
Overgrazing exhausted bunchgrasses that were important for forage,
and the range was impoverished to weeds. Meanwhile, railroads,
refrigeration, and the Panama Canal opened the door to eastern food
markets, and farmers began to see big possibilities. They turned to

increased irrigation for more dependable yields and for high-cash crops. Along rivers, owners held riparian rights and could ditch water to their fields. Groundwater was pumped from a scant twenty-five feet underground. Once people knew that this could become the richest farmland on the continent, the thirst for irrigation became insatiable. Small dams and canals were built early in the twentieth century and expanded with the establishment of irrigation districts. The Oakdale and South San Joaquin Districts developed reservoirs to water farms along the lower Stanislaus, but compared with the efforts to come, these early dams and ditches were the work of kids in a backyard stream.

The Central Valley Project and the State Water Project rearranged the water of California more than a million years of changes in climate could do. The strategy: take water from the Sierra snowpack and from the rainy north and divert it south to the 10,000 square miles of the Valley, and even farther to the drylands that would become Los Angeles, America's third largest city. Take water from where it is plentiful and supposedly unused to where it is scarce and in demand. Today the strategy is supported by data: 72 percent of the state's runoff is north of Sacramento, 77 percent of the water requirements are south of it. And it is bolstered by votes. In California's congressional delegation, twenty-four members represent southern California below the Tehachapi Mountains; nineteen represent the vast remainder of the state.

From a private and local function, the transport of water became a state and federal one. Power companies screamed socialism when generation of hydroelectricity at government dams was proposed. Local water interests fought against federalism, but Uncle Sam's offer was too good to turn down. Much of California's water quit flowing east-west and began flowing north-south in channels laid out by transit, in rivers dug by bulldozers and draglines. The State Water Project (SWP) now includes America's tallest dam, 770 feet high at Oroville on the Feather River. Nearly 2 million acre-feet of state water are delivered to San Joaquin Valley farms and to the cities, a figure that could double in the future (one acre-foot covers an acre with a foot of water and equals 325,900 gallons, the amount in a municipal swimming pool). Half a million acre-feet per year are shunted 600 miles to urban areas of the south by way of a 444-mile canal and a 3,000-foot, 300,000-horsepower lift over the Tehachapis. Urban growth in the south was encouraged this way. Assuming new reservoirs are developed, state officials project that 2.4 million acre-feet of SWP water will go south by the year 2030.

Delivery of 6.5 million acre-feet of water is provided by the Central Valley Project (CVP), a labyrinth of dams, canals, pumps, power generators, and ditches, first planned by the state, then built and operated by a federal agency, the Department of the Interior's Bureau of Reclamation. About 330,000 acres are irrigated in the Sacramento, San Joaquin, and Santa Clara valleys. The cornerstone of the CVP is Shasta Dam, built in 1945, 600 feet high, holding 4.5 million acre-feet of the upper Sacramento River. About $2.5 billion worth of CVP water projects were developed at no cost to the state, offering cheap water, interest-free, to the farmer. Another $3.5 billion (1979 price level) is authorized.

These projects gave California more large dams and more water storage than any other state, but at a cost. Over $6.4 billion has been spent on the SWP and the CVP, and the bills keep coming in. In 1978 the U.S. Department of the Interior's Office of Audit projected a $10 billion CVP deficit by the year 2038 if current repayment rates continue. Only 22 percent of the public investment may be returned in revenues. Annual CVP costs will have exceeded revenues in forty-five out of forty-seven years through 1995. CVP operations and maintenance alone cost over $30 million per year.

Unlike the Stanislaus Canyon, which remains mostly wilderness, the Central Valley has changed. Few places—maybe no place—of this size have changed this much. The drylands of the Valley were brown, but with irrigation water from the Sierra and the north, they are green with crops today. Dryland farmers switched to cotton, sugar beets, grapes, tomatoes, fruit, nuts, and rice. The Central Valley provides much of the nation's supply of broccoli, plums, lemons, almonds, olives, avocadoes, apricots, figs, and dates. With plenty of water, beef and dairy cattle have thrived (water for livestock feed and forage totals over one-half of all agricultural use, over 40 percent of California's total water use). Since the climate, soil, landform, and imported water allow almost any kind of crop to be grown, farmers can select the most lucrative. In the South San Joaquin Irrigation District, covering much of the lower Stanislaus, farmers work two thirds of the acreage for fruits, nuts, and wine grapes. About two-thirds of the Oakdale irrigation district is irrigated for pasture and feed for cattle.

The Central Valley holds 75 percent of the state's cropland and comprises 6,750,000 acres, an area twice the size of Connecticut. It is an outdoor hothouse. Californians grow 40 percent of U.S fruits and vegetables, and 25 percent of the nation's food. They have led the nation in agriculture for twenty-five years. In 1980 California agriculture earned $11 billion, and another $20 billion was earned in food processing, shipping, and marketing (tourism generated $19 billion in 1980). Agriculture is one of the largest money-makers in a state whose economy ranks ninth in the world, outranking the economies of Canada, Australia, or Brazil.

The three top-producing farming counties in the nation are in the

San Joaquin Valley. The Midwest may be the nation's breadbasket, but the Central Valley is the vegetable, fruit, and nut basket. Agriculture reached this status by using 85 percent of all the water used in California and is as dependent on irrigation as ancient Mesopotamia and Egypt were.

The Valley supports thousands of family farms and big agribusinesses. The largest 15 percent of the farms soak up 85 percent of irrigation benefits from public projects. Farmers using SWP and CVP water include some of America's biggest corporations: Chevron with 50,000 acres, Tenneco with 53,000, Getty Oil with 41,000, the Southern Pacific Land Co. with 38,000, and J. G. Boswell with 95,000 acres. The Tejon Ranch Co.—partly owned by the Times Mirror Co., which publishes the *Los Angeles Times*—owns 41,000 acres.

The economic boom resulting from government-supplied water is reflected in crops and also in land appreciation: undeveloped farmland has shot up from $200 to $2,000 per acre since SWP water arrived in the lower Valley in 1968. Appreciation on 20,000 acres comes to $36 million.

In the Central Valley, farming is industrialized: railroads tying together the ag-center towns; squads of teamsters driving double trailer-trucks; picking and processing equipment that replaces 100 hands; rows of tiny cottages for migrant pickers; aqueducts, canals, pipes, ditches, and snakelike siphons watering row after row; not tractors, but bulldozers pulling a score of plows; bulldozers leveling fields for irrigation; bulldozers parked in front of prefabricated steel barns; biplanes showering down a storm of chemicals; pump pistons banging along the rivers. Development on the land reflects big profits in food.

The Central Valley is not like the down-home dairyland of Wisconsin or Vermont, not like the rolling fields of Iowa or the pea country of misty Skagit Valley in Washington. The towns are different from America's traditional farm community of elm-lined sidewalks, white clapboard homes of two and three stories, a main street full of neighbors. In the Central Valley, the older towns have some pleasant residential areas, but most seem to be mainly shopping and transit centers. Streets are wide. The downtown districts have large Mexican-American populations. The urban fringe radiates out from the American asphalt environment of the commercial strip, with drive-ins, car washes, K-Marts, and neon blanketing the roadside for miles outside Stockton, Modesto, Fresno, and all the growing cities. Factories for processing and shipping food line the railroad tracks, gorging trains bound for Chicago and filling the bellies of trucks that snort down the street from Interstate 5, never far away.

Every summer Modesto celebrates "Graffiti Night," when people ceremoniously cruise up and down McHenry Avenue in their cars, an event harking back to *American Graffiti*, a film about the exploits of a

1962 California high school graduating class. Fresno gas-station windows are one-way glass, so that you can't see the attendant you're paying. In the Valley, you say "cee-ment" for "cement," and "am'nds" for "almonds."

The Central Valley is one of the best likenesses of rural feudalism in America. Many farm owners are absentees, living in San Francisco, Pasadena, Texas, or Saudi Arabia. They lease land or hire managers—mostly whites; migrant workers, including droves of illegal aliens, are hired during the busy harvest time. But many owners live on their land, and also hire a range of employees from managerial people to pickers. Class distinctions remain clear between Old Californians, Okies and Arkies who came after 1930, Mexican-Americans, blacks, and new urbanites who look as though they have come from Los Angeles.

Even more distinct is the cultural gulf between Valley people and other Northern Californians, such as people from the Bay Area. While each region sports diverse types, there are some typical features. One group wears running shoes, thongs, or Birkenstock sandals if they can afford them. The other favors cowboy boots and "Cat" caps or cowboy hats—Stetsons if they can afford them. One rides bicycles, the other horses. One drives VW bugs or buses, the other pickups. One touts energy conservation, trades the VW bus for a Honda CVCC, but still drives from San Mateo to Yosemite at will, maybe six times a year. The other cusses conservation and buys a new, roomy pickup. One group is hustled for est; the other for never-never land by Jehovah's Witnesses, who make the rounds once a month and canvass the Valley Greyhound stations. One group might include feminists, rock climbers, rock musicians, and Buddhists; the other, John Birchers, rodeo stars, fundamentalist Baptists, and Mormons. These, of course, are the extremes, but they are easily found in each respective area.

To the people of the Valley, the weekend migration from the coast to the mountains is an invasion. The urbanites roll down the Interstate in hordes, straight through the farming towns, and across the flats to the Sierra. They may stop for gas, a milkshake, or fresh fruit and vegetables on the way home on Sunday evening, but otherwise they stick to the public highway and traverse this foreign land just as fast as they can. They hardly blink an eye at the flat, fertile, dry valley that feeds America. People who hitchhike the route really feel the difference—this wave of one culture passing through the land of another. Especially when they get stuck thumbing in, say, Oakdale on a Saturday night.

Industrial agriculture. The billboards of the Production Credit Association don't call agriculture "farming." They call it California's "number one industry."

With that status comes political might. In Sacramento and in Washington, congressmen from Redding to Bakersfield occupy positions of high influence, dependent on the farm vote, and flush with the contributions of agribusiness. In 1979–80 Harold T. ("Bizz") Johnson of Roseville was chairman of the Public Works Committee in Washington. John McFall of Manteca was powerful on this committee and on the Appropriations Committee during his 1956–78 tenure. At the state level, the main path for water projects is the senate agriculture and water committee, occupied entirely by men and women from the Valley and the dry urban south. True to their constituents, Valley politicians always push projects for the supply of water. They don't just support them, they create and hustle and deal, because their reelection depends on it. Freshman Congressman Vic Fazio, representing the Davis area, raised $17,000 one evening when 170 farmers ate lukewarm suppers costing $100 each. Hundreds of thousands of dollars are contributed by agribusinesses to political campaigns.

In the Valley, water projects are a way of life. At Valley Springs, just north of the Stanislaus, they don't have a Valley Springs Lions Club. They have a Tri-Dam Lions Club. One of the main streets in Oroville is called Oroville Dam Boulevard. Some of the most used fishing sites are not along rivers but on canals. The largest sporting goods stores deal in outboard motorboats and waterskis for reservoir fun. Almost every day, Valley newspapers print an article about water and the various ways it is being shuttled around, making headlines as often as car accidents do, which is often. A sign over the main street in Modesto says, "Water, Wealth. Contentment, Health." ("In the Valley, they've got their own things going on," says Tom Hershenow, a native of Fresno. "They don't know that the Stanislaus Canyon exists. It's just not there. They're on the other end.") Along with the development of a mobile society that depends on cars, the growth of irrigated agriculture may be the most important chapter of California history.

The Stanislaus is a part of that history. When Sierra water leaves the Stanislaus Canyon, it is caught by New Melones Dam, then by Tulloch Dam and Goodwin Dam. What is left after irrigation diversions flows across the fertile Valley.

John Hertle's farm in the Central Valley sits right along the Stanislaus. Joseph Hertle trekked to Stanislaus County in 1924 from Germany by way of Argentina and Chile. He was evading old-country inflation and the draft. Immigration laws didn't allow him to come straight from his native Bavaria, where Hertles had farmed since 1710, but the man was persistent. He wanted to go to America. Hearing that one could emigrate to the United States from Argentina, Hertle took passage there, only to be stymied by more rules. Finally, he acquired a visa in Chile and boarded ship for California. Mark Dubois's great-grandfather and John Hertle's father were both old-world draft-dodgers, and both ended up in California.

Joseph Hertle hunted for a farm, and found dark soil in a dry valley. Near a river, he could rest assured that groundwater would be close to the surface and available for the dairy herd he planned to start. Hertle settled on the Stanislaus. With Old World frugality, the dairyman saved the $400 downpayment on a small frame house, and three years after he steamed into San Francisco Bay, Mrs. Hertle joined him.

Now, in the summer of 1980, it is fifty-six years later, and John Hertle, son of Joseph the immigrant, sits in the kitchen of a spacious ranch house, with a Mercedes out front and a driveway full of equipment. The downpayment on even a small piece of this machinery runs well over $400. The California land has been good to the Hertles. "My mother lives in that house down where the trees are," Hertle says. "I was born in the green place where you turned in, and my son John and his wife Carlene live right there." He points across a sundeck and an out-building to a smaller ranch house.

Hertle stands over six feet tall and is built broad and rough. One could easily guess him to be a California stockman. He wears blue jeans and could probably use the "men's cut" that Levi's advertises. I think he is the first farmer I have known who wears white sneakers, but this is California, and even the farmers are more casual and insist on being comfortable. John's wife, Carol, is serving up soft-boiled eggs and the second wave of coffee. The first came at 4:30 this morning, after John had tracked down a bellowing cow that got loose to give birth to a calf down by the river. Carol shakes her head, "We heard the cow mooing through the bedroom window, and I said, 'Oh no, here we go again, chasing the herd.' We've done that on a lot of cold, foggy nights, and I didn't need another. I'm glad it was just the one cow." Carol and John both smoke Camels most of the time, or at least when they're being interviewed for a book about the river out front—the river that floods, that has surrounded the house and left the fields sloppy wet.

A TV is set up in the kitchen. John heats another cup of coffee in a microwave oven, and Carol gets one for me. Sanka, actually, and she apologizes for being out of the real stuff. Two Saint Bernards, each larger than the newborn Holstein calf, look through a big sliding glass door, and one of them knocks with a mallet-paw but is ignored. Half a dozen sleek horses, the pride of this dairy ranch, graze between the homes of Hertle senior and Hertle junior.

Here is a scene of California farm life. An older, red-faced jolly man ambles in after knocking on the back door. He has some official role not revealed to me. I think he may drive the milk truck, because he and Hertle talk about a load that got spoiled and two trucks that are broken down. He leaves, we do a scant five minutes of interview, and John of John-and-Carlene enters. He is trim and wears a trucker/farmer style cap that says "Funks Hybrids." He smokes too. It is a cool morning for June in the Valley—probably 65 degrees—and the younger Hertle wears a blue vest of Eddie Bauer design, except that the chest pocket says "Albacillin Biodry TUCO," whatever that may mean in the lingo of agribusiness.

The older John Hertle is unequivocally a man of the Valley. Yet he likes to coax his horses into a big trailer behind the pickup and wheel up Sonora Pass to the headwaters of the Stanislaus's Middle Fork. He and family or friends ride back into the Emigrant Wilderness for a week of trout fishing and clear mountain air, loving that untouched country.

Hertle fished right here on the farm when he was a kid. "With an old Norwegian, Earl Stein, I'd fish out there for shad," he says. The pair would catch catfish and crappies too. Through high school, Hertle fished in the Central Valley Stanislaus, but no more. "I like to get away now for that," he says. So he goes to the top of the river and lets loose for awhile.

Hertle is one educated dairy farmer. University degrees are plentiful among the younger generation of Valley farmers, but not so common among his peers, aged forty-five or so. He went to Modesto Junior College, then the University of California at Davis, then U.C. Berkeley for Agricultural Economics. "I never expected to come back to the farm," he says. His first job was as inspector of fruits and vegetables for the state. "But I didn't like all the travel. I didn't like government work." Then, for three and a half years, he worked for the Modesto Milk Producers' Association. "But I wanted to be on my own." So the Hertles, now a family, bought land by the immigrant parents' farmstead and began milking ten cows. Ten. I look out that sliding glass door, and to the extent that I can see past the Saint Bernards, I recognize some small fraction of the eight hundred Holsteins the Hertles now own. A big dairy. Four hundred and fifty milking cows. Three hundred acres, and another hundred rented. Two men work full time just milking, and that is in addition to almost all the labor-saving devices high technology can economically provide. Yes, from scratch, John Hertle has done well. He worked hard through the fifties, sixties, and seventies, and now he has something to show for it.

"The first year nearly put us out of business." Hertle is playing back a part of the hardscrabble past. It is the part I am most interested in. The Stanislaus flooded in 1955 as neither the German nor the American Hertle had ever seen it do. "The land was washed and rutted, needed to be leveled for irrigation, and the river needed to be channeled so it would hold more water again. We couldn't borrow money from the bank. They said I should salvage what I could and sell. Go out of business." Give up. But this was not accepted in the Hertle family, or they would still have been in Bavaria.

"I went to the Production Credit Association for farmers, part of the federal land bank program, and they agreed on $3,000 so I could relevel. That gave us our chance at staying in business," he says.

The next bad flood was in December 1964. "It was not as high, but almost as damaging." Hertle remembers it well. The rains pounded, early snowmelt bloated the river, and it rose to rip out cottonwoods by their roots. The muddy current gained against the levee, scouring it. Hertle and a militia of local farmers hauled and dumped sand bags in a night out of a John Steinbeck novel, but to no avail. The levee broke. Time to get the cattle out. The horses were called from their pasture and drafted into service. John Hertle saddled up and drove cows from sodden fields. They wrangled 500 head Wyoming-style onto Highway 132 in the black of the soaking night. Hertle didn't lose any livestock, but a neighbor lost 150 head. The day after Christmas, thirty men worked with ropes, pulling stock out of the water. "A cow can swim for a day," Hertle says. Young John says I should have seen the one swimming in the flood with a rabbit on its back.

A large deck adjoins the Hertle house. It contains lawn furniture, a charcoal grill, and a table. A couple of glasses from yesterday hold water from melted ice cubes. Just like decks everywhere in California.

The front of the house faces the river. Although only a glimpse of the Stanislaus can be seen, the view toward the water is still uncommonly natural. There are girthy oaks, and birds screech and chatter in the tangled riparian forest. The other side of the house faces the barn and several acres fenced in almost up to the house. The cows feed in part of this area, and in the rest of it they stand around together switching flies during the daytime. The Hertle deck does not face the river. It faces the herd.

Hertle continues the flood count with one addition, January 1980. His oat field was hit, the one where the calf has just been born. "They haven't been a normal thing, these Hawaiian storms."

"Hawaiian?"

"Most storms come down from the north. But warm, wet ones now and then will come off the Pacific from the direction of Hawaii. In waves. Five, six, seven, eight, nine of them, one every twenty-four hours or so. Two or three are okay. After that, we're in trouble. They dump three inches of rain instead of half an inch. They melt the snow up high, and boom, here comes the water." In January 1980, there was a full dose of Hawaiian storms.

"The water was going to be real close to the other house," Hertle says, "so we got a bulldozer and pushed up a dike around it the day before the flood."

I ask Hertle if he has ever thought of moving off the flood plain, getting away from the problem. Especially after the first flood, when his investment was not so great, when the bank wouldn't loan the money. "No, never. This is our farm. I never gave it a thought." How about now? If he was starting now, would he get out?

"At my age, yes. At his age [meaning young John], no. The best land is the flood plain. Up at the end of the lane, we get fifteen tons of corn to an acre. Down next to the river, we get thirty tons, and it doesn't cost us as much to grow it."

Since 1937 the government has paid much attention to flood problems—over $10 billion worth, building dams, dikes, and levees, and digging channels. Many projects have paid off in reduced flood losses, but overall the destruction is worse. Each year high-water damage increases, the Army Corps of Engineers never catching up with the floods. The problem, analysts report, is that we develop the flood plain too much. We pretend that it is just like any other place, which is asking for trouble.

Spurred by environmentalism, shrinking economic expectations, taxpayer revolts, and water policy reform, a different view gained strength through the 1970s. Called flood-plain management, its basic point is that the flood plain is hazardous, to be used only in flood-tolerant ways. The federal flood insurance program, meant to soften economic losses, is a part of this. People pay premiums entitling them to payments that are 49 percent government subsidized when they incur damage, but they are eligible only if the local government prohibits new development in the hazard zone and requires flood proofing in the fringe zone.

Those involved in flood-plain management—planners, ecologists, economists, the Department of Housing and Urban Development, even the Army Corps of Engineers nowadays—are quick to say what should *not* be done in the flood hazard zone. No homes, commercial development, industry, hazardous waste dumps, landfills. "So what *can* we do?" irate landowners ask. All flood-plain management advocates reply with a list of open space activities, and right at the top is farming.

The flood losses of Hertle and his neighbors are no doubt significant. Lower Stanislaus losses in 1964 came to about $1.6 million. They were mostly agricultural, however, and on a relative scale agriculture is one of the low-damage uses. If you're going to do anything with the flood plain, farm it. That will result in the least economic loss.

John Hertle has just verified this view. His farm is as much a part of the flood plain as you can get. Just about all of the farm has flooded, except for the houses, which are on mounds of soil. The Stanislaus loops around the largest field, which is a low, fertile peninsula. Yet, Hertle says, it pays—fifteen tons versus thirty tons, and so forth. Over the years, Hertle has profited as much as, or better than, his high-ground neighbors. Hertle is not enthusiastic about flood insurance. It doesn't pay for agricultural losses. "The guy who works the flood plain takes a risk," he says. Simple as that.

John, Jr. needs to talk to John, Sr. about their silo, which is not upright and cylindrical, as some people would think, but sunk in the ground. It is a lined cavity, 300 feet long, 60 feet wide. "With our herd, you'd need a dozen or more of your old silos," John, Sr. observes. While they talk, Carol tells me about the day before. A mare was ready to have a colt, and it was Mrs. Hertle's job to keep an eye out. She visited the big-bellied horse hourly. Then, busy with something else, she skipped a run to the barn. Next time she checked, there stood the colt. "Everything was fine, almost always is, but we like to be there just in case she needs help," she says.

Hertle finishes the discussion with his son. It is nearly noon, and a pump needs to be turned on, one that draws water out of the river through a four-inch pipe into a ditch that branches across a pasture behind the manure pile and the animal waste pond. The river water is free—Hertle holds riparian rights, since he owns the shore. The dairy is also served by a Tuolumne River canal from the Modesto irrigation district. This water is almost free at $2.50 per acre. Not per acre-foot. Per acre, per year, no matter how much is used.

Returning from the river, we stop to watch a group of cows. Not just casually. Hertle is figuring which are ready for breeding. He determines this by their behavior. When ready, one cow mounts another. Depending on the enthusiasm of the top cow and the tolerance of the bottom one, the farmer knows which is fertile. Two are, three aren't. The two cows' numbers (attached to ear tags) are jotted down, later given to a hired man who takes care of these things.

This place is tuned to life cycles, to reproduction. The pregnant mare yesterday, that cow at 4:30 A.M., now these cows. So it is on the farm. Yet it is not at all back-to-nature. If Hertle misses a cow that is ready for breeding, he loses months of milk production from her. It's all very agriculturally economic. This is not Rousseau's peaceable kingdom, Louis Bromfield's Malabar Farm, or the Green Gulch Zen Center. These cows will get pregnant without even seeing a bull. They will be artificially inseminated with sperm that the farmer buys from an outfit with a name like "Golden Genes." There is a bull out back, but he is called into action only as a last resort, if more efficient and reliable methods don't work. Bulls are ornery, and artificial insemination saves the farmer the trouble of having them around.

So what does this have to do with the Stanislaus, anyway? Well, it makes me think of nature's cycles and rhythms, the inevitable waxing and waning of energies: reproductive, climatic, hydraulic. These alone, however, have little to do with the economics of farming. And Central Valley farming is primarily economics, very favorable ones.

It is not important that the river brought all that dark thirty-tons-of-corn-per-acre soil to the place described on a courthouse deed belonging to John Hertle. The soil is already there. To hell with this natural cycle of floods. Last spring the flood wiped out a whole crop of oats. Sixteen years ago, it killed 150 cows. Natural cycles are meant to be used if profitable, improved where possible, and eliminated where they destroy property.

Hertle says, "I first heard of New Melones Dam back about World War II, when my father said, "When they build that dam we won't have any more floods."

"After the '64 flood, I went up to the Oakdale irrigation board meeting to see what they could do about the flooding, to see what their release schedule was going to be." A news reporter was there, and he included Hertle's concern for flood control in his story. Another flood-plain farmer read the paper and called Hertle. After meeting with two more farmers, they decided to do something. That was how the Stanislaus River Flood Control Association started. Since then, a good part of Hertle's life has been spent getting New Melones Dam built.

Carol picks up a ringing telephone. It is another flood-plain farmer, who depends on Hertle for advice. The Stanislaus has been high due to spring runoff, and the neighbor wants to know if the water level will be dropping. "Yes, the river's going down," Carol says. She holds a hand over the phone. "John, it's May. She wants to know if she should plant her corn."

Hertle answers, "Tell her the river will stay down for awhile. They're having trouble with vortexing at New Melones, and they're finally going to cut back on the releases and raise the reservoir." New Melones Reservoir will be raised. The corn on the flood plain can be planted, but the Stanislaus Canyon will be drowned.

Another Central Valley farmer near the Stanislaus is Al Sorrenti. This year he is raising corn, wheat, and rice. Last year it was wheat, beans, and rice; two years ago it was tomatoes and beans. "This land can grow most anything," the farmer says. "Few people realize how much will grow here. We've raised forty tons of tomatoes to the acre. I tell out-of-staters what my yields are, and they look at me like I'm crazy. But it isn't easy. Farming is real competitive."

Sorrenti's father farmed near Fresno during the 1930s when people from the dust bowl of Oklahoma and Arkansas migrated to the Central Valley with high expectations. "Irrigation was cheap—a few dollars per acre, but because of the Depression a lot of farmers still couldn't pay, and they lost their water. When you lose your water, you lose your farm."

Al grew up on a dairy near Escalon, five miles from the Stanislaus, north of Modesto; then he moved to Santa Rosa. Eventually he returned to the Central Valley because crop yields are so much better there. Sorrenti addresses only quantity: "Ten tons of grapes per acre instead of two or three." For quality, most people agree that Northern California grapes cannot be beat.

Mrs. Sorrenti—Nella—came to California and the lower Stanislaus when she was twelve. Her father's dusty farm along Texas's Colorado River was taken by the government for a dam project in the thirties. "My dad thought we would find a better life out here," she says, and it seems they have. About 1950 Al and Nella paid $100 down on this farm, fifteen miles east of Stockton. A late model Mercury now sits out front. The home is neat and well cared for. Its interior style is 1950s suburban. Wall-to-wall carpet. Two deer heads mounted above the couch. There is a framed watercolor of ducks flying over a Central Valley farm that looks very much like this one, and probably is. A big TV is front and center and now shows "All in the Family." After a day of farm activity, Sorrenti is freshly showered. He is wearing new boots, the kind with soft tan soles, and a paisley shirt.

Sorrenti has Popeye forearms from fifty-five years of clutching tools and doing farm work. But that is not all he does. Like Hertle, he fishes for trout. He has tried his luck in the Stanislaus at Camp Nine. "It has its own beauty, but I like it up at six and seven thousand feet. That zone of granite, evergreens, and meadows." The upper reaches of the North Fork near Big Meadows and the Middle Fork at Kennedy Lake are his favorite spots.

"We have 240 acres," he says, "and two families work it. Our daughter and son-in-law live just down the road in the mobile home." They run a share of the farm, not quite in pursuit of the daughter's college majors of art and sociology (I'll bet she did the painting of the ducks). It is common, however, for many young people to return to Valley farms after they finish school.

"A lot of dairymen's sons stay," Sorrenti says. "There's a lot of work on a dairy. Most everything is mechanized nowadays, too, and young guys like it."

"Forget that handwork," Nella inserts.

Three more men—usually Mexican-Americans—are hired by

Sorrenti and his son-in-law at harvest time. Like Hertle, this farm owner speaks well of his Mexican labor. "If it weren't for them, the work wouldn't get done." Sorrenti's laborers are paid a minimum of $5 an hour, up to $7.50 (many others are paid the minimum wage and less). "I'll cut other corners, but cutting wages is not fair."

The Sorrentis have two other children. The youngest daughter is in college studying music education. Their son studied agronomy, and grows rice on nearby land that he rented, then bought from a family friend. Land purchases by young farmers are rare. "Criminey!" Al Sorrenti says, "It's $3,000 an acre, and today you can't even pay the interest. A lot of land is bought by foreigners—Arabs, French, Italians—all over, driving the price up. A young farmer can't make a start."

"Most of the district is small family farms," Sorrenti says. He means the Central San Joaquin Water Conservation District—a group of San Joaquin County farmers who organized twenty years ago to import water to their 67,000 acres. They are not yet successful. Where would the water come from? "Either the Folsom South Canal out of Auburn Dam on the American River or from New Melones Dam on the Stanislaus." Why do they need this water when they are already growing forty tons of tomatoes per acre? Why import water from the American or Stanislaus River when rice is already grown in flooded paddies that look like monsooned Thailand or rainy Louisiana? "Because groundwater is our only water," the deeply tanned farmer says. "In 1950 when we started here, our wells were 35 feet deep. Now we have to go down 140. A few feet deeper each year. In the drought years, '76 and '77, we lost 15 or 20 feet each. We need extra water so we can ease up the pumping, so the groundwater recharges as fast as we use it. Four or five other districts are just like ours."

Unlike John Hertle who suffers from too much water, Sorrenti can't get enough. This man and his neighbors farm without benefit of the public water projects, but not by choice. As chairman of the water conservation district, Sorrenti has gone to Washington twice and to Sacramento dozens of times trying to get water from the Central Valley Project before his groundwater gives out. He has encountered delays in the construction of Auburn Dam and in the delivery of water from New Melones. For Friends of the River and water reformers, he has little time. "It's a good thing we didn't have this element thirty or forty years ago fighting water projects. If we did, we wouldn't be able to flush the toilet or get a drink of water," he says.

Central Valley groundwater comprises far more water than all of the combined reservoirs and lakes in the state. Forty percent of the water used in the Valley is from underground. During the drought (1977 was the driest year on record), over half of the Valley water came from wells. Nine thousand new ones were drilled in 1977 alone. Over one-third of the water that is used statewide is pumped from underground aquifers, but as the tomato-bean-wheat-rice farmer says, the supply is running out. Overdraft averages 1.5 million acre-feet per year in the Central Valley, meaning 1.5 million more are sucked out than seep in. That's 480 billion gallons. During the drought (1976–77), farmers overdrew 5 million acre-feet each year, enough to cover the state of New Jersey with one foot of water. Throughout California, overdraft is about 2.5 million acre-feet per year.

This cannot go on for long, which is Sorrenti's point. First of all, the water is running out. Already some Valley wells near the Delta yield salt water. Secondly, energy is running out. It doesn't take much electricity to pump water from 35 feet, but 140 feet is a different story. Other areas of the nation share the problem: the Central Valley of Arizona, with its urbanized desert at Phoenix; the hot ranchlands of Texas; and the high plains for beef grazing in Nebraska and Colorado, where the Ogallala aquifer may be dry by the turn of the century. So far, most people aren't looking at the sustained yield of groundwater as a brake on food production or water extraction. Farmers don't generally say, "I can't grow rice because I'm overdrawing the groundwater supply." They just drill deeper, pay for more electricity, and make up the difference when they sell the water-intensive, cash-intensive crop. A primary purpose of the public water projects was to replace the use of groundwater in the San Joaquin Valley, but in many places that hasn't happened. Farmers can get more money by irrigating new land, so they do.

The way the landlocked groundwater farmers see it, they are competing with amply supplied neighbors, and depletion of groundwater is no reason to follow different rules or grow different crops. State attempts to regulate groundwater bring out farmers bearing pitchforks, and have gone nowhere in the state legislature. The growers say regulation is not the answer. New Melones and Auburn Dams are the answer, says Sorrenti. Once provided with subsidized water, the pumpers will lay off the aquifer, but until then, don't expect any changes. "There's hardly any money in dryland crops," Sorrenti says. What will happen, though, if the government doesn't bail out the groundwater farmers and the overdraft makes pumping prohibitive? "Then we'd have to cut back on production or turn to different crops." Some farmers might go out of business. Out here in the desert, when you lose your water, you lose your farm.

Overdrafting causes other complications. As in the coal country of northeast Pennsylvania or southern Illinois, subsidence plagues the land. Water miners, like coal miners, leave underground cavities behind. Overburden settles and eventually the earth slumps. Part of the Central Valley is quietly caving in as all that water is pumped out.

Once that happens, it can never hold so much water again. By 1970, 5,200 square miles of the San Joaquin Valley, an area the size of Connecticut, had subsided. West of Mendota, the land dropped twenty-eight feet. Expensive repairs were required on the Delta–Mendota and Friant–Kern Canals.

That's not all. The underground flow of fresh water toward the Delta (a salt water estuary) has been stopped, and the hydrostatic equilibrium has advanced inland. That means that salt water is pushing harder than fresh water, intruding from deep underground cavities. Stockton, population 137,000 in 1980 (only 110,000 in 1970) draws its municipal supply from groundwater being touched by the saline creep. This has also happened on Long Island, N.Y., in booming Florida, in Texas, in Europe, in Israel, and in Japan. The solution is basic—quit pumping out so much groundwater. How? By finding new sources, by conserving, or both.

An important concern is cost. Irrigation water from New Melones or any other new dam will cost the government $50 to $100 per acre-foot delivered. The RAND Corporation has estimated that water delivered through the proposed Peripheral Canal around the Delta will have a value of $245 per acre-foot. What do farmers pay? A normal minimum in the CVP is $3.50 per acre-foot. This can be decreased, however, if the government judges that the farmer doesn't have the "ability to pay." In the CVP, the average is about $7.50. The Westlands district pays about $8.50. Under the State Water Project, a common rate is $27 per acre-foot. Never $50 or $100. That means that the farmers' water is subsidized by the sale of hydroelectric power and, with the CVP, by the general taxpayers, most of whom live east of the Mississippi, and nearly all of whom do not live on farms. Even in the Stanislaus/Stockton district of Congressman Norman Shumway, only 9 percent of the work force are farmers.

How does a ruggedly individual farmer who is skeptical of big government look at the government subsidy of irrigation? "There are side benefits from jobs created," Sorrenti says. "For every dollar the farmer gets, seven go to the economy. The farmer gets $60 a ton for tomatoes. On the shelf, a can of tomatoes costs 45 cents." That would come to a retail cost of $1,600 per ton. "Somebody is getting a lot of money along the way. It's employing people. Then there's equipment, fertilizer, all the things the farmers buy. That money all adds to the economy. Income taxes are paid. That water all makes the economy of this county and state possible." John Hertle says that there are subsidies for highways, railroads, Chrysler, and Boeing. "Why not farmers? Why pick on one group when you talk about subsidies?"

Agricultural interests argue that everybody eats, and therefore enjoys subsidized water. According to the *California Water Atlas*, however, "Most of the subsidy is capitalized in the value of the land

and not passed forward to the customer in terms of lower food prices." In other words, the farmers benefit, not the consumers. To the extent that the subsidy does lower food prices, benefits are not necessarily enjoyed by those who pay. Rice, which uses huge amounts of subsidized water, is mostly exported to Japan and Korea.

There is another question: why subsidize some farmers but not others? Farmers of the Central San Joaquin Water Conservation District have not been much subsidized so far. Don't they have a right to scrap for Uncle Sam's contribution the way their neighbors have? How about the farmers of the East, a great agricultural region where you don't often have to irrigate? Some crops, of course, can be most easily grown in California. But how about the rice grower of Louisiana who is no longer in business because the Bureau of Reclamation, with the federal taxpayer's money, has made it so attractive to grow rice in the California desert for shipment to Tokyo? The populous East, via 1040 forms, has footed the bill to water crops in the arid West, offering a competitive edge that has put numerous farmers east of the 100th meridian out of business and guaranteed dependence on an energy consuming, coast-to-coast transportation system. The broccoli eaten by Philadelphians can be grown in Pennsylvania or New Jersey, but instead it is trucked or railroaded 3,000 miles from Stockton. Between 1944 and 1964, Southern cotton acreage dropped by 33 percent, while Bureau of Reclamation cotton acreage increased by 300 percent. Bean acreage has declined in the North, the South, and the unirrigated West, while bean acreage on bureau-irrigated land has doubled. Professor Charles W. Howe, former director of the Resources for the Future's Water Resources Program, and Professor K. William Easter, former Bureau of the Budget economist, have estimated that reclamation has probably replaced 5 to 18 million farmland acres elsewhere (see *Damming the West*, by Richard L. Berkman and W. Kip Viscusi [New York: Grossman, 1973]). All without so much as a whimper from the Eastern political delegation. Usually, all but two or three members of the sixteen-member Senate Interior and Insular Affairs Committee have come from the West. All of this is a complex part of the Central Valley and its agricultural water industry.

Given the choices of a new source or conservation, Al Sorrenti wants a new source—New Melones Dam. "It just blows my mind, the water that's washed out to the Delta," he says. "That water could be sold to return dollars to the federal government. It can be used to generate power, to raise a lot of food. What good is that water going down the river right now? That doesn't do anything for the economy." Whether it does or not is a good question.

The flooding experienced by John Hertle and the groundwater overdraft by Al Sorrenti are two problems affecting the Central Valley and the lower Stanislaus basin, thus far rich in the production of food. But there are more problems. Salt is building up in the soil. Salinization, one of the causes of the demise of the ancient Mesopotamian civilizations, is happening right here. The Bureau of Reclamation reports that about 400,000 acres are affected, and that more than 1 million acres could become a "barren salt flat." A $31 million loss per year could climb to $321 million.

Irrigation water captures natural salts, fertilizers, pesticides, and herbicides as it flows from field to field. Plants absorb the water and leave the salts and pollutants behind. This, alone, is troublesome. Making the situation worse, salts are often trapped by shallow or "perched" groundwater caused by underlying clay deposits or by overirrigation. Poisons concentrate, denying moisture to the plants and whitewashing the fields with the glaring hue of a man-made desert. On hundreds of thousands of acres, such conditions are steadily cutting agricultural productivity. This problem does not occur along the Stanislaus yet, but in other parts of the Central Valley, fruits, beans, and some other vegetables have been replaced with fodder crops that tolerate salt, though they bring less cash. But fodder can tolerate only so much salt.

What is the answer? The San Luis Drain, a canal that would channel the agricultural wastewater off the land, is partly built. Much more is proposed—300 miles in all. Problems are manifest, starting with a cost of $750 million to be shared by the state and federal governments. A larger project that has been proposed would cost $1.26 billion. Polluted water would have to be dumped somewhere. Then more water would be needed to dilute the discharge. Where will it come from?

People advance other strategies: increase the summer volume of the rivers, so that salts are carried away. Alexander Hildebrand, a retired engineer who now raises beef in the Delta, says, "You've got to have enough flow to carry the salt through to the Bay. If you don't, it's just going to sit there." He argues that if nothing is done, the Delta could become a man-made salt marsh, useless for food production. Hildebrand, national president of the Sierra Club in 1954, wants New Melones Dam so that the summer flow in the river will be higher and fresher, bringing less salt to the lower river and the irrigated land.

"Don't irrigate alkaline basins in the first place," says Cliff Humphrey, a student of Central Valley ecology. "I view the Central Valley as a production area, but here we're just asking for trouble." He points to the Tulare Lake Basin, lavish in salts, heritage of eons of evaporation from a landlocked lake. "Places like that should never be irrigated," Humphrey says. "We pump water out of the Delta to irrigate down there, which washes salt back into the Delta. Then we have to develop more water to dilute it."

Another approach, perhaps the simplest, most economical, and certainly the least destructive to the environment, is to decrease the volume of irrigation water, thereby importing fewer salts and reducing the problem of a perched water table. Some people suggest decreased irrigation water with periodic flooding to rinse salts away. For now, the experts have more questions than answers about salinization. Richard Howitt, an agricultural economist at the University of California at Davis, calls soil salinity, "The most underemphasized long-term problem in California agriculture." It may be the road to Babylon.

Then there is urbanization. Since World War II, California has been growing at breakneck speed. It still is. In 1950 there were 10.6 million people here. In 1980 there were 23.6 million. California is the most populous state in the nation, and government estimates indicate that it will bulge with another 7 million by the year 2000.

According to geographer David Hartman, one acre is converted to urban use for each ten new people. The developers target farmland that is level, accessible, and enjoys a good climate. The Soil Conservation Service reports that 27 percent of urban growth is on prime soils. In the Valley, land of prime soil, the percentage is higher. Each year 20,000 acres of irrigated land are converted to urban uses in California. The outskirts of Stockton sprawl with subdivisions, condominiums, and shopping centers that are paved over deep, dark earth—forty-tons-of-tomatoes-per-acre earth. Even closer to the Stanislaus, Modesto gobbles land the same way, and homes multiply in the corners of farms and on the edges of Valley roads everywhere. Cliff Humphrey advocates a string of new towns in the foothills at an elevation of 1,500 feet—above the inversion level that now traps automobile nitrates and perpetually hazes the lowlands in a yellow-gray pall of smog. "The Valley is one of the best places in the world for agriculture and we should reserve it for that use," Humphrey says. But other people don't want to sacrifice the foothills. "Keep their smog trapped down there," a Sierra resident says. "Why pollute the mountains with it?" State Senator John Garamendi of the Stanislaus district has advocated land-use policies that would protect agricultural lands from urbanization, that would encourage local zoning under state guidelines.

The Central Valley is where the water from New Melones Reservoir would go. The Stanislaus Canyon—Camp Nine to Parrots Ferry—would be sacrificed for Valley benefits of flood control, hydroelectric power, recreation, dilution of lower river pollutants, and perhaps groundwater recharging and fisheries. Now that we have seen the canyon and the Valley, it is time that we look at the dam.

CHAPTER THREE

The Dam

The debate over construction lasted thirty-six years, and here is the outcome. I stand at the bottom of New Melones Dam, looking up a scarp of limestone rubble, shell of the new mountain that blocks the river. The top of the dam is my horizon, 625 feet up, sixty-two stories, about as high as San Francisco's Transamerica Building without its tower, and a lot more permanent looking. Sixteen million cubic yards of dirt and rock, enough to fill 48 million wheelbarrows, or 2 million dump trucks, one of the larger piles of earth ever assembled by man.

The dam is in Iron Canyon, a dry, rocky gorge just above Tulloch Reservoir, about twenty-five miles east of Oakdale. It is half a mile thick at the base, with sides that taper inward to a skinny, flat summit where trucks sit, dwarfed like toys. (In December 1979, Mark Dubois kayaked from Camp Nine to Stockton, and he portaged this barefoot. What a climb!) In river time—9 million years so far—New Melones might be here just briefly, but for us it is forever.

People have said that California is above all one great plumbing system, and it holds true for the Stanislaus. A hundred years' evidence of water tradesmen is patent; they have done a job on this river, the New Melones part being just the latest in a century of change.

It is a big dam. We've come a long way from the Indians who lived along the bank and stuck their obsidian spears in the salmon. But they did all right. The year 1400 was probably a good one for the Miwok, because that is about when they found this place. With the salmon running, the natives had good years most of the time—1492, 1776, each year pretty much like all the others. The Miwok put up with the river's fickle lifeline, flood to drought. They went where the water was, hunting up high, fishing down low, always with the seasons. Fish, hunt, grind acorns. Fish, hunt, grind, collect fiddlenecks, pick berries. Meet the Nevada guys up at Sonora Pass and swap acorns for rabbits.

No reason for gold mining. You can't do anything with gold. The Miwok just lived, and the rivers just ran. And then . . .

Prospectors. Thousands of them. Armies of them, Mark Dubois's grandfather included. Eighteen forty-nine was a bad year for the Miwok. Things were changing. No space to fish down at the river. No space to live down at the river. Soon the river itself was changed, and, without it, a way of life was gone. Soon the Miwok were scattered, mostly dead. The Gold Rush was on, and with it, the history of water development on the Stanislaus began.

Angels Camp boomed with miners, merchants, and brothels, and drank itself short of water (perhaps only as a last resort) in 1850. The next year, locals formed the Union Water Company, and with dispatch finished a fifteen-mile ditch from the North Fork near Calaveras Big Trees. The Stanislaus has been tapped ever since. Neither development nor the bungling of it is new. The Union Water Co. engineer overestimated the amount needed, and the North Fork diversion flooded the gold claims that it was meant to serve. Miners wanted water, and they got a deluge. Eventually (nine years later), they cut an expensive 4,000-foot flume to release the overflow. Also organized in the 1850s, the Tuolumne County Water Company built several small dams in the South Fork basin and two larger ones at Strawberry and Lyons.

At the turn of the century, the builders were wiring California, and water development emphasis shifted from municipal supply and mining to hydroelectric power. The Utica Gold Mining Company installed a generator on the old Union Water ditch near Murphys, later constructing the Utica and Union Reservoirs in the canyons of the North Fork and Spicer Meadow Reservoir on Highland Creek, a tributary. Urbanites organized the Sierra and San Francisco Power Company in 1905. This was the era of Hetch Hetchy—the Tuolumne River Valley in Yosemite Park, where John Muir waged America's first great dam fight and lost to the city of San Francisco. Already the urban developers were stringing supply lines to the Sierra headwaters. The agricultural interests would follow with canals that would hook like lampreys onto every Sierra river. In the stunning land of high granite above Kennedy Meadows on a tributary of the Stanislaus's Middle Fork, the San Francisco Company built Relief Reservoir, where water was released to Sand Bar Reservoir, then channeled by flume to a powerhouse at Camp Nine.

Recognizing the need for public water systems if California was to grow, the state legislature passed the Wright Act of 1887, authorizing the establishment of local irrigation districts and offering generous provisions for bonds. Without adequate controls, the law invited abuse and fraud, and only eight of forty-nine districts survived into the twentieth century.

The lower Stanislaus districts, Oakdale and South San Joaquin, were formed in 1909. They jointly constructed Goodwin Dam in 1913, and later agreed to cooperate on Melones Dam, three-quarters of a mile above the New Melones site. After district members rejected bond proposals to fund Melones, officials garnered support from the Pacific Gas and Electric Company in the kind of public-private partnership that would become characteristic. Voters then approved the bonds, and in 1926 the dam was built; 211 feet high, holding 112,500 acre-feet of water, and producing 100.6 million kilowatt-hours of electricity in an average year, it provided 600,000 acre-feet of irrigation water per year.

The Federal Reclamation Act of 1902 had established the Bureau of Reclamation, which greatly expanded its powers under Franklin Roosevelt's New Deal. The call for a state role in water development, earlier rejected in favor of localism, also gained force.

Perhaps to prevent the federal government from encroaching on their role as water developers, perhaps in a simple continuation of old roles, the Oakdale and South San Joaquin districts planned four new hydroelectric dam sites in the 1940s and 50s: Beardsley and Donnells on the Middle Fork; Tulloch between Melones and Goodwin Dams; and Columbia, just downstream from the South Fork in the wild upper canyon of the Stanislaus. After dropping the latter site, sponsors named this the Tri-Dam proposal. The districts faced a jungle of impediments from Tuolumne County, which also wanted to develop the Beardsley site; PG&E, who eventually helped pay; and the federal and state governments. Federal agencies were split on the project in a pattern that would later intensify. The Bureau of Reclamation supported Tri-Dam. With New Melones in mind, the Army Corps of Engineers objected. As Secretary of the Army Robert T. Stevens testified to the Senate: "The Tri-Dam project would reduce the potential flood-control benefits creditable to New Melones Reservoir, with the resultant effect on the economic justification of the New Melones project possibly being so unfavorable as to postpone its construction indefinitely." In other words, you build Tri-Dam, and we might not be able to justify New Melones. But once Tri-Dam was approved and completed in 1957, the corps never raised this problem again.

That gives us at least five small dams and eleven major ones on the Stanislaus and its three forks; all the dams but the big one.

New Melones is a part of the Central Valley Project (CVP) of the federal Bureau of Reclamation. The project has been negotiated and changed, and doesn't have much to do with the CVP's main thrust of delivering irrigation water from the Sacramento basin to the arid San Joaquin Valley.

The Central Valley Project was first envisioned in the Alexander Report of 1873 to the federal government encouraging transfer of California water from wet places to dry. Under state engineer William "Ham" Hall in the late 1800s, state officials proposed developments that were rejected in lieu of local action. Water supply was a local concern, and turf was guarded with the provincial fervor more recently applied to zoning or fluoridation. Robert B. Marshall, an employee of the U.S. Geological Survey, privately published a report that he had written on his own time. The Marshall plan, grandiose and futuristic, proposed to divert Sacramento River water south in a scheme big enough to catch Californians' imagination and trigger government action. Through the 1920s, the state drafted studies that led to passage of the Central Valley Project Act by the California legislature in 1933. A Valley water lobby succeeded in putting through a statewide referendum approving the sale of bonds, but they were still stymied: the Depression bond market was in drought. When nobody would buy the bonds, Sacramento officials turned to Uncle Sam.

To initiate the CVP, Franklin Roosevelt approved $14 million of "emergency relief" funds for Friant Dam in 1936; subsequently Congress passed the Rivers and Harbors Act of 1937 authorizing the CVP's construction and operation by the Bureau of Reclamation.

Even after congressional action, definition of the project remained unclear. The Bureau of Reclamation assumed that it incorporated all the proposals of the State Water Plan, and they even proceeded to accommodate the project by augmenting California's "initial" and "ultimate" proposals. Early components were Friant Dam, Shasta Dam, the Friant–Kern Canal, and Madera Canal. Being broad in scope and containing an agglomeration of hardware, the CVP became a convenient hook where projects could be hung, half the justification battle already won. Bureau officials pointed to their open-door directive of "maximum conservation and beneficial use of the water resources of the Great Central Valley, California." More dams, power plants, pumping stations, and canals followed. More are yet to come. Maybe.

In the state's studies of the 1920s, New Melones Dam was first mentioned as a secondary site—in fact, barely discussed. Water planners found no need for the dam's conservation yield (irrigation water). The long-range State Water Plan later proposed thirteen reservoirs in the San Joaquin basin, New Melones being the largest and second most costly at $26.2 million. State planners proposed a height of 460 feet, a capacity of 1.1 million acre-feet. These figures would be juggled and mostly increased with aggrandized ambitions, generous appropriations from Congress, and the powerful influence of two federal agencies, the Army Corps of Engineers and the Bureau of Reclamation.

Established in 1795 or 1802, depending on the teller, the Army Corps of Engineers is the oldest public works agency and the largest engineering operation in the world. About 300 Army personnel and 30,000 civilians operate the civil works division, which builds dams. At any given time, the corps is working on about 300 projects: New Melones is only one of these. About 452 more are authorized, but not yet started. The corps is well entrenched, spending over a billion dollars a year.

At first roads were the main thing the corps built, but not for long. In 1852 Congress gave it responsibility for navigation—maintenance of harbors and rivers. This is how ocean freighters reach the Central Valley cities of Stockton and Sacramento. With the generosity and sympathy that followed floods in the thirties, the Flood Control Act of 1936 gave a popular job to the corps. They would try to stop the floods.

Corps responsibilities have grown, now including "investigating, developing and maintaining the Nation's water and related land resources, constructing and operating projects for navigation, flood control, major drainage, shore and beach restoration and protection, hurricane flood protection, hydroelectric power production, water supply, water quality control, fish and wildlife conservation and enhancement, and outdoor recreation," according to the corps's public information brochures.

The corps's role in California was unique because of the Gold Rush. Ravaged by hydraulic miners in the 1800s, hillsides eroded into streams, congesting them, clogging channels with mud and gravel, and creating flood hazards where none had existed. In their first display of political might, the farmers rebelled, ushering in laws against hydraulic mining in 1884. To correct the damage, state officials turned to the corps, which responded with channelization and levees that totaled 6,000 miles in 1980—San Francisco to New York and back again on a levee.

In 1927 Congress authorized the corps to do California river surveys (called "308" studies after a section of the act). Latitude was spacious. The directive: to see what the corps thought should be done. Specifically named were the Klamath, Mad, Eel, Sacramento, San Joaquin, and Kern Rivers. The corps interpreted the San Joaquin as including its tributary, the Stanislaus.

The other federal water agency is the Bureau of Reclamation, founded under the Newlands Reclamation Act of 1902 as a colonizing or settlement agency under Western enthusiast Teddy Roosevelt. The

Mother Rapid

Grapevine Gulch

Stanislaus below Bailey Falls

Stanislaus above Parrotts Ferry

Stanislaus above Grapevine Gulch

Stanislaus below Camp Nine

Rose Creek

Mother Rapid

aim was to bring families to unsettled regions of the West (the bureau operates in eighteen states), not to subsidize large farms or ranches. Safeguarding this point, the law stated that no federally supplied water would go to individuals owning more than 160 acres. But the law was often overlooked. In the Westlands water district near Fresno, the average farm exceeds 2,000 acres, agribusiness corporations being subsidized at about $1,500 per acre per year. In 1975 National Land for People (a group of small farmers) sued the federal government for ignoring the acreage requirement. The court ruled that the Department of Interior had to enforce the 160-acre provision, which prompted action by Interior Secretary Cecil Andrus and angry protests by corporations and farmers with larger holdings. With a lobbying effort costing a quarter of a million dollars per month, the corporations and large landowners won—reform legislation failed in 1980, and acreage exemptions continued.

The first multipurpose project of the Bureau of Reclamation was Boulder Dam on the Colorado River (Lake Mead) in 1928. This was also its first big project involving water to be used in California. The CVP was to become the bureau's main thrust in the state, however.

The bureau's role was expanded to include "multipurpose water development to meet diverse water needs of a maturing economy and an expanding population." That should pretty well cover it. Throughout the West, seven thousand full-time employees do this, and have spent over $8 billion, uninflated, since 1902. The bureau irrigates over 10 million acres, an area larger than Hawaii, Rhode Island, Delaware, and Connecticut combined, producing over 50 million tons of food a year. About a third of its water comes from the CVP.

Volumes speak to the history of the corps and the bureau. Glossy government literature provides the figures cited above and describes the achievements of the Army Corps of Engineers and the Bureau of Reclamation: 10 million irrigated acres; 646,000 California jobs; the Ohio River navigation system, which serves more commerce than the Panama Canal; and so forth. Other analysts have argued that flood-control expenditures by the corps have heightened flood damage; that more people drown in flood-control reservoirs than in floods; that bureau water is used to raise crops that the Department of Agriculture pays other farmers not to grow; but this is not my story. It is not my story that the corps's canals bankrupted railroads, which must be subsidized by the government to keep running; and that some bureau projects have dug up and drowned more farmland than they have irrigated. New Melones is a long story by itself.

In bureaucratic competition, the corps and the bureau both developed plans for New Melones; they fought over the right to dam this river. What with thunderstealing and one-upmanship between the agencies, the project grew and grew and grew.

The corps recommended a .45 million acre-foot (maf) reservoir. The bureau criticized the plan, recommending 1.1 maf to "conserve all possible water for irrigation, municipal and power use." (Eighteen percent of the CVP's East Side Division was to have been New Melones yield, but the East Side Canal has not been approved due to economic problems, including a lack of demand for the water.) The corps responded that the reservoir "should be constructed in such a manner that it can be raised in the future to provide the capacity proposed by the Bureau."

The corps's proposal for .45 maf was pushed by Congressman Alfred J. Elliott and was authorized by the Flood Control Act of 1944, six years before Mark Dubois was born. Approved cost: $6.1 million. As the act's title indicates, the purpose was to control floods. This was the key interest of the dam's supporters—riverfront farmers and the city of Stockton. Less than two months after authorization, the chief of engineers exercised his discretion and increased the project to 1.1 maf, later adding an unauthorized power plant as well. The corps still stressed flood control; the bureau still wanted irrigation. Battling between the federal superagencies intensified as each went public. Against the bureau's argument for greater irrigation use, Major General Thomas Robins replied, "If California would wake up and get the water first and then decide what to do with it she would be better off." Almost thirty years later, in Decision 1422 of the State Water Resources Control Board, the state of California would admonish the federal government for this strategy of act now and plan later.

Local groups, fearing a federal takeover and the 160-acre limitation, had no time for the bureau. The irrigation districts refused to die in a federalist era, still preferring to do the job themselves, the way they were handling Tri-Dam.

While the corps and the bureau sniped at each other and boosted their proposals, the Eisenhower era of fiscal accountability was reflected by Congress, which rose against the big bureaucracies. Eisenhower called Bureau of Reclamation projects "creeping socialism." Meanwhile, the state of California, finding that New Melones irrigation water was not needed, estimated the dam's benefit/cost ratio at .73 (for $1 spent, only 73 cents would be returned). It was not the last time that California would blow the whistle on the rambunctious federal developers.

The economics of New Melones were looking grim. The project had been authorized at $6.1 million, and by 1953 it was tagged $47.8 million (in 1978, the cost of the complete dam would total over $341,000,000; $1.2 billion with 7 percent interest over 100 years included). An economy-minded Congress directed that no construction should take place until the project's economic justification was determined, and in 1954 the corps reported that New Melones was in a "semi-deauthorized state."

All seemed quiet on the Stanislaus. A lull is common during times of unfavorable politics, and government builders are accustomed to waiting while politics change. Eisenhower would go; Kennedy would come in. And the economics of the problem would change too—at least on paper.

While the corps talked about New Melones being in a "semi-deauthorized state," they worked on a new justification. In 1957 they released an economic feasibility study for a 1.1 maf reservoir, expanding hydroelectric benefits and increasing income from irrigation. Interestingly enough, the new water yield doubled the 1949 figures with no increase in reservoir capacity. The 1957 claimed yield was, in fact, larger than the yield expected of a 2.4 maf reservoir in 1978. The project's "economic justification" was thus determined, as Congress had directed. Benefit/cost footwork aside, Congressman John McFall introduced a new authorization bill for the corps.

One could say that McFall is the father of the dam. He grew up near the river. Savvy is local politics, the young Democrat became mayor of the farming town of Manteca, later serving in the California Assembly. At thirty-eight, he was elected to Congress and flew off to Washington for twenty-two years, sitting on the Public Works Committee, the greenhouse of corps projects. He chaired the Transportation Appropriations Subcommittee, and in 1972 would be appointed House Majority Whip. McFall was the man to bring New Melones Dam to construction.

McFall's first bill failed to pass, in part due to opposition by the Bureau of Reclamation, which continued to plan for a swollen New Melones Dam of their own. Now that the corps had met the ante of 1.1 maf, the bureau increased its recommendation to a whopping 2.4 maf, halting the rising level of the reservoir just before it would submerge the Camp Nine powerhouse.

This counter-planning and bickering had gone on long enough. At this rate, nobody was going to get a dam, or, if they did, it would be increased to who-knew-what size. McFall, the corps, and the bureau negotiated. They turned to the "Folsom Formula," under which Folsom Dam on the American River was built by the corps and operated by the bureau, and reached a reasonable compromise. To avoid further opposition, the corps accepted the bureau's 2.4 maf. This was okay with McFall, who would later say, "The larger project will bring more benefits for my people." In fact, there is not much evidence that anybody but the Bureau of Reclamation cared about the size of the dam.

McFall then turned his attention to the home front. While the flood-control advocates encouraged the congressman, local opposition overshadowed them in many ways. Leaders of the Oakdale and South San Joaquin Irrigation Districts objected to the involvement of the Bureau of Reclamation. Newspapers condemned the federal presence on the principle that it was federal. The *Oakdale Leader* slammed McFall during the 1960 election: "John McFall has voted 100% in favor of those bills which limit our freedom of action on the local scene and in favor of federal domination of the local government." The foothill counties and PG&E were concerned about losing water rights or future development opportunities. Advocating local control of development, several chambers of commerce joined in opposing New Melones.

McFall argued that the big dam would provide "development of one of the finest remaining resource sites in the nation." The incumbent drew votes from beyond the Stanislaus basin and was reelected. "Opposition was largely limited to local irrigation districts who were concerned that a federal project would drain water from local counties to southern California," McFall maintains. Congressman Bizz Johnson, whose district then included Calaveras and Tuolumne Counties, joined McFall in the push for authorization.

On October 3, 1962, McFall's bill passed in the House of Representatives, and subsequently in the Senate, guided by California Senators Clair Engle and Thomas Kuchel. On October 13, President Kennedy signed the 1962 Flood Control Act, providing for New Melones and scores of other projects. The authorized cost of New Melones was $113,717,000, with the stipulation that the corps maintain an 8,000-cubic-feet-per-second channel on the lower river for flood releases. To mute local opposition, another rider reserved water for use within the "basin," with export of excess water only. A literal definition of "Stanislaus River Basin" means lands that naturally drain into the Stanislaus River. At a public hearing in 1980, however, McFall said that "basin" meant all of Calaveras, Tuolumne, Stanislaus, and San Joaquin Counties in the 1962 congressional districts of McFall and Bizz Johnson. Indecision and controversy would surround the definition, which was reduced to a political determination—the economic and political stakes were high in this question of who got the water.

Along with its size, the purposes of the dam were expanded to include irrigation, hydroelectric power, water quality, fish and wildlife enhancement, and recreation. McFall molded a broader base of support.

The congressmen had brought New Melones a long way—from .45 maf to 2.4, from single to multipurpose, from "semi-deauthorized" to authorized. This, however, did not guarantee funding and construction. Local opposition coalesced in the Stanislaus River Basin

Group. Attorney Philip Cavalero, their spokesman, argued against the massive reservoir, saying that the project was oversized and would unnecessarily drain millions of dollars from the CVP. Seventeen years later, California Resources Agency economist Guy Phillips would argue against the dam for some of the same reasons. Cavalero countered McFall with a proposal for a smaller dam. McFall's support persisted from flood-plain farmers, Stockton, and agribusinessmen who thought themselves beneficiaries of the water. But *The California Farmer* reported, "The only support for the federal project comes from organizations 200 miles south of the Stanislaus who hope to obtain any surplus water which can be exported from the watershed. . . . The only other active support is from several Congressmen who seem to want a monument to be remembered by—a $114 million taxpayer monument." In spite of the authorization, the antifederal people were entrenched. It would have stayed that way, but then came the flood.

On Christmas Day, 1964, leaden rains pounded the Valley and melted the early Sierra snow. John Hertle's description of what happened is given in the last chapter. The Stanislaus overflowed its banks, swamping farms and development on the flood plain. Damages totaled $1.6 million, mostly below Oakdale.

There is something about flooding, maybe any natural disaster, that evokes people's most generous reactions. Even in an age of taxpayer revolt, who objects when a governor or president declares a "disaster area" entitling people to government relief? After the Hurricane Agnes Flood of 1972, tens of thousands of federal grants went to the mid-Atlantic states. Owners of recreational trailers that sat along the Susquehanna River were handed $5,000 to aid their recovery. Commerce and industry used disaster checks to reopen their plants with hardware so modern that they hadn't known it existed until they went shopping after the flood. In Pennsylvania a statewide referendum to make even more money available to flood victims was passed without debate by a massive margin.

John Hertle says that the person who works the flood plain takes a risk. A risk that people tolerate: "This is our home; we can't leave this place." Digging out after floods is a tradition honored by the rest of us. People who go back, shovel the mud, and rebuild to face the next flood are described as courageous and determined, the stock that made America. The virtues of hard work, the calculated risk, and love of home are traditional values that surface whenever the floods do. Now, thanks to the corps and disaster relief, we can add the modern-day "values" of a welfare state.

"It is a view that combines arrogance and ignorance," says Lincoln Brower, ecology professor and flood-plain specialist from Amherst

College. Who are we to challenge a flooding river? Why doubt that floods will come? All you need is a hurricane; or two days of heavy spring rain; or seven, eight, or nine Hawaiian storms. Why do we keep paying the costs, over and over again? Johnstown, Pennsylvania, lost 2,200 people in a flood in 1889. Disaster hit again in 1936, the year that the corps was given the job of controlling these nuisance events. In 1977, when 87 more people were killed, the local governments didn't even have flood-plain regulations or flood insurance. They didn't think they needed them. And they didn't, if reimbursement was the issue—the taxpayers bailed Johnstown out again. They paid to bury the dead and rebuild. "People need help, yes," Brower says, "but what kind is best? Many people could relocate if they got a different kind of help instead of relief that ties them tighter to a future of more floods."

Here along the Stanislaus, both San Joaquin County (with its county seat of Stockton) and Stanislaus County were suspended from the Federal Flood Insurance Program because they, too, didn't comply with requirements to regulate land use in hazardous areas. In Stockton, as in other areas, the attitude toward the federal government was "pay for our water projects and leave us alone." After another flood disaster—broken levees in 1980—San Joaquin County reentered the insurance program. Stanislaus County also reentered the program in 1980, after resisting requirements to regulate subdivision and to notify adjoining municipalities about channelization or man-made watercourse changes.

At any rate, the community heart goes out to flood victims. They are usually solid middle-class people. What happened to them could happen to us. They were just unlucky with God, and when you're up against those odds you deserve to have the government on your side.

John McFall seized the political leverage that only the Christmas Day floods of 1964 could provide, and urged the drenched farmers to support New Melones Dam. Early in 1965, farmers joined in the first of a series of pro–New Melones organizations. It all began, as we saw in the last chapter, when John Hertle went to the Oakdale irrigation district and inquired about flood-control plans. They didn't have much. Farmers rallied around Hertle, and when fifty of them got together, they formed the Stanislaus River Flood Control Association, electing Hertle president. "No one else would take it," he says, "so I figured I'd do this for a few years and then it would be done."

It was this issue—flood control—that inspired local support, that stifled local opposition, that led to the dam's construction. Different reservoir sizes or flood-control alternatives were not considered. The strategy was straightforward—get New Melones built. Identical resolutions asking for the dam were adopted by the association, flood-prone communities, and the California Association of Soil

Conservation Districts. Alert in times of opportunity, the corps requested $1 million to start the project. This was not good enough for McFall, who elaborated on recent flood damage and urged Congress to better the corps with $1.5 million in 1965.

With dam construction seemingly assured, some people saw opportunities for improvements on the lower river. The State Department of Fish and Game took an interest in fresh water releases to restore the lower Stanislaus fisheries, especially the king salmon. They persuaded the corps to protect the gravel spawning beds by acquiring easements from farmers along the lower river, but eighteen years after authorization, easement acquisition would still not be complete.

The California Department of Fish and Game and the U.S. Fish and Wildlife Service asked for replacement of wildlife habitat that would be lost to the 12,500-acre reservoir. After battles with landowners, tedious negotiations, and delayed approval by the chief of engineers in Washington, agreement was finally reached on the purchase of 1,800 acres on nearby Peoria Mountain.

Water-quality improvement was a major issue and one of the most technically baffling. Releases would affect the lower Stanislaus, the polluted San Joaquin (which is one-fourth Stanislaus water), and the Delta—probably California's most complex water-quality system, which is dependent on the entire Sacramento and San Joaquin basins, the State Water Project, the Central Valley Project, salt water, and the tides. Standards were set for improvements in water quality: New Melones releases would dilute the solids and salts from erosion and the farmers' fertilizer, pesticides, and herbicides. This would benefit the fisheries and add fresh water for irrigation in the lower basin and in the Delta.

In 1970 Central Valley conservationists, primarily members of the Yokuts Regional Group of the Sierra Club, saw more opportunities. Through Stanislaus River Chairman Roger Gohring, they pushed for environmental improvements and a canoe "trail," with nine new access areas and lower-river parks to be bought by the corps. John McFall would call this the "string of pearls"—but it was more a string of perils to some farmers, concerned about encroachment on their lands. The corps said they would also build a four-mile kayak run by blasting and rearranging rocks in the river near Knights Ferry. In supporting the lower-river objectives of recreation, protection of wildlife through easements, water-quality improvement, and fisheries enhancement, the local conservationists added a special flavor to the New Melones project. The corps and others looked at this as a breakthrough in cooperation between conservationists and developers.

River enhancement below a dam was considered a progressive novelty in the field of water-resources management. John Hertle said, "To a person in San Diego, it probably doesn't make much difference that this river will have fresh water in it, but it shows that the project offers something to the lower river—it isn't just destructive like some reservoirs that only take water and offer nothing in return."

John McFall said, "The thing about New Melones about which I am most proud is that this is the first project of its kind for water quality. . . . The string of pearls parks are to be discussed and sometime accomplished, a greenway is being made along the river, and it was the first time a local environmental group was involved in the planning of an Army Corps project."

Final plans by the corps called for an earthfill dam 625 feet high, 1,560 feet across Iron Canyon. It would be the sixth highest dam in the United States; the only higher earthfill dam is Oroville Dam on California's Feather River. Filled to elevation 1088 ("gross pool" level), the reservoir would hold 2.4 million acre-feet of water, drowning 12,500 acres of land (an area about the same size as the city of Santa Barbara) and twenty-four miles of river under a reservoir with 100 miles of shoreline. The backwater would extend to Camp Nine and up the lower reaches of the South Fork and Rose Creek.

The corps calculated a 1979 benefit/cost ratio of 2.3 to 1, meaning that for every dollar spent, $2.30 would be provided as a benefit to someone. As designed, the purposes of the dam are downstream flood control, irrigation, hydroelectric peaking power, downstream fishery enhancement, downstream water-quality improvement, and flatwater recreation. To calculate benefits and costs, the Army engineers dealt with annual mean precipitation and runoff coefficients, acre-feet and reservoir capacity, standard project floods and intermittent region floods, kilowatt hours and dependable capacity, conservation yield and seven-year cycles of drought, dissolved solids and dissolved oxygen, ambient temperatures and diurnal temperature changes, road relocations, land acquisition, interest rates, and on and on.

For flood control, the dam would reduce flows to a maximum of 8,000 cubic feet per second, to be kept within channels and levees. Along the lower Stanislaus, 35,000 acres of agricultural and suburban land would be protected. Farther down the San Joaquin and into the Delta, 60 percent of the total New Melones flood-control benefits would go to helping cut damage on another 235,000 acres flooded by the San Joaquin.

Claimed irrigation benefits include replacement of irrigation water from Old Melones Dam and about 200,000 acre-feet each year to irrigate new farm land or supplement groundwater on lands already cultivated. To guarantee this amount throughout a seven-year cycle,

1.4 million acre-feet in the reservoir would be reserved for irrigation.

Hydroelectric capacity is projected at 455 million kilowatt hours. This is for peaking power, available about two hours per day in the afternoon, when electricity is most needed for air conditioners. A city of 200,000 people uses about as much electricity as New Melones would provide, if it were base load power (available all the time) rather than peaking power. One hundred kilowatt hours would be used to replace the yield from Old Melones powerhouse.

For water quality, New Melones would increase lower-river flows that almost disappear due to irrigation diversions. Polluted agricultural runoff would be diluted. Dissolved oxygen would be kept at a minimum of five parts per million, and dissolved solids from salt, fertilizer, pesticides, herbicides, cattle waste, and other sources would be kept at a maximum of 500 parts per million (they sometimes go up to 750 parts per million without the dam). Like water quality, planned fishery improvements were based on an increased downstream flow and lower water temperatures, with a primary interest in restoring salmon below Goodwin Dam. Other benefits were claimed for the lake itself, where both warm and cold water fisheries are proposed.

The final authorized use of the dam—recreation—was expected to initially exceed 800,000 people per year, climbing to 3 million. Facilities would be developed for motorboating, picnicking, and camping. Under federal guidelines, "area redevelopment" was later added as a project benefit, with the corps claiming $635,000 of annual benefits from employment.

In 1977 the corps listed the projected annual benefits as follows: flood control, $3,125,000; irrigation, $3,610,000; hydroelectric power, $10,380,000; water quality, $180,000; fish and wildlife, $650,000; recreation, $1,470,000; area redevelopment, $1,185,000. Total annual benefits were $20,600,000.

Virtually all of these figures would be challenged as New Melones moved toward construction, during construction, and through debates about partial filling.

The corps wasted no time in kicking off the project in 1965. With the first appropriation of $1,500,000, a ground-breaking ceremony was held. John Hertle served as master of ceremonies. Army Colonel Robert E. Math thanked the Flood Control Association and called the appropriation "a very significant step in the transformation of the New Melones Project from a mountain of paperwork to a real mountain of rock, steel, and concrete."

Construction finally began in 1966. Flood control was the main reason for support of the dam, and the major issues in the long debate had been localism versus federalism and the Army Corps of Engineers versus the Bureau of Reclamation. New Melones supporters had encountered no opposition because of the dam itself.

The environmental movement had not yet arrived; the wilderness canyon was a secret. Like the Colorado's fabled Glen Canyon, dammed in the 1960s, the upper Stanislaus was a place that few people knew about. The first known paddlers were a group of Sierra Club members in 1960; the first commercial outfitter appeared in 1962.

During the early New Melones debate, the United States had no Environmental Policy Act requiring environmental impact statements. The nation had no wild and scenic rivers system, no wilderness system, no coherent water policy. When plans were completed for the demise of the canyon, the green-and-white dynamo of a river, and the marble-cobbled beaches below 800-foot walls of white limestone, almost no one cared about the place, and nobody questioned the logic and validity of the corps's calculations. In all this debate over New Melones Dam, no one mentioned the place to be flooded, the land to be buried beneath hundreds of feet of slackwater. Nobody, that is, until Gerald Meral.

CHAPTER FOUR

For the River

Like many people in California, he came from somewhere else. Gerald
Meral grew up in Detroit, where whitewater churns only in laundry
tubs. The Boy Scouts introduced him to canoeing at age twelve. Later,
from the University of Michigan, he explored alder-bounded
streams—the Rifle, Pine, Père Marquette, and Au Sable. Meral's
paddling and rivering took a leap forward when he journeyed east to
Pennsylvania State University to do graduate work in biology. The
school is tucked away in the middle of the Appalachians, creek-by-jowl
with rock and rapid infested waters. The Moshannon was just over
Bald Eagle Mountain. The Lehigh and the North Branch of the
Potomac were a few hours drive away. The Youghiogheny, just
discovered by the river crowd, diverted Meral weekly. He began
paddling a C-1—a one-person whitewater canoe.

People mistake these boats for kayaks. They look much the same,
but with essential differences: the C-1 seems to sit higher on the water,
more of a mallard than a merganser. The paddler kneels instead of
sitting on the floor, and he strokes with a single-bladed canoe paddle
instead of the kayaker's double-blade. Mastering the whitewater canoe
is difficult at first, but a skilled C-1 paddler can tackle parlous water
with any kayaker. Some boaters prefer the C-1 because, being higher,
they see more of the holes and hard places ahead, but it is mainly
preferred because it is a canoe. Heritage and pride has sneaked into
this sport. A canoe culture thrives in this country, and Jerry Meral is
part of it. I ask him why he paddles a C-1. "Everybody at Penn State
paddled C-1's. I grew up with canoes. Why paddle a kayak?" he
asks me.

A canoe is almost the mark of an easterner. This is changing—canoes
are afforded new respect, and as the western whitewater crowds seek
new challenges, they will turn to the open canoe. In five years' time,

the rapids of California will be choked with these traditional boats, but for today almost everybody on western rivers travels by kayak or raft. So if you notice a C-1 on a Sierra river, there is a good chance that you are looking at Jerry Meral.

Like most active outdoorspeople, he is trim. Medium height and fairly broad, but not beefy, shoulders. Even when still, Meral gives the impression of a man in motion. His disheveled, curly auburn hair seems constantly swept back by the wind. Sitting at his desk, he seems headed downriver against an afternoon breeze. His beard is wiry and also blown back. His eyes are animated, coordinated with the tone of his voice. He is friendly, open, but businesslike; he moves quickly, and you can tell that he has a lot going on—a busy man.

The University of California had a good PhD program in zoology, and after graduating from Penn State, Meral emigrated to Berkeley, where the Detroit native would write a thesis about some fish from Costa Rica. In August 1967, the day after he arrived in California, he decided to go canoeing. Where? What is the West Coast equivalent of the Youghiogheny or the Cheat? Good whitewater he wanted. "I didn't know much of anything about rivers out here, so I called this guy named Scott Fleming who did Sierra Club outings. It turned out that a trip was planned for that weekend on a river called Stanislaus," Meral says.

Back then, Camp Nine to Parrotts Ferry was viewed as a difficult run. Being a responsible leader, Fleming wanted to be sure Meral was competent. Many western outdoorsmen seem to think of all easterners as dudes. "We talked it over," Meral recollects, "and decided it would be okay for me to go along." Okay indeed. Meral's C-1 descent of the Grand Canyon was preceded by only one other canoeist, his Pennsylvania paddling buddy John Sweet. And Meral was the first canoeist to paddle the whole canyon to Lake Mead. Meral was accomplished in running the Appalachian rivers, which are not so much water as rocks and steep stairs with you-better-get-off-your-ass left and right in between. Boaters call it "technical water." His leisure had been the New and Cheat Rivers of West Virginia, center of North American whitewater. Meral would do the first descent of the upper Tuolumne; the second of the now popular Clavey Falls reach, where the put-in was not yet named. It is now called Meral's Pool. Meral would be no risk on Sierra Club outings. Around flowing water, he would be a risk only to those building dams.

During the Stanislaus trip, a Sierra Clubber mentioned New Melones. He didn't say much, but it was enough to set Meral's eyes flashing. The whitewater biologist was ripe for a cause. "The Earth Day era was coming, and at Berkeley it was easy to get caught up in activism," Meral reflects. "I heard that a lot of good California rivers were ruined by dams. Then when I got here I saw it happening. First the Stanislaus. Then I learned the Tuolumne was threatened too."

The other paddlers thought that it was too late to save the Stanislaus. They would go elsewhere, if they could find an elsewhere. The Army Corps of Engineers would build the dam. Forget it. Who could buck the corps, a superagency with a billion dollars a year? Meral and a small group of boaters stoked their courage as if to run Clavey Falls and confronted a spokesman for the Army, who verified the theory of bureaucratic inertia—the project had come a long way, and it was too late for changes. But Meral was fresh to the scene—too green to give up, and too taken by that special place in the Sierra foothills. He had been washed by the Stanislaus up to his hairy neck as he crashed through Bailey Falls at high water—6,000 cubic feet per second—with only his face and paddle cutting air. Besides, he had not been involved in conservation battles, and knew no better. He didn't care about the odds. The odds had been against him leaving Detroit; against him making it down the Grand Canyon in one piece. Poor odds? Meral thrived on them. Little did Meral know that this initial opposition to New Melones Dam would grow and be heard around the country as a protest for rivers.

Meral joined the River Touring Section of the Sierra Club's Bay Area Chapter. Through the American River Touring Association, he met David Kay, a midwesterner who had also journeyed to Berkeley. Kay did public affairs work for ARTA, then managed the place. Later he would direct educational programs at the Environmental Defense Fund. Today there is a short quote on Jerry Meral's office wall by David A. Kay, who has returned to the Midwest: "Somewhere,/In the heart of man,/Is a place for wilderness."

While Meral's name was most known in the early days of the dam fight, Kay also played an important role. "Jerry had the facts," said Mark Dubois. "Dave, being gregarious, could involve people, and he knew how to describe the beauty and love of the river. Together they were able to kick the Stanislaus fight off with enthusiasm."

The two saw Norman B. ("Ike") Livermore, the head of the Resources Agency, appointed by Governor Ronald Reagan. Livermore had confronted the corps over the wildlife habitat that the dam would destroy: "It appears to me it should be the Corps' responsibility, in view of these clearly stated public goals, that if such mitigation, protection and enhancement measures are not incorporated in a given project or cannot be provided for in the same general region of the project, then the project should not be constructed." In other words, no habitat replacement, no dam.

Meral's concern was not that 1,800 acres on Peoria Mountain be bought for animals. Meral wanted to save the canyon. "New Melones is a terrible project and you ought to do something," Meral and Kay told Livermore, who responded by saying that the agency was a political creation with political constraints and that local opposition to the dam was the type of leverage needed.

Here was a view that would be met with again and again. To the dam's advantage, the Stanislaus struggle was regarded by many as a local issue. Livermore said, "Go see the counties." State legislators would follow the lead of local representatives. In Washington, the Stanislaus would similarly be regarded as a state issue. The California delegation, and in particular the Central Valley congressmen, would be all important. The river people were challenged to make the Stanislaus a statewide and nationwide issue; to convince people that everyone had a stake, that the river was nationally significant, and that federal tax dollars for New Melones were coming from everybody's pockets.

Disciplined in the methods of science, Meral spent nights analyzing and writing reviews, first targeting questions of local impact. He came up with the heretical notion that the project would be an economic burden, not a benefit, to the local people. They would suffer the disruptions of a construction boom and bust, with 683 workers coming and going in four years. After that, local communities would be inundated by motorboaters, highway bills, trash piles, and other demands for public service. Except for realtors, gas jockeys, and sheriff's deputies, who would get more business, the residents wouldn't get much of anything in return.

Meral's theories would be verified. A study by the California Employment Development Department would indicate that seven employees would operate the dam—not exactly a stimulant to local commerce. Thirty-seven people were expected to work on reservoir recreation during summer, compared to 150 or more who would be laid off by the rafting companies. Because of corps plans for stores at the lake, David Brennan of the local Economic Development District would later say, "there probably would be very little economic benefit to local merchants." A report by Brennan's agency would conclude that $10 million of local money would be needed by Calaveras and Tuolumne Counties to accommodate reservoir-induced traffic. Floyd Harris of the Calaveras County Chamber of Commerce would say that economic benefit from new visitors would be more than offset by traffic congestion. Calaveras County would have to deplete its highway budget for years by paying $1 million for the Parrotts Ferry Road realignment. Tuolumne Sheriff Wallace Berry would request six new deputies to handle the influx of visitors.

Kay and Meral scheduled meetings with the Tuolumne and Calaveras County Boards of Supervisors in 1969. "We made a terrible mistake in not coordinating with the Mother Lode Chapter of the Sierra Club," Meral regrets. "We invited them to come, but I didn't know anything about the politics of the club: chapters, groups, the national office, and everybody's different opinion." He shrugs his shoulders. The Mother Lode Chapter included the Yokuts Regional Group, which was deeply involved in supporting New Melones Dam and pushing downstream benefits. The split would generate confusion and division when the national Sierra Club opposed New Melones. Some local members remained steadfast in support of the dam and quit the club, including Alex Hildebrand, national Sierra Club president in 1954.

John Hertle heard about Meral's plan and warned the corps, urging that it be represented. Seems the dairyman missed nothing. The Tuolumne and Calaveras meetings marked the opening gun of the real Stanislaus fight. This was no petty battle over who would build the dam, corps or bureau, locals or federals. No negotiation over the use of reservoir water to dilute pollution, or the acquisition of public parks in a so-called string of pearls. Meral started the struggle to save the canyon. This was consistent with the environmental movement of the late sixties and early seventies, which was interested in preserving an ecosystem intact, rather than making do with proposals for development and then adding on environmental benefits.

To stoic listeners, Meral and Kay outlined their case, broaching issues that are still haggled over today. Kay spoke of the wilderness and the importance of the canyon to the local economy—rafting companies would do $2.7 million of business annually by 1978, much of the income filtering down through the local counties. Meral attacked the project from many sides, questioning the claimed benefits, arguing that a smaller dam could meet flood control needs, predicting that food surpluses and lower crop prices would result from the irrigation water, and charging that the corps overestimated flatwater recreation.

The Calaveras County leadership didn't budge. Before the 1964 flood, the county had been against a federal dam, but now that construction had begun, it was steadfastly behind it. Tuolumne County did not take issue with New Melones, though some people at the meeting did, writing to Secretary Livermore and asking for a full evaluation. With this support, Meral was successful in persuading the state to raise new questions, but Livermore's position was one of investigation, of playing devil's advocate, not of dam stopping. He was forerunner to other high officials who would oppose New Melones but stop short of decisive or risky actions to stop it. The list would grow to include the regional director of the Bureau of Land Management, an assistant secretary of the interior, the California attorney general, the chairman of the President's Council on Environmental Quality, the secretary of the interior, state senators, the governor, and the president of the United States. For strong river advocacy by the Resources Agency, Meral would have to wait a long time—until the era of limits under Governor Brown and Resources Secretary Huey Johnson, when the Stanislaus would be used as a symbol of waste and shortsightedness.

When the appeal to the local governments didn't work, Meral and Kay moved on to a new and bigger idea. They were setting a pattern: strategies for protecting the river would escalate, each unsuccessful effort spawning more ambitious, riskier ones. Meral had been involved in a Point Reyes petition drive with the eminent California conservationist Peter Behr. (Cliff Humphrey, whom Meral would oppose on New Melones, was also involved.) They had been successful; federal designation of Point Reyes as a National Seashore resulted, with protection against land development. Meral now launched a similar drive to save the Stanislaus.

This was the golden age of environmentalism. Congress passed the Wild and Scenic Rivers Act in 1968 and the National Environmental Policy Act in 1969. President Nixon scrapped the Cross Florida Barge Canal, a bôte noire of Deep South conservationists for a decade. Meral had his own black beast to slay. He and a growing band of river aficionados collected 100,000 anti-dam signatures for submission to the president. With the help of California Senator Alan Cranston's staff in Washington, Meral attempted to hand the petitions personally to Nixon's domestic aide, John Erlichman. "Stick'em in a shoebox and mail 'em in, is just about what they said," Meral recollects. The administration was unimpressed, and had other things to worry about. Round number two, lost. Local opposition didn't work. Petitions didn't work.

"What to do next?" Meral asked. The new National Environmental Policy Act mandated preparation of an Environmental Impact Statement (EIS) for any federal project. Such statements offer a way of assessing, objecting, appealing, and delaying. They give people a handle on development projects—an access point. In time, federal agencies would adopt elaborate guidelines for the preparation of statements, but in 1971 it was every planner for himself, and no one really knew what to do.

With NEPA in hand, the Environmental Defense Fund, a nonprofit nationwide organization, dragged the federal developers to court in 1971, suing the Army Corps of Engineers for an inadequate EIS on Gillham Dam on Arkansas's Cossatot River. Jerry Meral, Tom Graff, and Michael Palmer started a West Coast office of EDF the same year, and the C-1 canoeist brought the Stanislaus up. Attorneys Graff and Palmer agreed with Meral that the New Melones EIS was inadequate.

Along with the Cossatot action, the New Melones case would be one of the nation's first national environmental policy act suits to save a river.

The corps revised the draft EIS and released a report, five-eighths of an inch fat, in May 1972. Colonel James C. Donovan, regional engineer for the corps, boasted that it was "the best ever written by the Federal Government." The amount of information was impressive, and the first comments were complimentary. Then came the review by Palmer and Meral. EDF filed a lawsuit against Commissioner of Reclamation Ellis Armstrong. Palmer and Graff argued that the dam should not have been based on the Central Valley Project's unauthorized East Side Division, that the operational effects of the dam were not addressed, that economic analyses were incomplete, and that alternatives remained unexplored. Mainly they argued that the place where the irrigation water from the dam would be used was not considered. Standing with EDF were the Sierra Club, the commercial rafting companies, and individuals—including, of course, Gerald Meral. Russell Train, chairman of the President's Council on Environmental Quality, sent a letter to the Department of the Army indicating that construction should wait for a complete EIS.

The other side was formidable. Defendants included the commissioner of reclamation, the secretary of the interior, the secretary of the army, and others. Spokespeople for the dam joined in: agricultural water users, farm organizations, and the Stanislaus River Flood Control Association. The construction industry lined up: the Associated General Contractors of California, the State Building and Construction Trades Council, and the California State Conference of Operating Engineers (equipment operators). Finally, the defense was supported by local counties, cities, and individuals—including, of course, John Hertle.

Judge Charles Renfrew found the EIS inadequate because it failed to provide a "best estimate" of how the project's irrigation water would be used; however, instead of issuing an injunction as requested by EDF, the judge concurred with the corps and allowed simultaneous construction of the project and completion of the environmental statement. This illustrates what Resources Agency economist Guy Phillips calls incremental commitments. "The New Melones case is full of them, decisions which, separately, do not represent the whole project, decisions which are presumably reversible, but which lead to a point where people say, 'We can't stop *now*,'" Phillips observes.

Meral, Graff, and the others tried to halt the dam, but they failed. Meral says, "We knew NEPA was procedural—paperwork is the basic requirement—but back then we were hoping for what we called substantive NEPA, that a project wouldn't go through if the EIS showed how bad it was."

The lawsuit didn't stop New Melones, but it had an effect. The proverbial red tape delayed construction for a year. The Guy F. Atkinson construction company, the prime contractor, received 32 percent more money after the delay, even though the inflation rate in 1973 was only 6.2 percent. Most importantly, the forces of river awareness and environmental protection grew in 1973. Meral, Kay, Graff, and Palmer shattered the inhibitions against fighting New Melones. Because of *EDF* v. *Armstrong,* the public met the Stanislaus through the newspapers. But they also met it by being there.

The day of whitewater rafting had arrived. With its Stanislaus beginning in 1962, when Bryce Whitmore guided the first commercial passengers, the activity grew slowly, then flourished. It came at a time when people were searching for escape, for excitement, for the natural world. The 1960s and 70s saw a generation that was not satisfied to watch athletes on TV, not content as spectators, not sated with the schedule of sports in a gymnasium. Watered golf courses with groomed putting greens and motorized carts just weren't their style. They wanted to do other things. They wanted relief from security, and they found it in Rock Garden and at the Devil's Staircase. By 1972 there were a dozen rafting companies putting in at Camp Nine and taking out at Parrotts Ferry or Melones. Backpacking shops began carrying paddles, rafts, kayaks, and wet suits. Cigarette advertisements would feature mustached men of contemporary macho demeanor polluting the outdoors from a raft. George Wendt, owner of OARS, Inc. near Angels Camp, would be featured in a *National Geographic* advertisement for stamp collecting. Smiling faces in rubber boats would soon beam from the covers of *Sunset, Outside, Women Sports,* and *Sierra* magazines. Bobby Kennedy would raft the Colorado and Hudson; Jimmy Carter would risk his neck on the Middle Fork of the Salmon. Jackson Browne, Jerry Brown, and Pat Brown would raft the Stanislaus. So would film director Francis Ford Coppola. Rafting was the thing to do. For a little while, it looked as though the popularity of California kayak clinics might surpass that of est or transactional analysis (but, of course, it didn't).

Some of the Stanislaus outfitters and guides became dam fighters. "Not because running the river was their business," Dubois said, "but because they spent time on the river and began to feel it, to know it. It became our home, a part of us." Their guests saw the canyon, and the dogma of western water development was forever challenged; people would know that for every new California dam there was a price to pay. Many of those who rafted the Stanislaus concluded that the price was too high.

The Stanislaus and New Melones were also attracting the curiosity and talents of scientists and economists, who analyzed the proposal,

scrutinized its economics, and piled up evidence for the case that
Meral and Kay had begun. One of these was Dr. Richard Norgaard,
agricultural economist at U.C. Berkeley. With doctoral candidate
Thomas Parry, Norgaard—a retired Cataract Canyon river
guide—applied his discipline to the corps's claims.

Flood protection had been calculated in the 1950s for a combination
of projects—the New Don Pedro Dam on the Tuolumne, levees along
the San Joaquin, and the New Melones Dam. Benefits were then
averaged among the projects. Norgaard and Parry now argued that if
flood control had been figured just for New Melones, benefits would
be half the amount claimed. For irrigation, the corps assumed that the
water would be used for specialty crops—grapes, nuts, fruits, and
vegetables. Parry and Norgaard wrote that estimates of crop values
were high, citing a study by agricultural economists at the University
of California at Davis. For example, the engineers priced cotton at 32
cents a pound, though it was sold on the world market at only 20 cents.
Increased energy from hydroelectric power was figured as a benefit,
yet increased energy for irrigation pumping was not added as a cost.
For recreation, new flatwater activity was rung up as an advantage, but
the loss of river recreation was not considered. Benefits for water
quality were counted twice, Parry and Norgaard noted—once under
water quality and again under fisheries enhancement. Finally, they
addressed the discount rate: 3⅛ percent interest was applied to the
project's cost, instead of 6⅞ percent as recommended by the U.S.
Water Resources Council. (The pro-Stanislaus economists didn't even
mention the real cost of borrowing money in 1973, when the prime rate
was about 8 percent.) Instead of a total benefit-cost ratio of 2.5 to 1, as
claimed by the corps in 1962; 1.7 to 1, as claimed in 1973; or 2.3 to 1, as
claimed in 1979, Parry and Norgaard calculated a ratio of .31 to 1—a
miserable 31 cents on the taxpayer dollar.

Along with the Norgaard analysis, other information was collected,
other issues were raised. The dam fighters had become more
knowledgeable, their arguments more sophisticated, in contrast with
the day when rhetoric had been the ammunition of a dam fight. During
the very first struggle on the neighboring Tuolumne River in 1913, John
Muir had thundered against the proponents of O'Shaughnessy Dam
that finally flooded the Yosemite-like Hetch Hetchy Valley: "These
sacred mountain temples are the holiest ground that the heart of man
has consecrated. . . . These temple destroyers, developer devotees of
ravaging commercialism, seem to have a perfect contempt for Nature,
and instead of lifting their eyes to the God of the Mountains, lift them
to the Almighty Dollar. . . . Dam Hetch Hetchy! As well dam for
water-tanks the people's cathedrals and churches, for no holier temple
has ever been consecrated by the heart of man." In the Grand Canyon
dam fight of the 1960s, the *New York Times* carried a full page ad by the

Sierra Club asking, "Should we flood the Sistine Chapel so tourists can get closer to the ceiling?" But nowadays it takes more than righteousness and wilderness morality. It takes figures, ratios, tables. You want to fight a dam? Then you argue about diurnal temperature variation and dependable hydroelectric capacity. It is a war of statistics and everybody has his own. The river enthusiasts began digging, and they found what they were looking for.

Flood control: the project might benefit as few as 150 farmers along the river. It would be cheaper, the river people argued, to buy the flood plain ($70 million at $2,000 per acre in 1973) than to build the dam. Recreation: eleven reservoirs (plus the Delta) are within fifty miles; all but two are closer to San Francisco and/or Sacramento than New Melones. Fisheries enhancement: the California Department of Fish and Game did not oppose the reservoir, but stated that due to lower springtime flows, salmon population would be reduced to 10 percent if the reservoir were operated as proposed by the Bureau of Reclamation for full power and irrigation deliveries. Irrigation: a New Melones dam of 2.4 million acre-feet would yield only 200,000 acre-feet each year for irrigation. The American River's Folsom Dam, in contrast, holds only 1 million acre-feet and yields about 1.3 million acre-feet. This comparison would later lead Mark Dubois to his orange juice analogy: "At first, you squeeze and you get lots of juice, but the longer you squeeze, the less juice you get. Down to the rind, there's still some moisture, but it isn't worth the squeezing."

You want to fight a dam? Then you hire a hydrologist like Dr. Philip B. Williams, a San Francisco Englishman who studied the costs and benefits of the energy to be generated by New Melones. From the projected average year's 430 million kilowatt hours (kwh) of electricity, Williams subtracted hydroelectric power costs: 33 million kwh for construction and maintenance; 100.6 million kwh lost from the flooding of Old Melones Dam and powerhouse; the petroleum equivalent of 160 million kwh to be used for reservoir recreation; and 140 million for irrigation and pumping. Williams's bottom line? A net loss of 3.9 million kwh per year. "The main point," Williams stressed, "is not specific figures, but that 430 million kwh of energy to be produced is not the whole story. We need to look at the energy costs as well as production."

In a separate study, Williams analyzed theories concerning reservoirs and seismic activity. Koyna Dam in India, Lake Kariba in Zambia, Lake Mead in Arizona, and Hsingsengkiang Dam in China showed more and/or larger earthquakes after dams were filled. Geologists theorize that large impoundments trigger earthquakes due to weight and bedrock seepage of water, which may grease fault lines. (New Melones Reservoir, if full, would weigh 3¼ billion tons, not

counting the dam itself.) Near Oroville, home of America's highest
dam, a major earthquake—5.7 on the Richter scale—struck in 1975,
shaking the Department of Water Resources office in Sacramento,
and giving 700,000 people downstream reason for apprehension.
Stanislaus River advocates argued that seismic safety should be
addressed. Promoting safety, they would later cite the Bureau of
Reclamation's massive Idaho disaster at Teton Dam, which burst
without aid of earthquake, killing eleven people and scouring a Rocky
Mountain ranching valley for eleven miles. "Why extend a heritage of
dam disasters in California?" the river people asked. St. Francis Dam
in the San Francisquito Valley north of Los Angeles broke in 1928,
killing as many people as the legendary San Francisco earthquake.
Baldwin Hills Dam, near Culver City, partially collapsed in 1963; Hell
Hole Dam on the Rubicon River broke in 1967; the San Fernando Valley
earthquake brought about the near-failure of two dams in 1971.

Answering the allegations, the corps reanalysed the dam, "with no
preconceived opinion that construction of New Melones Lake should
be continued." While the challenges of Norgaard and others were not
directly addressed, the benefits claimed in the earlier Army studies
were again stressed. "Safety from flooding in the downstream areas
will promote better health, improve general living conditions, and the
economic gains will benefit the community by improving the standard
of living," it was reiterated. "The general effect will be to provide
opportunities for a greater number of recreation experiences in
the region."

"If the adopted plan for New Melones were to be revised
substantially, or if the project were to be abandoned, most of the
investment of public funds to date would be foregone," the corps
asserted. Incremental commitments, somebody said a while back. In
conclusion, Colonel Donovan reported, "I find that even if it were not
possible to completely mitigate the loss of the upstream whitewater
area, continued construction and completion of the New Melones Lake
would provide economic, social, and environmental benefits of such
magnitude that they would be a desirable tradeoff for the
environmental loss incurred."

Meanwhile, Meral remained a nemesis, jabbing with scores of letters
about any aspect of the dam. Details. He went up the tiniest feeder
streams of corps activity to find something wrong. You name it, Meral
raised hell about it. To the assistant secretary of the interior: "Several
rare and perhaps unique species are being endangered. As the area has
not been adequately studied, there is a very good possibility that other
rare and as yet unknown invertebrates may be within the project
area." To Colonel Donovan: "We note that the price of gold has not
only been raised officially by the U.S. Government, but has increased

notably on the foreign markets. This will undoubtedly mean increased viability for various mining operations." Meral and the miners were unlikely bedfellows, but help is where you find it. To George Weddell, corps chief of engineering: "We are glad to see that no clearing of any kind is proposed for the area between Camp Nine and Parrotts Ferry Bridge. We are disturbed, however, to see that clearing is planned for part of the river between Parrotts Ferry and Highway 49. This area is heavily used for river recreation, and should not be cleared as long as river recreation is continuing."

While the EDF case was still under litigation, another issue was debated, one that would temporarily prevent the federal government from filling the dam, and would work its way to the Supreme Court of the United States, prompting a landmark decision on states' rights.

Under 1967 California legislation, the State Water Resources Control Board (SWRCB or water board) is empowered to regulate the storage and withdrawal of surface water. They assign appropriative water rights, deciding who gets what. Going back to the Water Commission Act of 1917, a constitutional amendment in 1928, and other legislation, it is well established that water rights in California are assigned only if there is a "beneficial use" in the public interest. The SWRCB has authority to decide what the public interest is, and how it is to be served by water from rivers and reservoirs.

Nobody was exempt from the board's purview, not even the giant waterboy of the West, Commissioner of Reclamation Ellis Armstrong himself. Fifty-one bureau of reclamation applications were reviewed between 1938 and 1975. Though the board's authority remained unchallenged, the issue of state versus federal rights was near kindling and needed only a good flinty issue. Decision 1379 of 1971 established Delta water-quality standards that exceed federal ones. The feds were not happy, but they complied for the time being. Likewise, Decision 1400 of 1972 required flows in the lower American River that were greater than desired by the Bureau of Reclamation, which wanted to divert the water for irrigation. After complaining to the state on these issues, the bureau representative strolled into the water board office on the eleventh floor of the Resources Agency building in downtown Sacramento and asked for a permit to flood the Stanislaus Canyon. They were in for a surprise.

SWRCB Vice-Chairman Ronald Robie, an attorney by trade, took the lead in the state review. "My concern was for orderliness of the process," he recalls. "New Melones was moving toward construction without water rights from the state." The board had been dealing with other "in-stream" issues—meaning the use of water in the rivers (for example, fish) rather than out of rivers (such as irrigation). The Delta and American River decisions and the question of water releases from the proposed Warm Springs Dam (on a tributary to the Russian River) all dealt with in-stream flow *below* dams. For New Melones, the water board would make a ruling based on in-stream values *above* a dam.

To collect information and opinions, the water board held hearings on the New Melones permit. The result was eleven volumes of transcripts. People clamored for irrigation water, flood control, fisheries, downstream water quality. Already telegraphed in the EDF suit, the key issue was irrigation water and where it would be used. Vice-Chairman Robie raised the question on the first day of the hearings: "What we are asking for is a more particular statement of the place of use, in greater detail, rather than merely the gross area. . . ." He got a procedural response from the federal solicitor, who asked if the board intended to "depart from its past practices"—meaning the board's traditional disinterest in where the water went. Robie later explained, "The board hadn't evaluated the use of water in a given area before—the feds would say, 'It's to be used in the CVP,' and the state would say 'okay.' But other cases were less critical; in other cases we didn't have the upstream river values." At first Robie was not aware of these. "The values of the canyon came to me through Jerry Meral at EDF," he says.

The board had to determine that a beneficial use existed for the water, but the bureau could not show that the irrigation yield was needed. The board would not approve storage for irrigation without contracts or commitments, and the bureau didn't have them. In large part, the place-of-use mystery goes back to early CVP plans. New Melones was originally to serve the East Side Division, which died before birth. Now the state faced a proposal to store water for irrigation without a documented need, and without the East Side Division or any other means of delivery.

A resonant "no" came from the board in Decision 1422 in April 1973. The decision states: "The Bureau has presented no specific plan for applying project water to beneficial use for consumptive purposes at any particular location." Impoundment was approved only for prior irrigation rights, protection and enhancement of fish and wildlife (downstream), water quality (dilution of downstream pollution), recreation, and generation of power. Twenty-five conditions were attached to D-1422, including the nuts and bolts of outlet pipes and tree-cutting, but the main point was that the federal government could not completely fill the dam. Not now. "It was a surprise to just about everybody," Jerry Meral said. "It was a new idea, to have a dam and not allow it to be filled." Tom Graff was less enthusiastic. "If the board had turned down the application altogether, New Melones might not have been constructed," he believes.

To this Robie responds, "If it were a private party instead of the federal government, we would have turned down the application entirely. The problem was that Congress had legislated the dam's construction. It was the water board's job to determine the public interest, but it was hard to say 'don't build it' since Congress determines the public interest, too. It seemed logical to condition the permit the way we did."

The value of the canyon was specifically recognized in D-1422. "The upper river was very important," Robie says. The decision states that the canyon is a "unique asset to the state and the nation." Further supporting upstream qualities, the board's permit prohibits "the impoundment of water in New Melones Reservoir for consumptive purposes until further order of the Board following a showing that the benefits that will accrue from a specific proposed use will outweigh any damage that will result to fish, wildlife and recreation in the watershed above New Melones Dam." In other words, even when there is a documented need for irrigation water, its value will have to be greater than that of the canyon. Governor Ronald Reagan supported the decision: "I want you to know that I agree with the Board's decision which reflects California's desire for a balance between real water needs and environmental concerns. On the basis of adherence to this decision, I continue to support the New Melones project. It will provide flood protection and at the same time make available for recreational purposes the 'white water' stretches of the river for many years into the future."

While the EDF suit mostly failed, Decision 1422 mostly succeeded in protecting the canyon—temporarily. A state agency delayed the impoundment. Colonel Donovan of the corps argued against the decision, saying that partial filling would forfeit $5 million a year in power benefits. He also warned that during a drought there would not be enough water in the reservoir to keep its stocked fish alive. After the decision, the colonel said, "We hope we can comply with the state decision and still have a viable project. . . . The decision seems to offer half a loaf of bread to everyone, and if it can be followed, I would hope the environmentalists would drop their suit against the dam." The Bureau of Reclamation fumed, however. It immediately appealed the water board's decision to federal district court.

Already New Melones Dam was a symbol—one of state authority that the Bureau of Reclamation found untenable. Robie says that the case was unique in bringing public attention to upstream values—including the whitewater, which had never been recognized in the permit process. Later, the river and the dam would become symbolic of other issues as well: inequity in water pricing, destruction of wilderness, water conservation, and more. As an example or an indicator of values, the case would attract people of many persuasions, all seeing that this was not just another dam, not just another river.

The state lost the appeal in a decision by District Judge Thomas MacBride, but countered with another appeal to the United States Supreme Court, where California won in July 1978. The high court found that the state could require operating procedures provided the intent of Congress were carried out. The majority concluded: "The legislative history of the Reclamation Act of 1902 makes it abundantly clear that Congress intended to defer to the substance, as well as the form, of state water law. . . . While later Congresses have indeed issued new directives to the Secretary [of the Interior], they have consistently reaffirmed that the Secretary should follow state law in all respects not directly inconsistent with these directives."

Did this mean that Decision 1422 and the fate of the Stanislaus Canyon were settled? Far from it. The Supreme Court remanded the details back to a federal district court. Before it could act, the State Water Resources Control Board would have to specify the type of operations that it intended to influence. To help it do this, the Bureau of Reclamation would be required to submit an operation plan to the state in the fall of 1979. After the water board's decision, the court would decide if the state's intent were consistent with the intent of Congress when it authorized the dam. If so, California could dictate levels of filling for the specified operations (for example, hydroelectric power). But the district court was in Fresno and could be expected to lean toward the bureau's view. Appeals would be likely in any event. Meanwhile, New Melones reservoir could be rising.

In the long run, the water board's decision would probably not protect the river. If commitments for the irrigation water were found, and if the board could see irrigation and hydroelectric power outweighing upstream damage, then it could grant approval. And though the board performs a quasi-judicial function, it is a political entity; pro-New Melones politics could have a lot to do with future decisions.

Even before irrigation commitments, the canyon would face hazards over the next eight years, such as flood storage, the sympathy that floods bring, and the political hoopla that trails in their muddy wake. Just after high water in 1980, the California legislature voted to strip the water board of its legislated power. If it had not been for a veto by Governor Brown, the legislature would have rescinded the critical parts of D-1422.

Faced with failure in the EDF suit in 1973, and knowing that the water board decision would not be a final cure, Jerry Meral asked the recurrent question: what to do next? In late 1973, he needed to escape the strife, to get away from frenetic work at EDF. Meral and his wife

Barbara took a long weekend on an old scenic railroad, the Skunk line that pulls out of Willits and chugs over the north coast mountains to Fort Bragg on the ocean. He sat in the train, looking out the window, thinking about what he had hoped he wouldn't think about. It was true that every time a new Stanislaus strategy was planned, it was bigger, grander, more expensive, more exploitive of the lives of the people who were trying not to exploit the river. The risk would be greater, but the need more urgent. Time was running out on this nine-million-year-old, nine-mile river. "Why not an initiative?" Meral asked himself. "Let everybody in California vote to save this river or dam it."

CHAPTER FIVE

Promise and Despair

Beginning with a gleam in the eyes of Jerry Meral, the Stanislaus initiative flourished, with 30,000 volunteers collecting half a million signatures. Mark Dubois entered the dam fight and emerged from the statewide vote as a leader and spokesman for the river people. Friends of the River was born as a campaign organization. Supporting the dam, John Hertle and others organized Californians Against Proposition 17, managed by the Los Angeles campaign agency of Milton Kramer, whose imprint on the Stanislaus issue would be indelible.

Initiatives, like women river guides, hang gliders, and Governor Jerry Brown, are a California phenomenon. Nowhere else has the plebiscite become such a part of the balloting routine. "No on 9, It's a Losing Proposition," "Yes on 8 for More Housing," "No on 11, Stop the $100,000,000 Sting," and so on. Not just any question can get on the ballot. Over 300,000 registered voters' signatures are needed to qualify. Half a dozen questions often stare at the voting Californian from an ever more complex state ballot. The most celebrated was Proposition 13 of 1978, which reduced California property taxes by an average of 56 percent.

Like candidates themselves, the initiatives are prime material for ad men who reduce complex issues to slogans on neon-lit billboards bearing only a flashy color and six words. Most of the advertising seems to urge one to vote no. It makes sense when you think about it. Questions are brought up by constituencies as a last resort when politicians don't pass a law. The lobbies that held elected officials at bay also have the money to advertise heavily against initiatives. The "Sting" referred to above was a proposed tax on oil companies. They spent $5.6 million advertising against the question in 1980, versus $405,000 from the pro oil-tax people. The oil men won. During the seacoast initiative of 1972, $1.1 million was spent by oil companies, utilities, and developers to block regulation of seashore development, versus $216,000 by the environmentalists, who won anyway. But that was 1972.

Meral's idea brewed slowly for a few weeks in late 1973. Then he took a telephone call from Robert Caughlan, who asked to talk to people at EDF about fund raising. Meral agreed to meet with representatives of Caughlan's young advertising agency, called Roanoke.

One could say that Roanoke, like a shelf of political novels, is a child of Watergate. Unlikely parentage for an alternative ad agency, but here is what happened: Caughlan collected buttons. (Still does, with better than a thousand.) During the Watergate hearings, he took a shine to Sam Ervin, senior statesman from North Carolina, chairman of the Senate Investigating Committee. Ervin had no button. A celebrity without a button makes an opportunity, thought Caughlan. He sat around and talked about it with David Oke, a writer friend who also worked in film production at Stanford. The idea was just crazy enough to work in 1973. Caughlan and Oke commissioned an artist to draw the profile of double-chinned Ervin for a poster. Captioned "Uncle Sam," the same portrait was reproduced on a T-shirt and, of course, on a red, white, and blue button. On an otherwise newsless day, July 3, 1973, gregarious Caughlan and voluble Oke called a press conference. Fifty voices of the national and international media showed up, and the formation of the National Sam Ervin Fan Club was decorously announced. In a week, Caughlan and Oke were flying to Washington to be escorted through marble halls.

Did anybody enroll? Only 50,000 people. The fan club made print in the *Los Angeles Times, Newsweek,* and dozens of other newspapers and magazines. The two men hired the hard-core unemployed—some of their best friends—to mail Ervin paraphernalia and to rake in the cash. Salaries were skimmed off the top, but this was essentially a charitable enterprise. All profits went to appropriate causes: the American Civil Liberties Union and Common Cause impeachment drives against President Nixon. Thus was born the counterculture's answer to Madison Avenue.

Roanoke's founders would develop a pattern of alternating social causes and monied clients, feeding their consciences in turn with their wallets. They used office space at the Peninsula Conservation Center, where they heard that a kindred group, the Environmental Defense Fund, was searching for a fund raiser. That's when Caughlan called Meral.

When Caughlan and Oke met with Meral and Kay; they discovered that EDF was really thinking about a fund raiser on staff, not an agency. "Oh well," said Oke, "an afternoon trip to Berkeley is not much of a loss." But at the end of the meeting, Meral's eyes shone a little and he said, "How'd you like to go down the street for an ice cream cone and talk about a different idea?" Sure, Roanoke was up for anything.

"Ever hear of the Stanislaus?" Meral asked. No. "You guys conservationists?"

"Sure, but we've never heard of the Stanislaus."

"Well we have $14,000, 200,000 names and this idea for a river initiative. Think you'd be interested?" The money was Meral's own. All of his own, without much more in sight; nobody gets rich on an EDF salary. Stanislaus outfitters would later contribute from their rafting fees to repay Meral and Keith Roberts, another contributor, but for now they were on a limb as supple as a riverfront willow.

Caughlan had never floated a river—maybe never even swum in one—but, political type that he is, a statewide campaign sounded like a challenge. Oke had fallen in love with rivers a year before, when he had happened onto a Rogue River trip with a truckload of vacationing Grand Canyon guides, the craziest guides in the business, including a boatman named Don Briggs. Oke says he believes in a karmic flow of things: the Rogue trip, the idea to see EDF, Jerry Meral's cause, a statewide campaign for the Stanislaus, each step making the next one possible. There was a flow taking him this way. Yes, Roanoke was interested.

Meral, Kay, Caughlan, and Oke met at Caughlan's home to hammer out a strategy for raising 300,000 signatures to qualify for the ballot. It was 2 A.M. when everybody went home and Oke sat down at a typewriter to draft the very first letter. "Friends of the Stanislaus." No, that wasn't it. What's the Stanislaus anyway? A Polish Saint? "Friends of the River"—that felt right to Oke.

> *Dear Friend of the River,*
> *The Army Corps of Engineers hopes you burn this letter because it's asking you to do something they don't like very much. It's asking you to keep them from destroying one of the most beautiful rivers in our state. . . .*

Meral talked to twenty people as he put the initiative idea together. Congressmen, news people, political analysts, pollsters, attorneys, environmentalists. While talking to campaign strategists, he learned that advocacy should be positive, not negative. Better to be *for* a river than *against* a dam. Hence, the wording of the ballot: the specific language of Proposition 17 sought to put the Stanislaus in the California Scenic Rivers System, coincidentally axing New Melones as designed, yet allowing for a smaller flood-control dam. Meral thought that this would minimize confusion—if you were *for* the initiative, you were *for* the river, and you voted yes. But here lay fertile ground for muddling. "Yes" for the river meant "no" for the dam, so it was imperative to keep the two subjects straight. This vulnerability to confusion would not be lost on the river's opponents; they would exploit it to the hilt.

Meral met with Ed and Joyce Koupal of People's Lobby, a Southern California-based group for political reform that had pioneered California initiatives. Koupal put Meral in touch with Dennis Vierra, a People's Lobby employee, who was hired by the river savers to manage the Stanislaus campaign.

With Vierra coordinating the effort and Roanoke publicizing it, Meral built the arguments and spoke to groups of people. "He was not your charismatic leader type, not a Mark Dubois," Oke says. "But he was good at matching up resources, making connections. He knew the players and he was good at the arguments." John Hertle calls Meral a "formidable opponent." Modesto's pro-New Melones journalist, Thorne Gray, quips that Meral and he were the only two people who understood the project. Dubois calls Meral a genius. Milton Kramer, whom we shall meet shortly, was to call Meral "unethical," an accusation directed at only one other person before this contest was done.

Meral would prepare the information, the fact sheets, the rationale against the dam, then "give it to Shakespeare"—to Oke for editing or rewriting in his hard-hitting style.

Meral signed the checks. All of them. "I'm a real tightass on money," he admits. That explains the $14,000, which must have included nickels that this man earned back in his Detroit Boy Scout days. "We were not going to go in the red. Paying the bills is a good way to keep control over things. In all the controversy, we never faced a single challenge about finances, and it's a rare political campaign that repays every loan the way we did."

Early in the effort, the Stanislaus people met the campaign staff of Jerry Brown, entering his first gubernatorial bid in a close race against Houston Flournoy. Meral had the Stanislaus question added to a poll that was being taken for Brown. The survey showed that a majority of people would support saving the river. "Based on that poll," Meral says, "I felt we should not go radically into debt on the campaign."

David Oke's first Stanislaus letter asked for only four signatures and one dollar from each circulator. Later, Roanoke asked for ten signatures each. "The signature effort was incredible," Meral reflects. "To my knowledge nobody had ever done that well on a mail-back campaign, no one ever got signatures from every county in the state, and no one ever had so many volunteers.

"In some ways," Meral continues, "dam fights are the easiest for motivating people. They're so physical—there's the river, and it will disappear if the dam is built. The river doesn't just change, it doesn't fade away slowly by pollution or development; it disappears, gone. You get one shot, you save the river or you don't. It's not like a returnable bottle bill, where you can always try again next year."

The mail-back effort was unique at the time, but didn't overshadow the conventional, street-level petitioning. Tens of thousands of signatures were collected by teams of volunteers. From these efforts, a disparate group of people joined as Friends of the River. Boatmen and ecofreaks began learning the slippery ropes of political process. From their numbers came a score of people who would be prominent in the Stanislaus battle and in California river protection for years to come.

Don Briggs was a highway engineer for Colorado. In charge of statistics and data, he managed the raw material that justified the building of more roads and bigger roads, including projects like the Red Buffalo Tunnel that would have slapped Interstate 70 into the Eagle's Nest Wilderness near Vail. Briggs worked on that, and is happy it never got built.

With the Highway Department, Briggs learned a lesson that he would recall during the Stanislaus fight. "We were doing the After '72 Needs Study. In other words, how to spend the interstate highway money after the interstates are built. I was in charge of analyzing user data and I figured that the state had only 25 percent of the future needs, local areas 75 percent. The boss said, 'We're not going to get 65 percent of the money if we have 25 percent of the needs, so let's take another look at your basic assumptions.' We revised assumptions two more times until state needs hit 65 percent."

It was Benjamin Disraeli, then Briggs the statistician who identified three kinds of lies: lies, damned lies, and statistics.

Briggs reflects solemnly for a minute. He says, "In Colorado we were just apprentices in justifying ourselves. The Army Corps are gurus of it. They increased New Melones benefits by millions through one of the greatest engineering feats on paper—they changed the life of the dam from 50 to 100 years. In the Colorado Highway Department, we could justify building a new road on Pikes Peak. The corps could justify growing bananas there."

In 1967 Briggs and his wife signed aboard a Grand Canyon raft trip for a vacation. Only a few thousand people had ever been down the Colorado River. Guided by Bob Elliot, whose father founded the American River Touring Association (ARTA), the Briggs party saw no other people. Don talked to the boatmen—all under twenty except for Elliot, who was just over. Briggs said, "I wish I had done something like this when I was a kid." He was twenty-seven.

Three years later, Briggs ceased to be married and ceased to be a highway engineer. First, the department tried to fire him for having long hair. "Down to about here," he says, holding his hand below his right ear, indicating hair no longer than Edward Kennedy's before he became a presidential candidate. "For a year we played this game where the supervisor would say 'Cut it,' and I would, but just a little bit. Then one day he said 'Cut it or leave. There's us and there's them.' Funny, I always figured there was we. He said that everybody has individual rights but everybody must conform. I knew I couldn't budge another fuckin' inch."

Briggs hired an attorney. Highway department superiors unsuccessfully attacked the engineer's competence for five hours without a word about hair. The hearing examiner ruled that Briggs could not be fired, so they shuffled him, hard hat in hand, to an outdoor job on a survey crew. "I liked it," Don says, "until the bulldozers came to the I-70 corridor that I had surveyed in the foothills west of Denver. Nothing like seeing ten D-9's follow your survey line as they obliterate the landscape."

Finally Briggs quit his job. Eagle's Nest Wilderness, long hair, bulldozers. Enough. During these years, the engineer climbed rocks. Among other walls, he scaled 1,700-foot faces of Longs Peak in Rocky Mountain National Park. The ultimate, for a climber, is Nepal, for which Briggs bought a round-trip ticket. Friends threw a roisterous farewell party, but the next morning the man woke up and said, "I don't want to go to Nepal." Why? "Who knows? But after a party like that, my excuse has to be good." He called Bob Elliot of ARTA. "If Bob hadn't answered the phone, I'd have gone to Nepal and everything would have been different." Elliot answered, and Briggs asked for work in the Grand Canyon. "Any work. Scrubbing pots and pans, blowing up rubber ducks, teaching frisbee, anything." Elliot said okay, and the highway engineer-climber became a river guide at the ripe age of thirty-one.

Briggs was walloped by the Grand Canyon. "For the first time in my life I felt that I was a part of what was going on," he says. "Always before I had a lot of questions. Down there I didn't. I was just there, just living with no past and no future. It was fabulous." He says you have to go there to know what he is talking about.

After three trips on motorized rafts, Briggs and two other guides—Peter Winn and Kent Erskine—went north to run the Rogue in Oregon, picking up David Oke and others on the way. Peter Winn would later introduce Briggs to Ron Coldwell, then Mark Dubois. Kent Erskine would introduce his Marin County mother, Marty Kent, who was to be arrested in one of two known cases of civil disobedience to save a stream from the Army Corps of Engineers.

The American River Touring Association had just started running oar-powered boats in the Grand Canyon. This appealed to Briggs, but he didn't know much about it, so in spring 1972 he took ARTA training on a Sierra river called the Stanislaus.

It was spring of 1974 and Don Briggs was in the Proposition 17 signature business. He needed a few hundred thousand, so he started at the Co-op supermarket in Berkeley, the place where everybody got their training in collecting signatures. The Co-op was good for a thousand signatures or so, but soon the campaign had to branch out.

Briggs was not much aware of the FOR organization—Meral, Vierra, Roanoke, and so forth. He was just your basic hard-core signature getter, one of many. He and Bruce Simballa worked together. Another Grand Canyon guide, Bruce wore blond shoulder-length hair and a big disarming smile, and carried a corn-cob pipe, mostly unlit. People said that he would be the perfect mountain man in movies. "Goddamn Redford took my part," Simballa said of *Jeremiah Johnson*. He would later manage the FOR headquarters in Los Angeles—or he would try, in that massive blurred landscape of people and freeways that defied FOR organization.

"Bruce and I started moving our card table around," Briggs said. "We got on a bus and crossed the bridge to Market and Powell, then hit the financial district in San Francisco. Positive river energy was flowing. You know what I mean? You went for whatever you could get. What the hell. It was fun. A challenge." Boatmen never got so much culture: a Greek festival in Oakland, a Jewish bazaar in the Clement district of San Francisco. They hit the Marin Bluegrass Festival near San Rafael: "First day we had to pay. Then we figured out that employees had white caps, so we got a few and wore them through the gate on the second day." Briggs tipped his bogus cap as he breezed through the gate. Simballa's toothy smile was undeniably authentic, and Gracielle Rossi whisked through in between them. "We'd say, 'Save the Stanislaus.' People would sign and say, 'Have a beer,' or 'Have a joint,' and this went on all day." Briggs touches his brow at the memory. "We did Al Jolson routines to attract attention. It got so nobody escaped." If Briggs or Simballa bought a six-pack of beer, a package of tortillas, or a roll of duct tape for boat repairs, they got the cash register clerk to sign.

"The Starry Plough Bar in Berkeley was packed on Saturday nights. We looked around and didn't see faces anymore. We saw signatures. It was that bad. I said, 'How should we do it, Bruce?' Simballa said 'A skit.' So we got a shovel and hard hat out of the car and borrowed an army coat from some Starry Plough hippy." Creative drama followed. Briggs and Simballa played the role of the river and trees, and Bob Melville did duty as a general in the Army Corps of Engineers. "The piano player got into the melodrama, and when it was all done we gave a final pitch and everybody in the place elbowed up through the peanut shells to sign."

During the signature drive, Mark Dubois started on the dam fight. He had gone caving just after high school, and cavers take to limestone like hippies to the Fillmore during that year, 1967. In California, limestone means the Stanislaus Canyon.

The gangly seventeen-year-old stood on a white outcrop overlooking Mother Rapid, when an older friend said, "Down below they're building a dam." Californians grow up looking at reservoirs from pull-offs labeled "scenic overlook." Even with one-to-one slopes, bathtub rings, and mudflats, reservoirs are embraced as a form of beauty. Through the promotional hype of chambers of commerce, tourist associations, the Army Corps of Engineers, and the Bureau of Reclamation, reservoirs have become a definition of scenery. "So this will be another one," Dubois said. "Too bad, but dams are what we build in our society."

Then in 1970, David Kay, manager of ARTA, was stirring up the ranks of the guides, Dubois included. First, Meral's petition-in-a-shoebox to Nixon. After that, send letters. Send postcards. To Ike Livermore. To the Office of Management and Budget. To the General Accounting Office. To the editor of the *Sonora Daily Union Democrat* ("the DUD").

"Most river guides really weren't into knowing they could do something about the dam," Dubois remembers. "Now and then, we'd try to write letters, but most of us didn't think we could do it. I'd finish guiding a trip, and I'd say, 'Forgot to ask the passengers to write letters at the lunch stop.' Or I just wouldn't do it. The canyon is so beautiful and everybody has so much fun. Who wants to stop and talk about something like politics that most people think is ugly? Most people just didn't feel comfortable asking for letters.

"I heard about the state water board, but didn't know what it was. We went to the San Francisco Federal Building when the EDF suit was being heard, but it was these lawyers talking in ways we couldn't understand. I looked around and there was this nice man, Colonel Donovan. He was supposed to be the bad guy, and I couldn't relate to it very well."

With some river friends, Dubois went to a California Water Commission meeting in 1973. "It was all these old guys calling each other by their first names. I didn't know much about it, but it seemed like they were giving away projects to each other. 'Okay, we approved yours, now how about mine?' Then there was this other man. He got up and spoke for long-term vision. He said that the costs for pumping water would become prohibitive, that the Arab oil embargo was only the beginning. He said that until the price for using water reflects the cost of providing it, it will be wasted, and we don't have enough to throw away. He was dressed well and spoke clearly and was an encyclopedia of facts. He asked for a smaller flood-control dam at New Melones. One gray-haired member was snide and said that big floods can't be stopped by small dams. The younger man whipped back figures on runoff and reservoir size, saying that his alternative would hold any flood since the Pleistocene, when the glaciers melted. I asked who this guy was and somebody said, 'Jerry Meral.'"

So the two met. Dubois was slowly being drawn to the issue that would consume his life for years. News of Dubois had already reached Meral. "I heard about this tall guy and his brother who knew the caves." Meral asked Dubois to do a cave report for the Sierra Club.

Late in 1973, Meral and Kay spoke to an association of Stanislaus outfitters, asking for a dam-fight contribution of $2.50 from each river-trip customer. Since outfitters had already publicized their prices, the FOR donation would come straight out of profits. The river companies all agreed anyway. Dubois, Fred Dennis, and Ron Coldwell were there as unofficial outfitters since they were running the free etcetera trips for center-city youth. After the meeting, Meral asked Mark if he would be Sacramento coordinator for the Prop 17 qualification drive.

"How do I coordinate?" Dubois asked.

"You call up people and ask them to do things."

"A few hours a day?"

"Sure."

Other coordinators would be Gracielle Rossi for the Bay Area and Karen Klotz and Chuck Papke for Southern California.

Early in 1974, Mark and David Westphal gathered some river friends for a meeting with Dennis Vierra. "We were real enthused, but this guy sounded like a used car salesman and we wondered, 'Is this the way you save a river?' Vierra was real good at organizing though, and started us with the tools we needed." He told them how to get signatures. Where to go. Who to call. He gave them brochures titled "Deliver the River." They collected clip boards and card tables—the accouterments of Briggs and Simballa. But Mark's style was different. He never used white caps or hard hats or a hippy's army coat. He didn't have the craziness of a Grand Canyon guide. He would never ask for anything for himself—but he could get people to do things for this river of his.

"We went to a Joni Mitchell concert and collected hundreds of signatures. Then we went to a hard-rock concert and collected none. We really found there is a difference in the kind of crowds." This was taking more time than Meral had said. Dubois has worked mostly sixteen-hour days ever since he said yes to Meral. Streams of people were traveling through the Dubois house, FOR's Sacramento headquarters, where Mark lived and his father tried to. The neighbors wondered what was going on. Mark moved to a 23rd Street downtown apartment with Dave Westphal, who was sharing the leadership.

In a flurry, the Sacramento group beat the quota of signatures that Vierra had assigned. Dubois will take only a small part of the credit. "Doing it alone, I wouldn't have made it, but with Dave, we did." On June 27, 1974, FOR delivered 348,000 valid signatures to the California secretary of state. They qualified; then an additional 150,000 came in. River people, dam people, newsmen, most everyone was amazed. The Stanislaus had become a major California issue.

That was one side of the campaign. Everybody was a volunteer except Vierra, Caughlan, and Oke, and they worked part time. The entire Roanoke budget was $300 per month for four months, then up to $2,500 per month in the fall.

On the other side were the dam people—John Hertle and others in the Stanislaus River Flood Control Association—who had been involved in pushing for congressional appropriations and in fighting EDF. They didn't expect the momentum of the river people. "It was a renaissance of Earth Day," Cliff Humphrey said, though this time he was to campaign on the other side.

"We really didn't pay much attention to the qualification drive," said John Hertle. "We weren't very worried about it. What we hadn't realized was that it was more than a little group. It was a surprise to us that they made it."

Suddenly the river people had power, won by extraordinary and creative means, with some outrageous grassroots tactics. They were using the political system in a new style, distinctly their own, one that the Valley people did not identify with power. The river people had neither much money nor high influence. They were young, and looked like hippies, but the rag-tag river band had become a force to reckon with. What had they done to deserve power, to earn it? It was beyond the understanding of the dam people, who were guided by the massive inertia and conventional wisdom of California water development, by persuasive economic incentives, and by personal contact with politicians who were old friends. New Melones supporters held a traditional outlook on the control of nature for the benefit of man through the economy. The dam people blamed the controversy entirely on the commercial rafting companies. "Anybody who cares that much about the rapids must be concerned about money," said Fred Pollis from the Central San Joaquin Water Conservation District.

"It was a river, not love of money or jobs that was moving us," says Dubois. The people of the Valley and people of the canyon were generations apart, and now they would fight it out.

"We looked all over for somebody to carry our ball," John Hertle says. "Water groups, the chamber of commerce. We ended up realizing that we'd have to form a new, private group, but organized labor, the engineers' associations, and the chamber of commerce helped." To get started, a series of meetings were called, including one sponsored by the California Chamber of Commerce in Sacramento, where a whole cadre of water developers attended: the Bureau of Reclamation, New Melones contractors, the State Conference of Operating Engineers, the Association of California Water Agencies, the California Water Commission, and more. The Bureau of Reclamation stressed the need for "considerable and immediate funding." The immediate part would be provided through a $27,000 loan by John Hertle. The considerable part would come from contractors and big industry.

Californians Against Proposition 17 was formed at a meeting of contractors, union representatives and others at San Francisco airport. It was decided to hire a professional campaign management firm to fight the river people. This introduced one of the most dynamic and controversial figures on either side of the Stanislaus struggle, Milton Kramer.

"The guy knew what he was talking about, and he could run a low-budget campaign. That's why he was hired," says John Hertle. "A couple of the unions liked him. Other ad men were slicker, downtown types who wouldn't be that good for the general public."

"When he was hired he knew nothing about the issue, but he learned fast," says veteran Modesto journalist Thorne Gray.

"Out of all the characters in the Stanislaus campaign, he is the only one who really attracted anger and spite," says Dick Roos-Collins of FOR.

After Kramer accused Jerry Meral of being "unethical," Ron Robie said, "I don't pay much attention to what he says."

State economist Guy Phillips agreed with Robie. Responding to Kramer's general style, he says, "He's a PR hack."

"He's a professional," says Cliff Humphrey. A professional what? "He's spent a lot of time." Pause. "He's a professional PR person. He realizes there are ways to appeal to people. He is that kind of person, and on this issue he has become somewhat emotionally involved."

"He's a savvy, tough, dedicated guy," continues Hertle. "He will not work on an issue he doesn't believe in. He's like a bulldog and won't

Milton Kramer

Cliff Humphrey

John Hertle

Photo of dead fish used by Californians Against Proposition 17 in
campaign literature.

Californians Against Proposition 17 billboard

New Melones Dam

let go. He's had offers for better pay, but he won't take them." Kramer received $31,792 from Californians Against Proposition 17 between July and December 1974.

For myself, I say Kramer's good at what he does—getting people to vote the way he wants them to. Getting politicians to see it his way. And I find Roos-Collins's comment confirmed most everywhere.

Kramer is of medium height, heavy at the middle. The bushiness of his eyebrows is outstanding, and would no doubt be his leading feature to a political cartoonist. He is balding, and his remaining grey and black hair is slicked back tight against his head, further accentuating his eyebrows. When not expressing a jovial greeting or vituperative anger at those who disagree on the subject of a certain dam, his eyes have a saddened, bassetlike look. When lobbying or on TV, he dresses conservatively. Brown suit, tie. In his office, in a bank building in downtown Stockton, he wears an old knit shirt and older dress pants. This is the non-downtown look that Hertle referred to.

Milton Kramer was raised near Bishop, on the east side of the Sierra. While his address is Beverly Hills, he returns to the east slope often as a trout fisherman, setting his dry-fly in Glass Creek and Rush Creek. His eyes light up when he talks about it. He goes back in, away from the people. He loves it there. He has not seen the Stanislaus from Camp Nine to Parrotts Ferry. "But I've seen pictures of it from top to bottom," he says. "It's just another lower Sierra River. It's totally regulated by dams. If you want to see a natural Sierra River, look at the Cosumnes."

Kramer also fishes the upper Owens River. He says that his father was in on the dynamiting during the Owens Valley water war back in the 1920s, when William Mulholland's stupendously massive water delivery plan was put into action. Los Angeles stealthily bought water rights to the Owens River, then diverted it southward. The locals caught on late and dynamited the aqueduct, precipitating a vigilante struggle, in which LA detectives toted Winchester rifles and had orders to kill. The detectives won, Owens Valley lost, and today the city of Los Angeles gets 80 percent of its water from Owens Valley—Kramer's homeland— now reverted to desert.

He studied history and political science at UCLA. Watergate had nothing to do with the start of his campaign-advertising firm. It began in 1956, when Kramer represented a group of independent oil producers against major oil companies. I ask who some of his clients have been. "Ad hoc committees," he answers without elaboration. I ask what some of the issues have been. "Water issues," he says.

"My fundamental feelings go with the ecosystem concept," Kramer offers. "The only sound environment is a water-rich environment. New Melones will be good for the lower fifty-five miles of the river. The environmental side of this supports not putting the river in the wild and scenic rivers system. Those who want to save the nine miles upstream have a recreation argument, not an environmental argument. They overlook the fifty-five miles downstream.

"If you know something about history, the problems of the river are man-made. Before, in the summertime, the riverbed would get baked out. You didn't have the gravel spawning beds getting filled up with reeds. Twelve dams were put in, but none of them for major storage. Now, return flows [from irrigation] are warm. So how do you solve the problem? By providing year-round flow. Now we have problems of water quality, not in the Stanislaus but in the San Joaquin. Ninety percent of the salmon spawning beds are taken over by reeds and growth. One of the reasons we've lost riparian habitat is that people are farming up to the bank. Easement acquisition by the corps will stabilize the habitat. All these downriver benefits are passed off as minor considerations, but they are not.

"Seems to me that the trouble with trying to throw the banner of environmentalism around the nine miles is that the environment is not something that should be protected in its entirety; it is a matter of considering the enhancement of ecosystems which make it up. If you look at the Stanislaus and you know something about the history and background, you know that the problems are man-made as well as the whitewater.

"The real issue is, are you going to continue rafting or not? The nine miles represents nothing more or less than somebody's playground, which they resent giving up. When I was at UCLA, a professor said to know the difference: 'What's essential, what's important, and what's nice to have?' While recreation is important, it shouldn't take precedence over the growing of food. And I think wealthier nations have an obligation to help those at subnutritional levels." We do not discuss the types of crops to be grown with New Melones water— grapes for wine, beef, almonds, peaches, cotton, and rice exported to Japan, where malnutrition does not run rampant. It is clear that Golden State agribusinessmen do not want New Melones water for crops exported to Bangladesh.

Without my prompting, Kramer again brings up the Cosumnes River, a scenic little stream south of Sacramento. "It's natural and unique. It is the only western Sierra river without a major storage or diversion project. The only way you can raft it in August is with a four-wheel-drive vehicle, because it's bone dry. That is what the Stanislaus would be like without the PG&E pipe that your wild river comes out of." Kramer is talking about the pipe that intercepts water

up above and diverts it to a power plant, then returns the water to the
river at Camp Nine.

The *California Water Atlas* shows what the flow of the Stanislaus would
be without dams. During the average year, there would be enough
water to raft except for three months. I ask Kramer how the
Cosumnes compares to the Stanislaus. "About the same," he says.
"All these western Sierra streams are about the same." Kramer is
thinking of seasonal flow patterns, but in size the rivers differ greatly.
Bulletin No. 1 of the California Department of Water Resources gives
the Cosumnes 374,000 acre-feet of annual runoff; the Stanislaus,
1,210,000 acre-feet.

The implications are endlessly arguable. True, the Stanislaus's flow
would be erratic without upstream dams. Sometimes rafters might
sprain their ankles walking through riffles. False, you could navigate a
four-wheel-drive in the riverbed. But why does Kramer imply that the
upstream dams are so terrible relative to the wild river proposal? What
difference does it make that upriver dams make electricity and also
enhance the summertime flow of the Stanislaus?

After being hired by Californians Against Proposition 17, Kramer
took a poll to see where people's sensitivities were. Are you against
dams? What do you think makes a wild river? Other questions. The
results showed that people did not consider a river with sewage plants,
dams, and diversions to be wild. At one place or another, though not
in the canyon, the Stanislaus has all these. "We also knew the public
was environmentally conscious in 1974," Kramer says. Jerry Brown's
poll showed that Californians would vote to save the canyon.

Kramer forged a pro-dam strategy to beat the environmentalists at
their own game. Californians Against 17 would stress the downstream
water quality, fishery, and recreation improvements New Melones
promised. They would not, of course, mention the Central Valley
Project's Trinity River Dam, where environmental assurances were also
given, but where the salmon run was cut as much as 90 percent when
the dam began operating. On the Stanislaus, there is concern that
downstream environmental improvements may not be delivered, or
may be preempted when they conflict with the needs of agribusiness
or Los Angeles. Kramer says that it would be contempt of court for the
corps to violate the lower-river environmental program on the
Stanislaus. But in a discussion of California water needs, James Cook,
regional planning officer for the Bureau of Reclamation, said, "When
the going gets tough, people will get the water, not fish."

To hammer home the need for improved dissolved oxygen levels in
the lower river, Californians Against 17 discovered a photograph of

dead fish—stinking rotting carcasses all over the place. They sent it out in information packets and to congressmen. The caption said, "fish killed by oxygen depletion in the Stanislaus." I asked Kramer where the photo was taken. "On the lower Stanislaus," he replied. "You'd have to check with the *Modesto Bee* for details. That's where we got the picture." I checked with the *Bee*. They had a tough time finding the photo because it had been cropped from a much larger print, but the *Bee* staff was cooperative and returned my call: the fish had been killed just below the Simpson-Lee paper plant at Ripon. One hundred thousand fish died from a chemical spill, not from oxygen depletion. Thorne Gray, the *Bee* reporter on both the Simpson-Lee and New Melones stories, said, "New Melones will improve San Joaquin water quality from agricultural runoff, but nobody ever said it would clean up pollution from industries or cities."

Kramer later denied knowing the real cause of the fish kill when he began using the photograph. At any rate, his strategy stressed downriver environmental improvements, and was backed by the chemical-spill shot. It also said the river wasn't really wild. Indeed, the campaign charged that the whole wild river argument was a hoax. "It *was* a hoax," Kramer says. "Still is. You can't have a wild river if it is not free-flowing!"

I have seen the river, and geologists have told me that the Stanislaus has been flowing for nine million years. "Why isn't it free-flowing?" I ask.

"Because the water in that section comes from two reservoirs, a pipe at Camp Nine, and a powerhouse in the summertime."

"But if you look at the water in the canyon, is it flowing?"

"Don't try to pin me down with that kind of rhetoric. In a natural state, the canyon would be dry. So the only reason that water flows in there is like in a sink that is turned on. Is that free-flowing?" Kramer is mordant. He is getting worked up. Somewhat emotionally involved, as Humphrey said. "The only time the water in the canyon flows is when the power plant is on," and with "on," Kramer strikes his desk with his fist. "That matters, because if the plant were shut down permanently there'd be no water there. Then it wouldn't be free-flowing, would it?"

It would be free-flowing. There just wouldn't be as much water in the dry season. And nobody ever said a "wild" river had to have lots of water in it all the time. Kramer's point is that the dams upstream affect flows in the canyon, making the water higher and more runable in summer. Therefore, the river is not wild. My point is that there are no dams in the canyon itself, and its water moves right through unimpeded.

Let's look at another river. The Colorado probably attracts more
river hype than any other waterway in America. It begins in the
alpine meadows of Rocky Mountain National Park. All the way
across the state of Colorado it grows, dropping to the sea faster
than its mountains, and the canyons deepen. Grown muddy, it slices
through red Utah canyons like Westwater and Cataract, names that stir
boatmen's (and, of course, women's) adrenalin. It is 1,400 miles long,
but what everybody remembers is the Grand Canyon. The Colorado
River made the Grand Canyon, and each year 14,000 people (this is
25,000 fewer than travel on the Stanislaus) cruise down it for ten days
in a rubber boat, dory or kayak. Many people recall their Grand
Canyon trip as one of the best times of their lives.

Is the Colorado a wild river? For 226 miles, there is no road along it.
Hermit Falls has fifteen-foot waves. Lava Falls is one of the more
challenging drops in the West. The golden walls of an inner canyon
climb straight up for thousands of feet; then cliffs rise 3,000 feet more
to Arizona's Kaibab Plateau. Beaches, caves, waterfalls, a blazing
summer sun. The Colorado through Grand Canyon is thought by
many to be the preeminent wild river in America. The canyon area is
a National Park, one of our oldest.

The Colorado also comes out of pipes. Lots of them. It has barely
splashed off the Continental Divide when it is caught in a reservoir,
and some of it is directed to Denver via a tunnel through the Rockies.
Then there are low dams, maybe a dozen, and tributary dams like
those of the Stanislaus—only there are dozens and dozens on
the Colorado. Just above the Grand Canyon put-in at Lees Ferry is
the Bureau of Reclamation's Glen Canyon Dam and power plant,
the Colorado's very own Camp Nine pipe. The river is regulated by
God and the U. S. Department of the Interior. So is it wild?

There are thirty National Rivers designated by Congress—waterways
with outstanding qualities, protected by the federal government.
Dams are not allowed on the particular section of river so designated,
but they may be permitted above it or below it. This national wild and
scenic rivers system includes many streams with upstream reservoirs:
the Rogue, Delaware, Skagit, Allagash, Rio Grande, St. Croix, and
more. Congress doesn't even ask about upriver impoundments. It is a
superfluous question. If upstream regulation by dams made a river
ineligible for the California state scenic rivers system, four of the five
charter members would not be members at all: the Klamath has Iron
Gate dam, the Trinity has the Trinity and Lewiston dams, the Eel has
Van Arsdale dam, and the lower American has the Folsom and Nimbus
dams. But Kramer says that the Stanislaus is not eligible because there
are upstream dams, which is why Californians Against 17 called the

wild river proposal a hoax, the message they broadcast loud and clear to the voters in November 1974.

"It's not free-flowing because it has an artificial source," Kramer says.

"The snowpack?"

"No, that is the point you miss. It is not the snowpack. That would only be true in two or three months of the year, and the rest of the time it would not be true."

"Do they make water at the power plant?"

Pause.

Kramer says, "Doesn't it defy credibility in the mind of the ordinary guy to talk about a wild river that is fed by a power plant? I think it does. Our picture of that power plant providing that water is one of the main reasons that editorial boards all over the state went against the proposition.

"The Congress functions on the basis of public opinion, and so what is important is not what *I* say or think is a free-flowing river," he continues. "Not what *you* think is a free-flowing river. It is what the *public perception* of a free-flowing river is. I don't think that showing a picture of a dam and a power plant supplying the water fits into the public's perception of a wild river."

Of Milton, Cliff Humphrey says, "He realizes there are ways to appeal to people."

With Kramer as the PR pro, Cliff Humphrey was the environmental spokesman for the dam people. "Anybody can like the river, that's not the fight," Humphrey says. "I don't like dams, but they can be useful."

Humphrey grew up in Chico and Stockton, then studied Human Ecology at Berkeley and did an "individual major in interdisciplinary studies" at San Francisco State. He was active in the peace movement at Berkeley, then formed a group called Ecology Action (not to be confused with the Washington-based group, Environmental Action). He traveled back and forth across the country talking up individual action, recycling, buses, bicycling, and the political process to fledgling environmental groups. Humphrey became an Earth Day leader, and in Berkeley on April 22, 1970, he took the first sledgehammer swing at an old car, symbolizing the enemy. After this, he took a job in Modesto, not far from the Central Valley Stanislaus, organizing and running a recycling center. So the Valley had its own "environmentalist."

Humphrey is now in his early forties. His sandy hair is medium length and a little ruffled. Liking the river is "not the fight," Humphrey says. What is? "There is no other place on earth like the Central Valley," he begins. "The Valley is fertile and hot. Crops can be grown year-round. Surrounding mountains keep insect pests out. This area should be designated for production. John Muir's Central Valley is not here—that price has been paid. There are no more antelope or grizzly bears. Let's use this area and make less pressure on other places. Things grown in the Valley will replace petroleum products. Cotton instead of polyester. Oil is running out, and we'll turn more to the land. It just needs water."

Now we look at Central Valley agriculture. Huge dams. Pumps using more power than the dams generate, carrying water 400 miles from its source. Bulldozers all over the fields. Trucks and trains carrying produce 3,000 miles. Rice being shipped to Japan. Fossil-fuel–based fertilizer that is a staple of Valley crops. Automated picking equipment, gasoline-powered drying equipment. Pesticides, herbicides. It may be the most energy-intensive agriculture the world has known. This is what New Melones Dam will help to perpetrate. How does this fit into Humphrey's scheme?

He says, "Don't assume I support or approve of the way the Central Valley has been irrigated in the past. I do not. And hydroelectricity is just for making mischief. . . . Economic growth is capital punishment— that's an old slogan we used at Ecology Action. Economically, it will be feasible to dam every river for power, but that is unacceptable.

"Water should not be pumped for irrigation. That is not an efficient use. The Central Valley Project will make more money if they sell municipal and industrial water to Los Angeles, but that's a mistake. They'd have to pump it. In my opinion the whole LA basin should look like a Mexican courtyard. All the yield of New Melones could be put into gravity-flow and used locally. I would oppose the filling of New Melones for the delivery of water by pumping anyplace."

Humphrey advocates changes in the way the Central Valley is run today. "It's valid to look at changing crops. We should irrigate only soils that are sweet and will drain.

"We need an integrated plan for the Valley, to stop urban sprawl." Humphrey advocates new towns in the foothills to reserve Valley soils for farming and to let people settle above the inversion layer that causes pollution to be trapped in the Valley. "We have to be responsible so we don't destroy systems we're dependent on. We should grow materials in the most efficient manner.

"Looking at food production, my personal opinion is that every city will have around it an ideal climate—a protected area for vegetables and fruit. Grains and meat will be imported. Then, emphasis in the Central Valley will be on chemical feed-stock crops. Fiber and pure chemical crops will increase as petroleum is used up."

Humphrey is expecting extraordinary crop values. He foresees a day when fruits and vegetables will be replaced by higher-value chemical crops. He doesn't mention the replacement of livestock, which now preempts two-thirds of all agricultural water supplies. He expects plenty of cotton as a replacement for synthetic fiber, even though cotton is the third most water-consumptive Valley crop. I ask if he considers the efficient use of water as part of "efficient" agriculture.

"The overdrawing of groundwater and the soils that are slowly salting up are problems that have to be attended to. To me it's an unspeakable future if we dam the river and salt the land both."

So how does all this relate to New Melones? "New Melones will provide a reliable source of water through almost any drought. That is 75 percent of my reason to support it. We need a water-rich system. If we have only a minimum amount of water, there may not be enough return flows to support secondary effects—hedgerows and valley habitat. We need enough water to flush salts through."

"Does this amount to trading the canyon for Valley hedgerows?" I ask.

"Yes, it's more diverse in the Valley. To have the Central Valley support growth, some other habitat will be denied."

"With an issue like this, I relate in a big context," Humphrey says. "Other people relate to the floor of the canyon."

"If New Melones and other projects are used to assure farmers their status quo—a continuation of cheap, subsidized water—how will the reforms ever come about?"

"It's not possible to use New Melones as a hostage to get price increases," Humphrey says. "It's not big enough to be a hostage."

With Friends of the River on one side and Californians Against Proposition 17 on the other, battles of verbiage and statistics began. Here are some of their arguments:

Californians Against Proposition 17:

"By the November election $80 million will have been spent in construction. This will be wasted if the project is stopped."

Friends of the River:

"Why waste another $200 million? We agree with Gubernatorial candidate Houston Flournoy that the Army Corps should suspend construction to prevent a waste of money should the high dam be halted. Instead, the Corps organized multiple shifts to work seven days a week so that as much money as possible can be spent by November."

Californians Against Proposition 17:

"Since 1972, a tiny, misguided group of rafting hobbyists, joined by several commercial rafting companies, have fought the dam."

Friends of the River:

"Proposition 17 and protection of the Canyon is endorsed by environmental, political action and tax reform groups."

Californians Against Proposition 17:

"New Melones will generate an annual average of 430 million kilowatt-hours of electricity, enough to supply the combined cities of Pasadena and Santa Monica."

Friends of the River:

"New Melones would provide only one-third of 1% of California's energy needs. Only peaking power would be available, two hours per day."

Californians Against Proposition 17:

"Every spring there is some flooding of the agricultural lands along the lower Stanislaus. Average flood damage is more than $1 million per year and a twenty year flood [i.e., the worst flood likely in a twenty-year period] would cause $10 million in damages."

Friends of the River:

"A 200,000 acre-foot reservoir would allow additional storage space for the most severe floods."

Californians Against Proposition 17:

"If Californians innocently vote to place the Stanislaus in the 'Wild Rivers System,' they will have been deceived into permitting one of the most blatant special interest grabs ever carried off in this state."

Friends of the River:

"Flood control will offer protection to only 150 farmers; irrigation will benefit only 300 farmers. Millions of subsidy dollars will be given to these groups."

Californians Against Proposition 17:

"New Melones will provide inexpensive public recreation for hundreds of thousands of Californians."

Friends of the River:

"River recreation costs the taxpayer almost nothing, but the recreation facilities for New Melones come to $65 million, plus interest, plus operating expenses, plus the recreation share of reservoir construction costs. Motorboating is the only kind of recreation you can have in the reservoir that you can't have in the river."

Californians Against Proposition 17:

"If the dam is not built, agriculture, gravel mining and pollution will continue to destroy the lower Stanislaus."

Friends of the River:

"Pollution problems should be solved at their sources. Improving the lower river is no excuse for destroying the upper river. A smaller dam could provide all of the environmental benefits to the lower river."

Californians Against Proposition 17:

"Tourism and recreational employment will contribute millions to the economies of the four counties, becoming a major factor to inspire beneficial commitments to environmental and recreational preservation, and balancing the area's present heavy reliance on its agricultural economy. The Army Corps projects initial use at 320,000 visitor-days per year, later rising to 4 million."

Friends of the River:

"Facilities have not been developed at nearby reservoirs because there is not enough demand for them. Yosemite National Park draws only 2.5 million people per year. A mud-ringed reservoir will hardly be more popular."

Californians Against Proposition 17:

"The Stanislaus is only 5% of California's Class IV white-water. There are 259 miles of this class in the state. The river is not unique."

Friends of the River:

"Should we quarry granite at Yosemite since it is only 5% of the Sierra Nevada? . . . There are 1,500 large dams in California. This is one more we don't need."

In the end, it would not be figures or analyses that would count, but advertising, and for that you need money.

Like the Miwok, river people are a migratory lot, and after the spring qualification drive, many of the volunteers left for the rivers where they worked as guides. They couldn't continue as volunteers without pay forever. Briggs and Simballa returned to the Grand Canyon. Dubois, Westphal, and dozens of others spent the summer on the Sierra rivers, and the struggle for the Stanislaus was all but forgotten. "Looking back," Dubois says, "a lot could have been done to build support during the summer." Californians Against 17 hired Kramer, acquired funding, and plotted their campaign.

Dubois had always wanted to do a river trip the whole way from Camp Nine to San Francisco. One night in September, five friends of the river brainstormed and asked, why not a 200-mile voyage to kick off the fall campaign? Roanoke agreed that "Row for the River" would invite publicity, and would raise funds if the paddlers and rowers could persuade sponsors to pay by the mile—a row-a-thon. So they did it. One hundred people started with the frothy canyon run. Then a score of kayakers portaged around the old cement of Melones Dam; past the foundation of New Melones, where construction crews herded fleets of belching diesel machinery rearranging the walls of Iron Canyon; and over Tulloch and Goodwin dams. From there they kayaked through fifty miles of Central Valley farmland; on down the San Joaquin agricultural conduit; through the Delta checkerboard of land and brackish water, and into San Francisco Bay. It took them eight days. Among the twenty were Fred Dennis, who had started etcetera with Dubois; Dave Westphal; and Bruce Simballa. Jennifer Jennings, Robin Magneson, and Kathy Meyer also paddled to the white foggy city, and would later fill important positions with Friends of the River. Steve Luke made the trip with a cast around a broken leg. Sixty more supporters joined at Tiburon; then the eclectic armada of five rafts, eighty kayaks, canoes, four sailboats, a wind-surfer, a three-masted schooner from the Oceanic Society, and a floating army truck crossed the choppy bay to Aquatic Park. Gracielle Rossi arranged for fireboats, a marching band, and 1,000 people to herald the voyagers. The river people felt strong and elated and sure that they would win on November 5. If only saving their river had been as easy as traveling it.

There were no funds for mass-media advertising, so Friends of the River's campaign was door-to-door. Droves of young people hit the streets with the Stanislaus gospel. Briggs and Simballa went to a World Series game and leafleted. They went to 49ers football games—actually, to the parking lots. A hot-air balloon flew over the crowds with a banner reading "Yes on 17."

River trips for newsmen would have employed an army of natty PR specialists if this had been an industry or government campaign. Guided by the simple premise that anybody who saw the Stanislaus would support it, two trips per week were run for the media and VIPs. "One of the best things that Friends of the River ever did was to offer a raft trip to anyone who could hold a pencil," comments David Gancher of *Sierra* magazine.

"When we saw the articles coming out, it looked like we had it made," says Dubois. "All that good coverage. What we didn't know was that editorial boards are different." By hard knocks, Friends of the River would learn much about the power of the media and who wields it.

As the campaign rattled on, each side touted a list of endorsements. Californians Against 17 boasted the State Chamber of Commerce, the AFL-CIO, the County Supervisors Association, water agencies, most local governments, construction companies, the State Building and Construction Trades Council, and other groups. The state assembly and senate passed resolutions urging completion of the dam.

The Metropolitan Water District of Southern California (Los Angeles) joined in, and some local farmers winced, wondering who would get the New Melones water. "We're fearing the same thing the people in the Owens Valley feared," said Al Sorrenti.

The California Council for Environmental and Economic Balance, headed by Edmund G. "Pat" Brown, voted to support the dam, though for "personal reasons" the former governor, father of Jerry Brown, abstained. The elder Brown rafted the canyon on one of the FOR publicity trips and was enthusiastic. He lost a sneaker while swimming through the rapid called Wino Swim. He swung from the big rope above Razorback. He was standing on the shore at the rope swing when another group of rafters drifted by. Somebody yelled, "Hey Governor, your fly is open," and everybody laughed together. Tom Graff of EDF later said, "If Brown had supported 17, it could have made a difference. He was such a booster, so beloved by business and industry, that his support would have been an unmistakable signal to water interests that all bets are off, we are in a new era of water development."

Supporting Proposition 17 and FOR were the California Planning and Conservation League, People's Lobby, American Rivers Conservation Council, American Whitewater Affiliation, the California Native Plant Society, Americans for Democratic Action, the California Tax Reform Association, and others. A memorandum was sent to local government leaders from San Francisco Board of Supervisors President Dianne Feinstein and the mayors of Beverly Hills, San Jose, and Santa Clara, attempting to counteract pro-dam publicity.

Each side battled to cancel the other's endorsements. Local groups opposed the wild river, while their state and national counterparts usually supported it. The Stockton Audubon Society opposed the wild river, the National Audubon Society supported it. The Ecology Action Education Institute in Modesto (Cliff Humphrey's group) was against it; the Environmental Policy Center was for it. The Associated Sportsmen of California and the Stanislaus Speleological Association opposed it; the Northern California Council of Fly Fishing Clubs and the State and National Speleological Societies supported it. The Yokuts Group of the Sierra Club was against the wild river; the National Sierra Club was for it.

Presidential candidate Jimmy Carter supported the proposition at a Los Angeles fund raiser in October 1974:

> In many of the Corps of Engineers' dam projects around the nation, the benefit/cost ratios have been grossly distorted. Data and premises on which project approvals are sought are erroneous and outdated. False justifications of projects are attempted.
>
> Every corps project that was initiated many years ago should be thoroughly evaluated and computations should be confirmed by the General Accounting Office. This would insure the saving of billions of dollars in taxpayers' money and hundreds of miles of irreplaceable and precious wild rivers.
>
> A recent GAO analysis of the Sprewell Bluff dam project on the Flint River in Georgia indicated vividly the fallacies in existing Corps of Engineers analysis procedures. Construction costs were underestimated, extremely low interest rates were assumed, nearby lakes were ignored, population projections were exaggerated, environmental damage was concealed, power production estimates were based on overloaded generator ratings, no archaeological losses were included, and major recreation benefits were claimed in spite of official opposition from state and federal recreation agencies.
>
> Similar distortions exist in the New Melones project. I strongly urge California voters to support Proposition 17.

Too bad there were only a dozen people at the Los Angeles meeting.

Carter's example, Sprewell Bluff Dam on the Flint River, had been successfully fought. This stream slices a narrow valley through the Appalachians' southern tail in west-central Georgia. Its sharp rapids excite rafters and canoeists. Seeking to stop the dam, Georgia environmentalists had appealed to Governor Carter, whose people studied the project, and reported over-optimistically estimated benefits and underestimated costs. They discovered what Briggs discovered during Colorado's After '72 Needs Study: justifications can be fudged. Against the legislature's opposition, the governor cut support for Sprewell Bluff, killing the dam, at least as long as Carter was in power.

Carter, himself an engineer, had no love for the world's largest engineering outfit. As presidential candidate, he said that he would put the corps out of the dam-building business. Time would show his statement to be as overly optimistic as the corps's estimate of the benefits of Sprewell Bluff.

Jerry Brown supported Proposition 17. Back in May, the gubernatorial candidate had gone on a see-and-support-the-Stanislaus trip. Larry Orman guided him down the river on high water. "We had one and a half hours for the trip," Orman recalls. "The day before, the guides tested for speed—seventy minutes. The trip was sort of a coffee break, a rest between political speeches. We had an oar boat—the safest kind—but when we got to Camp Nine, Brown looked at a paddle boat and said, 'I want to go in *that*.'" Behind Brown, Jerry Meral thought "Oh no," and shook his head emphatically at Orman. But Orman was powerless. Candidate Brown wanted to paddle. Forget the big hole at Widowmaker. So off they went in a woolly descent through willow-high water and souse holes capable of burying a campaign, notebook-clutching newsmen included. Meral, with all his experience, had never paddled a raft. He and Rob Caughlan sat up front, Brown and a Los Angeles *Times* reporter sat in the middle, and Orman took the back. They hit the hole at Widowmaker and the governor-to-be almost fell out. Everybody almost fell out. Brown didn't talk much, but in squishing sneakers at Parrotts Ferry he said, "If we can get along without a dam the size of what the Army Corps of Engineers wants, I think we should." In the summer he was "studying the issue," then emerged to say, "I support Proposition 17. The $270 million allocated for building the dam could be used to fight pollution and to create more jobs . . . than would be created due to construction of the dam."

On election eve, Brown argued for the canyon. He spoke of the river and its meaning—more than recreation. He touched on some of the features that show the power of place: "It's a matter of values. That whitewater may not add up in an accountant's mentality, in a corporate executive's suite, but in the year 2000 when we have skyscrapers and a plexiglass society, I think you will want your children to be able to ride down a white river and look at the beauty of the mountains and look at the beauty of California instead of seeing a sixty-two-story dam."

Milton Kramer said, "The nine miles represents nothing more or less than somebody's playground, which they resent giving up. Talk about a unique canyon or how you feel about the canyon in lyrical terms, but the real issue here is, are you going to continue whitewater rafting or not?"

But Brown was not talking about a playground. He was saying that the canyon represents historic California. And if we want to know it and remember it, we need to keep some of it around. "It isn't just jobs that draw people here," says state economist Guy Phillips. "This is a place that you can define, a land that shows something special. Lose that and you've lost California."

Stanislaus River historian W. Turrentine Jackson, professor at the University of California at Davis, summarized the Proposition 17 campaigns as follows:

> Friends of the River's approach fell into two categories, one emphasizing hard information, the other imparting a moralistic fervor reminiscent of the classic environmental crusades. . . . The Californians Against Proposition 17 campaign, as the name of the organization implies, was chiefly negative in nature, opposed to the ballot measure but not necessarily defending the New Melones project. Much of its campaign was designed to denigrate Friends of the River and only indirectly to support the federal flood control and reclamation project.

As the campaign wound to a close, the battle was reduced to rhetoric. "Stop the Wild River Hoax, No on No. 17," dam proponents advertised on billboards. "There may never have been a more moot issue in a wild and scenic river fight," said Howard Brown, executive director of the American Rivers Conservation Council, but Kramer and company sold their line with devastating impact.

As Kramer said, their most crucial effort was visiting newspaper editorial boards. Along with his dead fish photo, Kramer carried another of the Camp Nine Powerhouse with water being dumped via pipe into the river. "Those who saw that picture opposed the wild river designation," said Kramer. "What makes it whitewater most of the year is not a natural flow but the periodic artificial release of water from a PG&E power plant," the *San Francisco Chronicle*'s editors wrote. They compared it to Disneyland. The *Los Angeles Times* stressed the other part of the pro-dam strategy—that New Melones was the best thing for the environment: "Several Sierra Club groups actively support the project, and Alex Hildebrand, a former two-term national president of the Sierra Club and now a Manteca farmer, said last week that New Melones would provide 'more ecological and recreational benefits than any other water management project of which I am aware.'"

Kramer, Oke, and Dubois agree on one thing—that the editorial stance was a crux of the campaign. "Eventually we saw a lot of the editorial boards," Oke says, "—too late." Kramer, Hertle, and Thomas Shephard (their attorney) had left their stamp, and decisions had already been made.

Friends of the River recognized that Southern California, with its teeming population, would decide the election. They knew that the attitude south of the Tehachapis was not much aligned with river preservation. First, there are no role models. The Los Angeles River was relegated to a concrete channel before this generation of voters was conceived. Bus drivers are trained in the dry Los Angeles River bed—it is like a freeway without cars. Second, this is a culture addicted to long hoses, powerful spigots, and frequent flushes. People pretend it is not desert and landscape their homes as in Baltimore or New Orleans. But they are not oblivious to the water's source—dams. No dams, no Los Angeles. So dams are good. Response to the 1977 drought shows something of attitudes to water: north of San Francisco, Marin County cut water consumption by 60 percent. The East Bay cut consumption by 40 percent. There was community spirit in conservation efforts. In Los Angeles it was business as usual. The Colorado River supply remained plentiful. They swept the sidewalks with hoses, not brooms, pushing dirt around with a scarce commodity—snowmelt from the upper Owens and the Colorado.

San Francisco and Los Angeles both subsist on rivers from the Sierra. Construction of Hetch Hetchy began in 1914, only one year after the Owens Valley aqueduct opened. But attitudes were different, maybe due to an environmentalist minority in the north that was stronger than the environmentalist minority in the south.

FOR's biggest problem was that Los Angeles's pacemakers are the mass media. The river people found that television, radio, and newspapers were the only way to be heard. "How do you canvas the freeways and a desert of strung-out suburbs?" Briggs asks. "You can't take a campaign to the streets when there aren't any."

With lots of spirit, lots of guts, FOR volunteers headed for Los Angeles like a pilgrimage of would-be rock stars. Briggs, Simballa, Sue Bassett (another Colorado River guide), Dubois, and many others went south. For their guerrilla war against the mass media and massive billboards, they created banners from bedsheets bought at Goodwill. Simballa sewed them together on a treadle machine at the ARTA house in Vallecito. "It was real grassrooty," Briggs says. Letter stencils were cut from refrigerator-box cardboard. Forty of these banners were trucked south to help persuade the Los Angeles voter to save the canyon.

Just off Olympic Boulevard, Friends of the River rented a two-bedroom apartment as staging area and nerve center for FOR

South. Fifty people were in and out. Twenty-five slept there one night. The landlord caught on and suggested that they graduate to more appropriate quarters—get the hell out! Even under duress, Simballa's grin is impregnable, and he negotiated a sleeping limit of ten.

There were teams for sniping. That's when you staple posters to telephone poles. John Cassidy, B. C. Rimbeaux, and Marty Booth were the fastest snipes in the West. Without the complete halt required of stop signs or normal dismounting, Cassidy would drive his relic of a step van past a vulnerable pole, while Rimbeaux and Booth grappled from the door in high and low formation and bam, hit the creosoted standard with posters and staples.

Trained and accomplished in the science of highway engineering, Briggs took charge of placing sheet banners along freeways. First stop, as any engineer knows, was the district CalTrans office to acquire flow maps for "a, ah, consulting job." Then came strategic selection of routes, and a proper peppering of bedsheet sites. Most major freeways were covered, which was quite an accomplishment. Briggs had an uncompromising policy of avoiding overpasses where the vital message might fall onto a car and blind its seventy-miles-per-hour driver with the message of a yes vote. Banners were hung from buildings bordering commuter arteries and inside wire-cage pedestrian overpasses, where commuters needed to raise only their eyebrows to learn of a river needing their vote.

Of course, the heat came. The police didn't know much about the Stanislaus—not even the Polish saint part. They didn't care much for the banners, and had generally been brought up without much sympathy for guerrilla tactics. On a North Hollywood Freeway overpass there had been an insidious problem with suburban youngsters heaving stones onto traffic. Police were on the lookout, and spotted Cassidy, six foot one, and Briggs, six foot two. The problem seemed more serious than previously thought. Two officers shuffled uncomfortably. They scanned the scene in an instant, as police officers are trained to do. No rocks, just a bedsheet. This piqued the heat's curiosity. "What in hell . . . ?" Cass, never short on words and wit, reasoned that so long as FOR was there doing sheets, kids wouldn't be skipping stones off commuters' windshields. The cops listened with interest, but didn't buy it. No sheets in North Hollywood.

"We did two Halloween pranks," Briggs confesses. "We hung a sheet from the bottom of a 'No on 17' billboard. And once we slapped bumper stickers on a fleet of *LA Times* delivery trucks."

There were lighter moments. ("Best trip I ever had to LA," Briggs says, admitting that he enjoyed the place.) But that doesn't diminish the intensity of the campaign. "We were all working sixteen and eighteen hours, day after day. We were sure we would win. Absolutely sure." The polls, however, showed FOR sagging in their battle of pamphlets against television, of newsmen disagreeing with editors, of recycled bedsheets that contradicted billboards.

A TV and radio blitz was scheduled for the last days of the campaign. TV, of course, by the dam people; radio by the river people. Television ads blistered: an older woman almost in tears down by the water, saying that the rafters were taking her river away; narrators documenting the "rafters' rip-off" and predicting a "slow polluted death" of the river; airplane footage of the pipe that gushes water back into the river at Camp Nine, accompanied by a credible voice that said that the conduit creates the whitewater. The advertising hit hard. Kramer saw to that.

Paul Newman and Charlton Heston became river people, donating their voices for radio ads. But in the end, it came down to money. The river people had $238,126 to finance their effort, including the qualification drive in the spring. The American River Touring Association was the grand patron, gleaning $18,724 from customers—all contributions under $100, most of them $2.50.

The dam people collected over $400,000. Up to election time, only $281,699 was recorded, including $50,000 from the dam's general contractors—Guy F. Atkinson Company, Gordon Ball Inc., and the Arundell Corporation. Only after the election was it revealed that another $150,000 had been contributed by the Melones contractors. As the prime dam supporters, their role was safely hidden from the public eye until after everyone had voted.

The New Melones contractors had what you would call an interest. Not only here, but in other corps projects, too. The Atkinson Company was finishing the $65 million Cochiti Dam on the Rio Grande in New Mexico. Atkinson, Ball, and Arundell had a $45.9 million contract on Mississippi's Tombigbee River—another river targeted for rescue by the environmentalists. Just north of the Stanislaus, the three contractors were building the foundation for an even larger dam on the American River at Auburn, where they would again encounter the dam pest, Jerry Meral.

FOR received no contributions of $5,000 or more. Californians Against Proposition 17 received thirteen from Los Angeles, San Francisco, Texas, Ohio, Pennsylvania, Oregon, and other corporate headquarters. Here they are:

Melones Contractors	$175,000
Guy F. Atkinson Co.	$25,000
California Construction Achievement Program of Sacramento	$12,500
Construction Industry Advancement Fund of Southern California	$12,500

Peterson Tractor Company	$10,050
Reclaimed Island Lands (farming company)	$10,000
Construction Industry Advancement Fund	$10,000
Morgan Equipment	$10,000
E. I. DuPont de Nemours (manufacturing)	$10,000
State Building and Contractors Trade Council of California	$5,000
Goodyear Tire and Rubber	$5,000
Texaco	$5,000
Pacific Gas and Electric Company	$5,000

Rob Caughlan charged that the corps was running a "high-paid welfare system for construction workers." He admitted to pro-dam charges that rafting companies would benefit if the canyon were preserved, "but so would the public by saving $200 million from a wasteful dam."

The financial records are clear: FOR was supported by rafting companies and many individuals; Californians Against Proposition 17 was mainly funded by contractors who built the dam.

While the pro-dam TV ads were running and the pro-river radio spots were playing, FOR people were doing what they could in Los Angeles. Outfitter's busses hauled reinforcements down from the north, 120 people. The telegram format is not patented, so David Oke drafted a message in this style and volunteers slipped them under thousands of doors in the dead of night before the election. With daybreak the river people collapsed in the ARTA bus and rolled for hours northward through the hot Valley on November 5 to vote in their districts.

All of the river people were invited to Joanna and Bob Rabkin's home in Alameda to watch the televised returns. As at Camp Nine, anticipation was high when fifty volunteers crowded around the tube. They were jubilant with the first returns from Northern California, the water-rich, environmentalist region where FOR had always held an edge. Some people even congratulated themselves and left. Optimism was intemperate, but then came the other areas. By three to one and greater margins, the Central Valley and foothills backed the dam. Southern Californians, as predicted, were the pivotal group. Their early returns opposed the initiative. Their later returns opposed it. As the hours wore on, the spirit in the Rabkins' living room sank lower and lower; and by late that night the outcome was clear. The south went slightly over 50 percent for the dam. The initiative lost, 47 percent to 53 percent. The river got 2,576,000 votes; the dam, 2,891,000.

The canyon lost. Friends of the River lost. Most people cried. A few tried to be strong, to say that they could do it again, but the energy was gone, replaced by hard, unmitigated despair. Men and women drifted away into the early morning darkness. Many of them never returned to fight for a river.

"First I felt the pain. The river," Dubois remembers. "But then a greater hurt came for those friends, many people who were never involved in the political system before. It was an era of cynicism and they didn't want to bother, they didn't believe their effort would make a difference, but they did it anyway. They said they would try working through the system and they poured themselves into it. They worked their hearts out. They gave all they had, then saw that the winning was bought by money. It was somehow a rip-off of the human spirit."

What went wrong? "We started out ahead," David Oke says. "But then came billboards. Then came the endorsements of newspapers and the TV and everything else that money can buy. With the advertising came the confusion and by then there was nothing we could do."

"Aw, baloney," says Milton Kramer. "I don't know what the confusion was. The ballot said do you want a wild river designation or not."

Oke continues, "The other side knew we were ahead and they knew they had to capture our votes. So they dressed their position up like ours. Most people really didn't care about the lower river. When they heard a 'save the river' pitch they assumed it meant save the river from the dam. The dam proponents made a vote for a government gift of flood control and cheap irrigation look like a vote for the environment."

"Voters were fooled," says Caughlan. "Friends of the River's phones rang for a week with people apologizing for voting the wrong way."

"We were comfortable with the public relations," says John Hertle. "The dam will give the higher summer flows needed to save the lower river. When you're in a political campaign you use political slogans and political bravado. It was obvious the general public was environmentally sensitive. Since the lower river would be enhanced by the dam, that made a better case, and it was the truth. We were comfortable with what we said and thought it would be effective with the public."

State Senator John Nejedly, from Walnut Creek, announced plans to curb false advertising in statewide proposition campaigns. As chairman of the Natural Resources and Wildlife Committee, he believed that the opponents of Proposition 17 had deliberately tried to deceive the public. He also pointed to advertising in other initiative campaigns: opponents of the Coastline Conservation proposition in 1973 had used billboards that called on the public to "Save the Beaches" by voting no. Opponents of a campaign reform proposition proclaimed, "Save Free Speech, vote no." Steve Perryman, a Santa Clara lawyer and former captain in the Army Corps of Engineers, had asked the secretary of state to take steps to "correct the confusion created by the misleading Proposition 17 billboards."

Brent Blackwelder, director of the Environmental Policy Center in Washington, says, "For opponents of Proposition 17 to call the regulated flows of the Stanislaus 'artificial' is to perpetrate a fraud on the California voter."

"They ran a deceptive campaign," says Oke.

"Hogwash," says Milton Kramer, his face getting beet red. "I regard it as a personal insult when people say the campaign was deceptive. Look at this, an *LA Times* editorial on Proposition 17 in which they urged a no vote. Look at this—an editorial from the *San Francisco Chronicle*. They use the words 'saving the river.' We meant the fifty-five miles of lower river and we were right and accurate and the papers bought it and used the language. Are you also trying to say we fooled some pretty erudite editors? Do you think that they were deceptive too? Maybe you'd like me to tell the editor of the *Los Angeles Times* that you think they were deceptive. Do you think every major newspaper in the state was deceptive?"

"The media has too much power in this country, simple as that," says Oke. "The media is incredibly irresponsible on political issues. The side that gives them the best hook gets the best coverage."

The *Los Angeles Times* editorialized against the proposition, but also against the pro-dam billboards. The *Time*'s editors wrote,

> Cliff Humphrey says he is "very comfortable" with the billboards he has sponsored opposing Proposition 17.
> That's interesting, because the billboards seem an absolute betrayal of the truth to us. We too, oppose Proposition 17. But to call it a "wild-river hoax" and to suggest that the proposition would result in pollution is a resort to tactics that have no place in responsible democratic campaigning.

The *Sacramento Bee* also editorialized against the billboards, saying, "It seems that every election campaign brings forth the worst in some people and organizations."

Thorne Gray, journalist for the *Modesto Bee,* had covered the issue for years. After studying it, he became a supporter of the dam, and he knows more about it than almost anybody. Gray is also a rafter of note; on the Tuolumne, down below Meral's Pool, is Gray's Grindstone. I ask the journalist to react to accusations that the pro-dam campaign was deceptive. He retorts, "What was false? Was anything they said false?"

> False: Contrary to truth or fact; erroneous.
> Deceptive: Having power or tendency to deceive.

Why did the dam supporters say "Save the river, vote no," instead of "Build the dam, vote no?"

Oke further analyzes the loss: "We should have raised the funds we needed to hit every major media market. We needed TV and billboards in Southern California. We should have gone to editorial boards before they did. We didn't have the cohesion we needed, especially in Los Angeles. We needed two organizations, one in the north and one in the south. We shouldn't have peaked so early.

"River people are free spirits and they look like it too. That makes personal contact harder. River folks are so incredibly idealistic. Idealism doesn't win political campaigns unless it's channeled to the streets. California is bigger than most nations. It's too big for a street campaign.

"The river itself is the best sale; next would be a person who stands for the river. We should have made Mark a media star. With all his potential for swaying people it would have worked. 'Gentle Giant of the River.' He was a personality people could relate to. He, of course, would never have it that way. He never wanted to be a star. He was uncomfortable with it.

"A lot of idealism was dashed to the rocks," Oke concludes. "Another initiative might have worked but I couldn't do it. Most people were just burned out."

The week after the election, FOR contracted the widely respected polling firm of Corey, Canapary and Galanis to survey voters. Just how confused was the public anyway? The conclusion: "On election day, November 5, 1974, the majority of voters in California intended to vote against construction of the New Melones Dam and Reservoir on the Stanislaus River."

"Hogwash," says Milton Kramer. He laughs. "Those surveys don't mean a hill of beans. I can write a survey questionnaire that will get you whatever results you want. The way you ask the question and the people you ask make all the difference." I ask if Kramer has seen the survey questions and the profile of respondents. No. "The election speaks for *itself*." He accentuates his point by using his fist on his desk again.

Hertle says, "The loser always says the public was misled."

The Corey, Canapary and Galanis report continues, "As of the survey period more voters opposed the dam than favored it . . . Confusion caused by the wording of the ballot proposition itself and by the advertising resulted in the defeat of the wild and scenic river initiative."

The survey showed that confusion was pervasive, affecting people on both sides. Of those voting yes (for the wild river and against the dam), 24 percent meant to vote no. Of those voting no (against the wild river and for the dam), fully 46 percent meant to vote yes. Confusing indeed. Those figures suggest the whole election was a farce. The net result—*about 60 percent of the people who voted intended to vote for the wild river and against the dam*. This was the vote that guaranteed construction of New Melones.

Jerry Meral would soon take a job as deputy director of the California Department of Water Resources and would fade from the Stanislaus battle. Dubois, who had emerged from the campaign as a Friends of the River leader, went to Central America, where he traveled with friends and explored rivers and caves for two months. The other hundreds of river people scattered. The dam builders had won. It seemed that the river people had gone for broke, lost, and disappeared. That was mostly true, but it wouldn't be for long.

CHAPTER SIX

Return to
the River

The river kept running with green peace and white speed. Water
hissing on sand, rattling the brush and flooding willows that twitch
in the current. Rapids washed the roots of the alder, flinty points of
limestone, gold miner's rusty cables, and last night's tracks of the
raccoon and fox.

The river brought feelings of excitement and peace and its power.
People ran with the river in a flight back to nature, to a God, no less, to
old times filled by the sun and birth, of growing and dying and back to
birth again. This was Eden, but other people thought differently.
Paradise was to be swapped in a bargain between farmers and
the government.

The river brought people to the canyon once more at Thanksgiving,
1974, three weeks after the defeat of Proposition 17. Dubois rowed a
raft and wondered what he would do. Seventy other people who had
worked on Prop 17 kept their hope, but didn't know what to do about
this river that was not supposed to run much longer. They camped on
the big, smooth beach above Razorback Rapid at Grapevine Gulch
where a creek drops from the rim, and they looked at the wild river
that had been called a hoax. Not Dubois, but others talked of violence.
Striking out. How much fantasy, how much reality, who knows?
Explosives homemade from a ton of fertilizer and some fuel oil—the
philosophy of Hayduke, novelist Edward Abbey's creation, who blows
up the bulldozers and the draglines that chew on the wilderness, and
even has plans for the Glen Canyon Dam. I first heard of the Stanislaus
River from Jennifer Jennings in 1976, in a Washington, D.C. restaurant,
when she said that violence against the dam would not surprise her.
But most people tried to put the river out of mind. Go kayak the
Salmon, bum in Mexico, make money, smoke some grass, guide on
the Tuolumne, graduate from college, take a job with the state, enroll

in law school, raise a family, raise a garden. People quit the Stanislaus, not because it died, but because they expected it to die.

For one man, however, the river's silence behind a dam could not be accepted until it actually happened. Dubois said, "After a few months I realized the river wasn't gone yet, that something could still be done." After all, Jerry Brown had won the election in which the Stanislaus Canyon had lost, and Brown opposed the dam. While Atkinson, Ball, and Arundel carved the foothills under Army Corps of Engineers supervision, Dubois was traveling in Guatemala with some friends, knowing that he would not quit the Stanislaus, but not knowing where this doggedness was taking him.

He returned to Sacramento, but Meral and Kay were gone. Caughlan, Oke, and Vierra were gone. Westphall, Briggs, Cassidy, and the others were gone. Nothing was left but frayed posters and a box of "Deliver the River" brochures. The place was dead. You can't have a dam fight with one person. But Dubois was not alone. Jennifer Jennings was also ready to resume the fight.

Jennifer grew up near Folsom, a tiny old town twenty miles upriver from Sacramento at the edge of the Central Valley, immortalized by Johnny Cash's prison song and by the Bureau of Reclamation's Folsom Dam, where Sacramento goes motorboating. She discovered rivers at an early age. As soon as she could balance a two-wheeler, she peddled down to the American River below the dam and leaped into the cold water with her squealing sisters. Her grandparents had migrated west in the early days, just after the 1906 San Francisco earthquake, which gives the family fair tenure in California.

After starting college at Chico State, she transferred to the University of California at Santa Barbara, which seemed a little more progressive; then to Davis, which seemed less like Southern California. Hunting some spice and adventure as an escape from the humdrum geography and heat of the Valley, Jennifer signed on with the Davis Outdoor Adventure Co-op. One sweltery weekend in 1974, they piled into a van and cruised down I-5 to Lodi, up Route 12 to San Andreas, south on 49 to Angels Camp, east on 4 to Vallecito, then down the low-gear, snakey twists of Camp Nine Road to the Stanislaus put-in.

Seeing the canyon, Jennings couldn't understand burying it. "Can't they see . . .?" She was narrow-minded about what she regarded as narrow-mindedness. There is a special stubbornness about her. She allows no slack to foe or friend alike. She was ready to get involved.

She telephoned FOR during the Prop 17 campaign. Mark answered the phone and maneuvered quickly, as if to catch the smallest of eddies behind a limestone boulder. He encouraged Jennings as he encourages everybody. "Sure. Right-right. You betcha. Come on down." Jennifer worked on the campaign and paddled her first kayak in row-for-the-river. She organized the 1974 Thanksgiving trip.

In the winter of 1975, Jennifer and Mark talked. Bruce Simballa came by, and they decided what historian Stephen Mikesell would say six years later: Proposition 17 didn't resolve New Melones Dam. Prop 17 hardly resolved a thing.

"What was that river in Georgia? You know, the one that what's-his-name saved when he was governor back there?"

"Carter, you mean Jimmy Carter."

"It was the Flint River. Carter stopped that dam on some bluff."

"Sprewell Bluff."

"Well, why can't Brown do the same thing?"

Around the same time, Doug Allen, a Georgian-gone-Coast who had helped Roanoke during the last months of the Prop 17 campaign, contacted Dubois. Having seen Carter save the Flint, Allen thought Brown could save the Stanislaus. FOR took off on new wings. "Send letters to Brown," was the word.

Bruce Simballa spent all summer on rivers, and in the cool rainy winter he took shelter in bars. Throwing darts and drinking beer one evening in Sacramento's Fox and Goose, Simballa ran across a bargain on an apartment, and the next week FOR had an office and a home at 1611 S Street.

Even though the name, Friends of the River, had been born on David Oke's typewriter, it had been solely a Prop 17 label until now. Dubois, Jennings, and Simballa began a second phase of FOR that would keep the organization trundling along. A third phase would bring added professionalism—Brad Welton, Tom Burton, Dick Roos-Collins, hold buttons on telephones and so forth—but that comes later. If Dubois, Jennings, and Simballa hadn't gotten together, it would all have been over, and the Stanislaus would have been forgotten forever.

Arguing to reopen the New Melones debate, Dubois said, "New Melones may have been a good idea when it was first authorized, but the times have changed. Can we admit that? Can we admit that good ideas from before may not be good ideas now?"

Twelve thousand letters were sent to Governor Brown between June and September by people urging a halt to construction. The problem, of course, was that Brown is a politician, and no matter the hoax, the postelection poll, and the old ideas–new ideas argument, the river had bellied up in the hustings. As Milton Kramer said, "The vote stands by *itself*."

Even though the appeal to Brown was unsuccessful, the 1975 determination of Dubois, Jennings, and Simballa again fired people's optimism, much like the earlier efforts of Meral, Kay, and EDF that snapped people's inhibitions against fighting New Melones. Once again, there was a rallying point.

Alexander Gaguine arrived in the very unpromising land of Friends of the River, 1611 S Street, Sacramento, after three years of wandering.

The son of a Washington, D.C. lawyer, he grew up in a big red brick house crowded with azaleas off Connecticut Avenue. He graduated in psychology from George Washington University in 1972, when times were turbulent with the war, counterculture, drugs. Droves of young people drifted for lack of direction, and for fun. Gaguine drifted, too, feeling that he had to escape from Washington, where he heard too much of "Go to law school." Essentially, he ran away from home.

In 1973 Gaguine was hitching through Utah, and a Grand Canyon river guide gave him a ride. River guides are talkers, and the river sounded good to Gaguine. A few weeks later, he arrived at Lees Ferry, a put-in for Colorado River trips, where he advertised himself as a grunt, toting outfitter's black bags from tailgate to rowing frame. He always asked if they "needed a crew," which is what he had heard Chesapeake Bay sailors say at the harbor in Annapolis when he was a kid. After five days of grunting, he strapped on a Mae West, hunkered down on a big rubber boat, and disappeared into the mile-deep canyon.

Gaguine would never be the same again. "If you start canoeing on the Delaware River, it's pretty neat," he says. "If you start rafting on the American River, it's pretty neat. But if you start on the Grand Canyon, it just blows you away. People come off that trip and say, 'That changed my life.' There's so much beauty and perfection. To realize that it exists adds such a huge new dimension to what you thought the world was."

He apprenticed as pot scrubber, tended to the ammo-can john, then graduated to boatman. In one of those times around the fire when guides talk about rivers (night after night after night), another boatman, Bob McGavern said, "When you go to California, you've got to see the Stanislaus."

Ka-smack. Gaguine and Debbie Dohm, a San Francisco nurse, took a screaming leap from the Camp Nine Bridge. That was their sudden introduction to this Sierra river. Gaguine had worked two seasons on the Colorado, Green, and Yampa Rivers, where the flow is violent and the standing waves are one story high. Debbie had been a passenger of Alexander's on a Grand Canyon trip. Now, in a tiny raft, they bounced from granite to limestone, crashing and burning on down the river. They remained together, testament to something or other. They headed up north and ran the Rogue in the same duckie, with only one black bag to keep a week's worth of gear dry.

The California river scene impressed Gaguine. Proposition 17 seemed a sure win. "Who would vote against saving a river?" he asks, mimicking the naiveté of those halcyon days. "The war was over and all these people were saving the river; it looked like the Age of Aquarius. There was a solid community of people, and out here there were women guides." Then the initiative lost, and the community collapsed.

In 1975 Gaguine rowed the Stanislaus for OARS, Inc. After the season, he took an internship at the Integral Urban House of the Farallones Institute in Berkeley, where people developed the technology for energy-efficient, ecology-minded urban survival—solar heat, greenhouses, fishponds, windmills, that sort of thing. A dam fight over the Tuolumne River was brewing in 1976, and Gaguine became involved from his new Berkeley base. Helping to collect postcards to politicians, he argued, "They just did in the Stanislaus, now they're after the Tuolumne." At a public hearing, he saw this big guy he recognized from the river. "When you run into Mark Dubois, you remember him," he says. After the hearing, Gaguine wanted to talk about the Stanislaus, but Mark was busy rounding up half a dozen people for a trip to Fosters for ice cream.

A few months later, Gaguine heard of a Stanislaus River bill by State Senator Peter Behr. To offer help, he called Mark, who invited him over to the FOR office/house. "You betcha, right-right, come on over whenever you can." Gaguine was ready to leave Berkeley anyway, so he grabbed his backpack, and in four hours he arrived at the FOR office in Sacramento. "Seeing the country, that's how we all got started," he says. "But ever since I met Mark Dubois I haven't seen much country. Not the landscape part anyway." Gaguine was caught by the special energy of Dubois. "In three days Mark said, 'Why don't you be college coordinator.' Two weeks after I met him I was on TV. I've been on TV ever since."

Today is July 17, 1980. Alexander Gaguine picks up the telephone at FOR and convinces somebody to come to the Bureau of Reclamation hearing tonight, where comments will be heard about the supplemental Environmental Impact Statement on the delivery of New Melones irrigation water—the result of the EDF suit in 1973. It sounds as though Gaguine has also talked this person into a new membership and a $20 donation. He hangs up, then diplomatically handles a call from an anti-draft leader who is irate because somebody put an FOR poster on top of his anti-draft poster on some bulletin board. Then he offers Ronnie James hasty mailing instructions for the latest Stanislaus Action Alert that he has written. Gaguine expresses himself as well as David Oke and has technical expertise to boot; but mostly, he is an organizer.

He rounds up people, starting them on jobs, tipping them on how to approach whomever they are approaching. He coaches volunteers who will visit congressional offices: "The tone should not be aggressive. Go in there respectful but firm. Let them know you'll be watching, that in their district we're strong. In their district [in Northern California] they may have nothing to lose by protecting the canyon." Gaguine coaches on the tactics of rallying, for he has staged a dozen rallies over the last five years. They are one of his favorite things. Give Gaguine a choice, and he will hold a rally every time. He coaches on civil disobedience.

He smiles often, but just barely—just enough to mean congeniality to some people, cockiness to others. He testifies ad lib at the hearing: "People have lived in that canyon for thousands of years. Now 90,000 people go there to lift their spirits. It is very much a part of their lives. This is a place that people love. I think that everybody here can understand that there is a piece of land that you can love." There are many farmers in the audience. Gaguine is not trying to convert the anti-canyon crowd so much as make his own people feel good, to draw them together and into this struggle. He drives back to the office in the battered FOR Datsun pickup. "What I want to do is move out to an organic farm somewhere," he says not too seriously, "but I can't quite get away from the Stanislaus," and he smiles.

Except for the survival of FOR, 1975 was the pits for the river people. Not that they didn't try. In September, 1,000 opponents of the dam under construction rallied at the state capitol. After Judge Thomas MacBride's ruling against Decision 1422 of the State Water Resources Control Board, Governor Brown asked U.S. Senators John Tunney and Alan Cranston and the dam's father, Representative John McFall, to amend a congressional appropriations bill to protect states' rights in water management. They refused, the senators still smarting from 1974, when they had urged a similar rider but were trounced by Bizz Johnson, a powerful Central Valley congressman. Twenty-five state legislators, including the president of the state senate and the speaker of the assembly, urged the governor to continue to fight for states' rights in water resources. Then, on January 26, 1976, State Senator Peter Behr introduced his bill.

Behr comes from the big city—72nd Street on the Upper East Side of Manhattan, where he was born in 1915, making him one of the most senior friends of the river. His urban outlook was balanced by the idyllic Appalachians of New Hampshire, where young Behr spent summers. "My grandmother there romanced me into a lifelong affection for the outdoors," he says. Growing up in New York, you might accept a world that is less than natural. Quite a bit less. When you grow up in New Hampshire, you might get a bellyful of trees and warblers and tumble-rock streams. When you grow up in both places, you've got the makings of an ardent environmentalist. Behr saw the before and the after. The with and the without. The gritty wheels of Newark industry and the clear mountain morning.

In 1940 he passed the New York bar exam, joined a large Manhattan law firm, and then abruptly embarked for the Pacific and World War II. Behr told me he was a deck officer. I didn't know exactly what that meant, so I looked up his record in the California Legislature Handbook and found that he was a lieutenant commander. After the war, he returned to New York, but the fancy office soon palled. He had lucrative opportunities with his banker father, but Peter was a pioneer and resisted the lure of security. He headed for the Coast, settling down in a law firm in San Francisco and a home in Mill Valley in 1949.

Even back then, zoning was a hot issue in Marin County. "One of the supervisors said that if a man wanted to raise hogs in the neighborhood, he should do it," Behr remembers. "People asked if I'd run for his position. I left for a vacation in Mexico and when I came back I discovered they had qualified me. I was stuck." It was the first successful California recall election against a county supervisor, and that is how Behr entered public office.

Today, Behr sits in the Sand Dollar Restaurant at Stinson Beach. His eyes are bright blue and he is tanned from his natural habitat—the Marin outdoors. Weathered like a Plains Indian, he is topped by a Robert Frost crop of snow-white hair. Behr sips coffee and says, "Another cup if you would, please," to the waitress, who smiles. He is wearing khaki pants, sneakers, and a chamois shirt, and obviously enjoys retirement from the elected responsibilities he tended from 1961 on.

Marin was Behr's sweetheart, and he did all that one man could to keep its hillsides green and its seashores free of boardwalks and fences. To save Point Reyes from development, Behr mustered the petition effort that inspired Jerry Meral to collect his shoebox of signatures for the Stanislaus. Point Reyes is now a national seashore. Behr fought against the gutting of Frank Lloyd Wright's only public building, which some people wanted to change from a civic center to a hospital. Throughout his career, Behr managed to be both a liberal and a Republican. "Some of my colleagues suggested I be more honest and change my registry, but I was born into it." With a twinkle in his eye, he says, "I decided to stay and reform the party so it could continue to exist."

In 1970 he ran against State Senator Jack McCarthy, whom nearly everyone would agree to be a non-conservationist. Behr won, drove to Sacramento, and introduced a state wild and scenic rivers bill. Just like that. So what about the macro-plumbing culture of California, CVP, SWP, agribusiness, the timber lobby, LA thirst, hydroelectric power, a century of water development? Behr is so polite you wonder where the guts are, but there he was, a freshman senator going against the momentum of water hustlers since Ham Hall in 1890. The audacity to beat it all was that none of the rivers to be protected were in his district. Well, he lost. But only the first year. The second year he pushed again and butted heads with Randolph E. Collier, dean of the senate, who introduced a stalking-horse in the shape of a toothless scenic rivers measure intended to filch votes from the Behr bill.

A strange practice (though not the only one) of the California legislature is that two contradictory bills can pass. All those legislators who wanted a good wild rivers system voted for Behr's bill; all those whose careers could not weather the wrath of Randy Collier voted for Collier's bill, and there was considerable overlap. Both bills cleared the senate and assembly and landed in tandem on Ronald Reagan's desk. If you've seen one wild river, you have not seen them all; Reagan signed Behr's bill (both being Republicans), and Californians suddenly found themselves with one of the finest state wild and scenic river systems in the country.

It was one of the best—still is—because it named five rivers and scores of tributaries as immediate members of the system, instead of simply authorizing studies and perhaps designating streams later. Moreover, it authorized state management plans with some authority over riverfront development and watershed management (most state river acts only encourage local zoning). Included were the Klamath and its tributaries, the Scott and the Salmon; the Smith and all its feeder streams; the Trinity and the Eel and their major tributaries; the lower American in Sacramento, and the North Fork American above the proposed Auburn Reservoir. The weightiest inclusion was the Middle Fork of the Eel, where the Dos Rios dam was projected as a part of the State Water Plan (Collier's original bill did not include protection for the Eel). Governor Reagan's withdrawal of support for that project is one of his outstanding environmental accomplishments. The dam will be reevaluated in 1984. All of this, of course, happened before Proposition 17. This is the scenic river status that a successful initiative would have brought to the Stanislaus.

Well, how did Peter Behr find out about our river? "Oh, you couldn't avoid it. They were cruising around all the time. Mark stopped in at the office one summer day in 1975—he had reached the stage where he knew the telephone wasn't worth much. Then Jennifer asked if I'd like to go for an outing on the river."

What did the senator think of the Stanislaus? "It has a surprising variety of scenery. The archaeological sites are priceless." Behr pauses. "That can mean they have a very high value, or that they have no assigned value at all." What did he think of Dubois? "I found him quite charming, simple without being simplistic. Back then he knew the Stanislaus had to be saved. He didn't know the legislative complexities, but he worked things out. He is somewhat of a folk hero among his contemporaries, and it is astonishing to be a folk hero among folks."

About Behr, Dubois says, "He always inspired us. He showed us that 'yes, people can make the system work.'"

The senator was angry about the MacBride ruling on Decision 1422. "So far as our water rights are concerned," Behr said, "California will become a colony, ruled by our federal bureaucracy." During the river trip with Jennings and Dubois, Behr said, "If you find you can't get the governor to act, and I don't think you will, then we can try legislation." The senator later drafted a bill to put the Stanislaus in the state scenic rivers system and introduced it in January 1976 as Senate Bill 1482.

Legislative counsel for the state warned that the bill, by itself, would not keep the federal government from flooding the canyon, any more than Decision 1422 had. This view was supported by concurrent events in distant North Carolina, where the state tried to stop a hydroelectric dam on the South Fork of the New River. State scenic river status did nothing to reverse a Federal Power Commission license for the dam. North Carolinians were, however, successful in adding their stream to the national wild and scenic rivers system, and the American Electric Power Company's permit was revoked. With federal protection, the New River of the southern Appalachians flows free today.

Behr persisted anyway. State scenic river status would be a convincing step, he reasoned, in getting federal officials to respect state policies. The Army Corps of Engineers almost always dropped proposals that triggered official state opposition. Further, state scenic river status would reinforce the water board's case in their Decision 1422 appeal, destined for the U.S. Supreme Court.

Jennifer Jennings persisted too. "Jenny could talk to senators and assemblymen. No one else could work so well at that level," Dubois says. She visited lawmakers' staff, office to office, amassing Behr-bill sponsorship by one-third of the senators and one-third of the assemblymen. Paul Richardson, who had earlier been an aide to Peter Behr, joined full time as FOR organizer and lobbyist for the bill.

Mark Dubois, Larry Moss of the Planning and Conservation League, and Peter Behr toured newspaper editorial boards. "It didn't do much good, but it was lively," Behr recounts. "We were up against the usual water lobbyists: farmers, cattlemen, irrigation districts, water districts, Westlands—agribusinessmen who were probably the hopeful recipients of the liquid loot."

The Behr bill had to clear the senate natural resources committee, on which the Marin County senator secured four of eight votes. FOR targeted committee members Rubin Ayala of San Bernardino and Albert Rodda of Sacramento. The Behr bill was considered the "last and best chance" to save the Stanislaus Canyon.

Debbie Dohm, Nancy Magneson, John Cassidy, Bruce Simballa, and Alexander Gaguine hit Los Angeles again to generate constituency pressure on Ayala. They slept at the University of Southern California Ecology Center, where they met Tom Burton, who would later become a FOR researcher.

Meanwhile, the dam people mobilized against the bill. New Melones supporters elected John Hertle and Cliff Humphrey as cochairmen of a new pro-dam group under the crafty title of "People of the River," with the same pitch as Prop 17—build the dam and save the river. Milton Kramer was rehired, and letters were sent to legislators: "SB 1482 reads like an environmental measure, but it would be an environmental disaster."

Through the spring of 1976, the two groups vied for crucial senate committee votes. In the week and a half before the committee voted in May, Rubin Ayala was barraged with 1,200 letters supporting the bill. For thirty-six hours before the vote, Senator Rodda's telephone rang an average of once every thirty seconds with canyon supporters calling. Yet neither Ayala nor Rodda supported the bill. Ayala said, "The people who say that the dam will destroy the only whitewater river west of the Mississippi should realize that the whitewater that exists there now for recreation was created by the Tri-Dam project of 1958 . . . the New Melones is simply not going to cause the irreparable damage to the environment that many have been led to believe." The Behr bill died in committee without ever reaching the senate and house floors, where FOR had strong sponsorship.

What did Peter Behr say about the loss of the Stanislaus scenic river bill? "Like England, we can gain comfort from some of our symbolic defeats. If properly perceived, they can harden one's resolve. Like hammered metal, we either shatter or harden. Hopefully, the environmentalists aren't brittle."

Mark Dubois met with Jerry Meral, and they went for a long quiet walk. "Well, it looks like the Stanislaus is over," Meral said. It was not a question of brittleness. Meral was not brittle. Dubois was devastated.

"My mentor, this genius," Dubois said. "Jerry was saying that it was over. Jerry, who always had some new creative thing to do." I asked Mark if it was like being left on his own, like growing up. "Yes, like being thrown out of the house. Like being told, 'Here's the world. It's all yours.'"

Defeat of the Behr bill in May 1976, marked a turning point for Friends of the River. Meral's recurrent question, what to do next, brought stony silence. In June the river people met to mull over their future. Among them was Brad Welton.

Jerry Meral

Mark Dubois at FOR

Debbie Dohm

Brad Welton

Jennifer Jennings

Don Briggs and Nancy Magnesen
at rally

Peter Behr

Alexander Gaguine

Welton's father had been an avid outdoorsman, running a summer camp in Maine, where Brad lived for five years and got an early start canoeing on the Rangley Lakes and the Kennebec River. While in graduate school at Albany State, Brad took a summer job with the Bureau of Land Management in Washington, D.C. After graduating from Albany in 1973, he planned to enroll in law school in California, but early in the summer he talked to his old supervisor at BLM, who offered him a very special opportunity.

Most of the BLM's domain is sagebrush or tundra, but with some striking exceptions. Wilderness rivers cover its Alaska territory like a trellis. Specialists were hired to deal with these. BLM manages part of the popular Rogue River in Oregon, for which they have sponsored research and management plans galore. But in California, the agency had another river in its care, about which BLM knew little, except that it was popular. Officials wanted to know more, so Welton's boss asked him if he would spend seven weeks in the Sierra foothills, counting faces, interviewing visitors, and identifying problems at a place called Parrotts Ferry. Brad said "sure," and he was off to the Coast.

On his second day at the river, Brad's BLM host took him to a small trailer that sat along the Stanislaus just above Parrotts Ferry. The ranger wanted Brad to meet these people: Ron Coldwell, Fred Dennis, and Mark Dubois. A few days later, Brad was going down the river with fifteen delinquent kids from Sacramento, Mark Dubois, and Nancy Magneson, who lived with friends in a cottage across from the trailer. The group called etcetera was recorded in the Brad Welton book of Stanislaus statistics.

When the survey was completed, BLM officials were amazed at the amount of whitewater use on the Stanislaus—maybe the most in the West, certainly the most of all BLM rivers. From that point on, the agency was deep in conflict and indecision about the wild river and the big dam.

Brad went to law school in Sacramento and San Diego, helped on Proposition 17 and the Behr bill, and passed his bar exam. Involved in tennants' rights, he applied for a job at the Sacramento legal aid office, but they needed women and minorities. "Mark was encouraging and I liked Alexander a whole lot, so I went to work for FOR in 1976." Welton got $250 a month—all of it needed to repay school loans. He would become the central organizer and manager of the Stanislaus Campaign in 1979, after earning a reputation, like Dubois, as an intemperate workaholic.

At the June 1976 meeting FOR survivors talked. And talked. Democracy is a hallmark of this establishment. Everybody has a say. Nobody leads, follows, or focuses, and the discussion is interminable. If you're concerned with efficiency, it can drive you stark raving mad, but an iron hand would shatter with this group. This is the way they do things. We shall skip the marathon of preliminaries that night at 1611 S Street. The outcome was that Friends of the River would organize as a continuing lobby to save rivers all over California—from the undammed Smith to Bakersfield's Kern; from the vacationer-packed Russian to the wild canyons of the Feather; from Redwood Creek to Zabriskie Wash in Death Valley.

Kathy Meyer would edit a newsletter called *Headwaters*. Debbie Dohm and Nancy Magneson would build the membership. What membership? FOR had none. It had staff, volunteers, contributors, but all this time it had had no card-carrying members. "Well, anybody who had given us $10 or more was then considered a member," Debbie said. "We had these names all over the place on little slips of paper." Nancy and Debbie alphabetized them in a Rolodex, and an annual membership was established. By 1980 it would swell to 3,000. FOR's budget would hit $200,000, one-third coming from membership; one-third from outfitters; and one-third from T-shirts, Tom Lovering's fund raiser at his outfitting store, and other odds and ends. Nancy and Debbie filed ten yards of papers and reports. Laurie McCann later organized a board of directors.

"We talked about goals for awhile," Gaguine recalls, "then came up with a list. Mostly Bill Center rattled them off and they sounded good so we said 'sure.'" Nancy Magneson added the most remembered river-saving goal—to have fun doing it.

The committee of twelve found no drought of endangered streams. They plowed into Auburn Dam, which was under construction on the American River. FOR organized local opposition and publicized seismic hazards. After the Oroville earthquake in 1975, the Bureau of Reclamation contracted for multi-million dollar seismic studies that eventually would show Auburn to be unsafe. FOR exposed a U.S. Geological Survey report that documented the hazards, and a map that illustrated the lowlands that would be scoured if the dam ruptured. Along with the governor, 700,000 people lived in the area shaded on the map. Public support for Auburn Dam waned.

Under Bill Center's leadership, FOR fought a chain of dams advanced by the El Dorado irrigation district on the South Fork of the American—California's second most popular whitewater at that time. Under Welton's leadership, they wrestled plans to plug the brilliant North Fork of the Stanislaus in four places.

Gaguine said, "The North Fork case snapped us together as a group." The Calaveras County water district proposed to build the dams and sell the hydroelectric power to the Sacramento Municipal Utility District (SMUD). Brad Welton stormed a SMUD board meeting and demanded public review of the public utility's plans. Gaguine,

Dohm, Fox, and others induced 600 people to pack an auditorium for the next SMUD meeting. "It was just before Christmas," Debbie Dohm said with a giggle. "Six of us dressed up in Santa Claus outfits sewed by Ronit Rieser, and we leafleted in downtown Sacramento. 'Ho, ho, ho. Don't let SMUD rip you off.'" They were chased from the door of one reputable retailer, who thought Santa should stick to promoting merchandise. FOR orchestrated criticism of the dams by economists, and threats of lawsuits by attorneys. Brad organized the experts; Alexander got out the grassroots support.

"We just steamrolled," says Gaguine, with a cocky smile. SMUD dropped the plan, and never picked it up again. A vote was later taken in Calaveras County, where the North Fork dams would be built. At first residents barred the projects, but five months later, after the water district and developers had advertised, the county people voted two to one to build a modified project. Now, in 1980, the scrapping continues over a stream that is among California's most beautiful.

The Stanislaus Canyon was not forgotten. Brad Welton filed suit against the Army Corps of Engineers, which had no environmental impact statement for the new bridge under construction at Camp Nine. State agencies also protested, saying that Decision 1422 limited filling, so that the new bridge would not be needed for a long time. Maybe never. Why waste $2.1 million?

While the corps met some of the National Environmental Policy Act requirements, it disregarded the argument about Decision 1422. Joe Countryman, assistant to the chief of engineering for the corps, argues that the project had been authorized. "We had no reason to wait. We don't just decide to build or not build something on our own." The bridge was delayed one month.

FOR forced special investigations of the rare harvestman spider, which lives in a cave to be flooded. They persuaded the corps to study potential arsenic pollution from gold mines to be flooded by the reservoir. Joe Countryman admits, "The dam fighters had incredible resourcefulness. They used up all their tools, but then they found more."

Tom Graff of EDF found a study done by Woodward and Clyde—seismic consultants—that indicated that faults capable of eight points on the Richter scale might lie within three or four miles of the New Melones dam site. Headlines said "Ignored Report Tells of Quake Danger to Dam." The corps then hired the consultants, who carried out a $300,000 study and reduced their hazard estimates.

After the Behr bill, FOR tactics still filled a garage, but strategy was lean. There was no Jerry Meral–type plan for saving the Stanislaus. It was hit and miss; comment on reports whenever public comments were in order; raise hell if you could find a detail to raise hell about.

The river people didn't yet realize that this was Congress's dam, and that to change anything but fragments of the corps's plan, Congress would have to act in a bold way to save the river. Congress would have to make this a national wild and scenic river, but that is getting ahead of the story.

To lobby against appropriation of annual construction money, Jennifer Jennings flew to Washington, where she served up a bucket of embarrassing licks about price escalation and those buttery benefits versus costs, but nobody cared. Jenny got upset when Congressman Joe Evins, in a Tennessee drawl, tried to figure out her marital status while she testified.

"It's Ms."

"How is that spelled if I might ask?"

"It's spelled MS. What difference does it make whether I'm married or not?" Jennings retaliated. She would not surrender her feminist pride for the sake of getting straight to the Stanislaus.

"Well you look very young," he answered.

"I wouldn't be any older if I was married."

The Southern gentleman, who may or may not have been married, did not vote the way Jennings asked.

Appropriations for New Melones remained unscathed, and up at the river the contractors barreled ahead. In September 1976, they poured concrete around the clock for six days and nights to form a 16,000-ton surge chamber that would fill with water to equalize pressure when the powerhouse was shut down. In November the Archie Stevenot Bridge on Route 49 was completed at a cost of $15 million, named after a Mother Lode native who led efforts to preserve local historic sites.

Adding to the river savers' problems, there was the drought. Beginning in 1975 and running through 1977, it was the driest spell since John C. Frémont had started jotting down notes about California weather. The Sierra Club scheduled outings to the silt-crusted granite of Hetch Hetchy Valley, this being the first time it had not been a watery tomb since the days when John Muir had roamed there with biscuits and black tea in his pack. The hills were parched to kindling. Bark beetles, loving the dryness, infested and killed many pines. While turbines squatted silent in the cement basements of dams, nuclear energy advocates argued the fickleness of hydroelectric power. Near Escalon, Al Sorrenti's well-driller, more than a familiar sight by now, pounded twenty feet deeper to strike water. People in Marin County conserved 60 percent, because they had to. While Friends of the River waged last-ditch efforts to delay the dam, reservoirs were hardening chalk-dry, with scrawny Herefords picking at rare tufts of grass where water was supposed to be.

Peter Behr criticized the management of the reservoirs, contending that we squandered the water when we had it; that the Bureau of

Reclamation didn't operate the dams as planned; that more water should have been held back, instead of being sold dirt cheap early in the drought. By allowing shortages to worsen, the dam-building agencies assured vigorous demand for new dams. "The demand for water in this state is insatiable," Behr said. "To pay for the dams, at least in part, water is stored to be sold, and it will be sold, whether it is prudent or not, because the corps and the bureau are catering to their own constituencies, and don't want to let them down. So dams and delivery systems, like underground aquifers, are foreordained to be overdrafted."

The FOR office was moved from 1611 S Street, near the state capitol, to a residential neighborhood—to a home offered at low rent by Dubois's mother (donations from other people have included a truck, a motorcycle, a ten-speed bicycle without a back wheel, a subscription to the *Bee*, a patched raft, scrap paper from Grady's print shop, a rusty file cabinet, and ten ears of corn from an anonymous Central Valley farmer). Mark and Alexander were leery of the move. "We'll be too far from the capitol," they complained. Debbie, Nancy, Laurel Nesbitt, and others said, "Let's move. Over there we'll have more room. We need it. We can have a garden and a yard for people to sleep out on." They moved, people slept out, and the lobbyists pedaled bikes.

The place is a very basic, one-story stucco house, furnished with donated furniture that looks, well, like donated furniture. Several pieces grow leaner by the month, as people sit in them and squish out stuffing through ruptured upholstery. An ancient leather-covered chair was once easy, is now emaciated. Its springs poke at the visitor like the bony spine of a Forty-niner's mule. Debbie, Laurel, and Nancy painted the dark walls light, then decorated with river posters. News clippings surround the commode. A library of pamphlets is available to visitors. Food and overnight floor space are available to all volunteers.

At FOR headquarters, which once housed eight full-time residents, they do not have the low-tech sophistication of Gaguine's Integral Urban House in Berkeley, but they do well. The only time the furnace is turned on is when somebody sneaks past Dubois to the thermostat and ups it to 60. Soon enough Dubois turns it down again. Dishwater goes on the outdoor plants, except those to be eaten—there is something or other in the soap, even the biodegradable kind from the Sacramento Co-op, that makes it an unwanted additive to the organic garden. The FOR composting system is more elaborate than its filing system, and is pursued with more consistency. On occasion, people not living at the house partake of compost-pile benefits, importing their garbage and stirring it into the rich black brew maintained by Dubois. The organic refuse will grow squash, chard, and tomatoes to nourish river lovers next year. The bathroom shower drain stays plugged (except for very occasional scouring), and the accumulated water is dipped by bucket to flush the toilet. One sticker on the wall reads, "Don't shower by the hour." Another says, "Shower with a friend."

Outside, the yard gets a little brown in summer—the color of the foothills in June—because it is not watered much. It is ecologically diversified. Weedy. The back yard is screened by a wooden fence that hides a border of vegetables planted mostly by Dubois, the only continuous resident since 1978. Mark is always talking about playing in the garden. It provides therapy for him and food for everybody. Thou shalt not buy any commercially grown, pesticide-laced produce that you don't have to. The American River, with its belt of green, only a ten-minute bike ride away, is Dubois's other therapeutic place, a river park the whole way through the city.

Out back there is a garage—Dubois's office and quarters. Covering a picnic table, his papers bear hand printing so small that only a few interpreters can read it. Is he conserving pencil lead? Red and blue telephones sit among the papers. In the house, Ronnie James continually answers calls, yelling out the bedroom window to the garage, "Mark, red phone," or "Mark, blue phone." Faded placards from a dozen Stanislaus rallies organized by Gaguine and others are tucked in corners and wedged behind shelves. Friends of the River T-shirts are warehoused among outdated files and reprints of magazine articles about the river. A homemade table of three-quarter-inch particle board is always covered with stuff. The garage's spare design and its open door and windows (plastic is tacked on in winter) give the impression of your basic structure in a less consumer-oriented culture—say Mexico or the Hoopa Reservation; but inside Dubois may be working on state water resources control board testimony, or hashing water-pricing policy over the telephone with Gray Davis, the governor's chief of staff, or Leo Eisel, director of the Federal Water Resources Council. Mostly though, Mark talks to people about seeing politicians, always building their enthusiasm and helping them to organize their thoughts for a visit to Congressman Don Clausen or Senator Cranston.

"It sort of freaked out the neighbors at first," Debbie Dohm says. "We expected it. Then after some of them came over and visited, we got along real well." Mostly. One neighbor squealed to the city codes officer when carpenters of FOR were remodeling the garage into Dubois's office suite. They had to halt construction, which, along with Mark's spare tastes, partly explains the less-than-posh environs.

"We were getting spending money—food money—from Tom Lovering, the treasurer, but only when we needed it," Debbie recalls.

Always full of good humor, she dramatizes FOR austerity in a squeaky animated voice: "Tom, can I please have two dollars?" Once they were settled into the new house, staff were doled out a regular allowance —five dollars a week. "Mark, of course, never took his," Debbie says. "Then in 1976 we got salaries of seventy dollars a month." She raises her eyebrows at all the things you can do with such a bulging wallet. They even went to movies now and then.

In my Stanislaus files, there is a promotional piece by the State Building and Construction Trades Council, urging opposition to Proposition 17. It reads, in part, "Through use of this technique local projects of any kind, whether it be water, electric power, transportation or housing, can be picked off one by one by well-financed pressure groups." The council was talking about FOR before the five dollar allowance.

Why did they do it? "Love of a river," I hear over and over.

Laurie McCann, who would become a co-director of the group said, "What it comes down to is that the river's still alive, and death is a negative factor."

"It's a spiritual place." Debbie Dohm says. "It's the first time I worked for something I really believe in. It was exciting, people were supportive, and things were getting done. There were real good times, a wild enthusiasm." Part of it was just plain fun.

Peter Behr says, "Their lifestyles are such that they aren't used to money—not that they don't want it. FOR began with a deficit and will expire with a deficit, but not because of it. It is unique among organizations; money doesn't matter. I'm convinced they can live on nothing. They must be fed by the birds."

Tom Graff, attorney for EDF says, "They're a pretty unusual group of people. Folks who will band together. They're pretty damn good. Some of the antinuclear groups have old-time radicals, but there is no young environmental group like FOR. They're non-sexist too: Fox, Schifferle, McCann, others—they've had some persuasive women and good lobbyists."

In 1977 Brad Welton worked hard on the Tuolumne River defense, opposing a federal energy regulatory commission license that would have allowed the city of San Francisco to plan new hydroelectric projects. He spent much of his time in San Francisco, and so rented a Berkeley apartment that served by default as an FOR work center. Soon Catherine Fox, Dick Roos-Collins, and Nicole Magneson were doing river work in the Bay Area. A San Francisco office was opened at Fort Mason Center—a military base converted to offices, meeting rooms, exhibition space, and theaters for non-profit ventures that include everything from children's festivals to Japanese martial arts and a Zen restaurant called Greens, where Jerry Brown sometimes eats. Etcetera, the Oceanic Society, and other groups have offices in these old three-story military buildings that end at pilings in the Bay.

FOR was becoming more professional. They had four telephones. They had Welton's legal expertise. Catherine Fox specialized in fund raising, directing the Friends of the River Foundation, and Dick Roos-Collins brought an analytical touch blended with a feel for publicity.

Activist tactics were not abandoned, however. In August 1978, a walk for the river was held, with sixty people participating off and on, fourteen of whom trekked six days from Camp Nine to Sacramento to focus public attention on the Stanislaus. At the capitol, outside Jerry Brown's window, they planted a toyon tree from the doomed lower canyon below Parrotts Ferry. Cathy Duncan was walk-mother, and laughs about the night the town manager of Jackson gave them permission to sleep in the local park. "He didn't tell us that the automatic sprinklers start at 1:00 A.M.," she says. Serving as Los Angeles media coordinator for the walk, Tom Huntington started working with FOR. He was a Southern Californian, who had started running rivers in Oregon, where he had gone to college, then guided for OARS. Huntington would become a leading grassroots organizer and a mainstay of FOR enthusiasm.

Talking about the changes in FOR, Thorne Gray of the *Modesto Bee* criticizes early efforts during the Proposition 17 struggle—the approaches that Roanoke took. "Instead of selling the values of the canyon, they were on the offensive, fighting the corps and the farmers. Now it's different. When Mark got on board after 17, they switched the story, talked about the river and that place, and the tragedy that these things have no stated economic value. Mark tells that story and tells it in a valuable way. His sincerity is obvious. He put the argument on the footing it should be on.

"FOR is a formidable opponent," Gray continues. "Tom Burton and Dick Roos-Collins are really sharp characters. Then they hired Phil Williams, who is a genius in his field of hydrology. Mark can walk into anybody's office; he has access. People are happy to say they're his friend. It is an immense conflict, and Mark is a giant up against other giants—engineers who are trying to master the river."

Mark's father, Noel Dubois, who has written letters to editors about the extravagant waste of money on water projects, has an old mining claim in the Trinity Mountains up north, where Mark and his brother Gar spent vacations and came to love the outdoors. They'd hike and mess around and dig for gold a little. Then it was caving and the river. Mark has had only two jobs besides this one in the FOR garage. He

once filled jugs in a bottled-water plant, where he was faster than a
new machine that the manager had just installed. "I moved fast," Mark
says, "but also broke a few extra bottles." Today Dubois talks about
being stronger than machines—the bulldozer type. Being stronger by
being weaker. "This spring I was walking through a meadow up above
the canyon and I looked back and saw wildflowers that I stepped on. I
felt bad, then thought, "I could have been on a motorcycle. I could
have been in a jeep. Or I could have been on a bulldozer." Dubois does
not plead innocence. By being alive, we consume resources, sucking
some of nature dry. "There is a place where we all make trade-offs, and
I'm trying to minimize that."

In April 1980, Dubois stood barefoot in a conference room in
Washington, D.C., and half joked about cutting rubber trees to make
shoes. A month later, at Camp Nine, he was helping a river guide load
gear. They didn't have enough "hoopy"—nylon cord used to tie gear
into the raft. Dubois held a six-foot cord in front of a ten-foot load and
said, "Good practice—how to get by on less." While no one else is as
Spartan as Mark, he sets an FOR image both in lifestyle and in
Stanislaus tactics.

The tactics are what Thorne Gray means when he talks about Mark
coming on board after Proposition 17. "Back during Prop 17, it
sometimes didn't feel good to me, and I'm just now starting to see
why," Mark says. "It feels like the environmental movement overall
has made a key mistake in finding scapegoats, in attacking the other
side, not respecting them as people." He says "people" softer. "Now
they're shooting back, and they can do it better. We need to learn to
help them understand us, to work together more. You get back what
you give to people. Give hate or anger or accusations, and you get that
back. This doesn't mean turning around. It means giving them the
opportunity to change. We met with some of the farmers and found
that we agree on 80 percent of the things we talk about.

"Where does trust start? We have to trust each other to make it in
this world, and now there is almost no trust anymore. It has to
start someplace.

"Last fall I was in the canyon and saw the geese flying south. I've
heard that they fly in formation because it's easier; it takes them less
energy for their long journey. They have the same goal. I didn't see
them biting each other's backs. One goose alone would have a tough
time. A flock of geese will make it in the long run, but we might not."

For Dubois, this is not a dam fight or a river battle. He doesn't
usually use those words. He is not fighting. It is not a combative thing
for him. It is doing what he believes in. He quotes Mahatma Gandhi
something like this: "If the other side doesn't agree, then you haven't
won." He says, "Our strength is in what we love. We don't have to be
noisy. We need to show what we love.

"I'm starting right here with this river, but healing the planet is the goal." Dubois gives this signal that he will never be done. He has jobs to look forward to. It is not likely that he will have time to work in a bottled-water factory again.

"Gandhi says there is enough for everybody's need, but not for everybody's greed. The *Global 2000* study by the Council on Environmental Quality shows that with everybody trying to reach our standard of living, disaster is coming. At our rate of consumption, there just isn't enough to go around. We need to change."

What will happen in the struggle for the Stanislaus? "Something new is needed—people refusing to allow destruction to happen, saying 'no' when they see it. Peaceful resistance and a change of commitment is needed, saying 'yes' to the positive alternative that will help us in the long run."

CHAPTER SEVEN

The Case
for Compromise

First, in 1966, the Army Corps of Engineers built the overlook—the
visitors' observation area. You get nowhere without good PR, and, as
a rule, people thought that the construction of a dam was beautiful.
Then came access roads, a work headquarters complete with a runway
for the general's airplane, and a low-level intake structure. At the dam
site, the canyon was scaled by stripping away all the vegetation, soil,
and loose rock. Then commenced the scraping, blasting, carving,
bulldozing, truck loading, and transporting of earth from just above
the New Melones dam site to the site itself. Dirt and rock were
crammed tight into Iron Canyon. Networks of hairpin switchback
roads were pounded by trucks. Pick up a load of dirt, dump it on the
dam. Pick up a load of dirt, dump it on the dam. Those drivers for Guy
F. Atkinson Company must still twist the bends of that dusty route in
their sleep. They spent four years hauling dirt to make that dam. By
mid-1976 a last-ditch effort to halt construction was beyond the realm
of possibility. The dam would be finished.

When the Proposition 17 struggle was being waged, construction
was 20 percent complete. During the Behr bill debate, it was 40 percent
complete. By October 1978, the whole thing was done. What chance is
there of saving a river after a dam is built? Someone in the field of
water politics has said that once they move that first shovel of dirt
you'll never get them to put it back. That is largely true, but the Cross
Florida Barge Canal was one-third complete, with $50 million spent, in
1971. A dam had been built and channels dug along the Withlacoochee
River. The next step was to dredge the river-swamp of the Oklawaha
to create a big ditch, impoverishing Florida for a barge shortcut
between New York and Houston. The environmentalists were
supported by central Florida developers, because the canal would
hemorrhage away groundwater needed for booming Florida

development. The Environmental Defense Fund and Florida Defenders of the Environment filed suit, and the canal was stopped by President Nixon. Jimmy Carter requested $13 million in 1978 for reclamation—to put the rivers back together again. In another Florida case, the Everglades Jetport was partly built, then halted because of its brutal effect on the Glades, Florida groundwater, and wildlife.

Closer to home, San Francisco's Embarcadero Expressway is a testament to the power of changing minds. Three lanes wide and two tiers high, it would have connected the Oakland Bay Bridge and Interstate 80 to the Golden Gate Bridge and points north. The freeway would have been elevated above ground, arching along the waterfront, where it would disrupt the city least. The entire Marina district would have been cut off by the expressway. Fisherman's Wharf would have been leveled or truncated. There would be no view of the Bay without a foreground of concrete and steel. The people of San Francisco said no, and today the Embarcadero Expressway hangs in the air unfinished. They are considering its demolition.

But the change of mind doesn't always come in time. Planned in the 1950s, Tellico Dam blocks the Little Tennessee River today. It is one of thirty major dams built by the Tennessee Valley Authority, one of sixty-nine in the Tennessee basin. As in the New Melones case, environmentalists were late on the scene. Why always late? Because most dam fighters are a product of the environmental movement of the 1960s and 70s, when the science of ecology began to rival that of engineering and other competitors. Some people think that going to the moon showed us how small earth really is. We have consumed the wild, the natural places of North America. Now we sit with a shred of tapestry, and the remainder seems worth saving to some people.

The environmentalists pointed out that Tellico Dam would flood the last large section of the Little Tennessee, would drown one of the finest trout rivers in the East, flood rich farmland, bury sites sacred to the Cherokee nation, and doom a species of life—a small fish called the snail darter. It is only two inches long, but still a whole species, no other like it. When this news arrived, Tellico was almost built.

Through the courts and a contorted legislative process lasting for years, the dam was halted, first by an injunction under the Endangered Species Act, then through a congressionally created "God Committee," authorized to determine if a project is worth the extermination of a species. The committee said it wasn't. Members Charles Schultze, chairman of the President's Council of Economic Advisors, averred that Tellico would not pay for itself in any case. S. David Freeman, director of TVA, opposed the completion of the dam too. The Cherokee and the environmentalists cheered.

But Congress will be Congress. Tennessee Congressman John Duncan amended the Public Works Appropriations Bill of 1978 to fill Tellico no matter what. No other laws apply. Forget the Endangered Species Act. Forget the National Environmental Policy Act. To hell with an economic evaluation that was properly done. Just fill it, fill it. In a legislative process that lasted about forty-five seconds, the bill passed. Carter signed it, TVA shoved in the cork, and the valley disappeared. The Little Tennessee is gone, down there somewhere in the murky deep with the graves of the Cherokee and a species of small spotted fish.

So what does all this have to do with the Stanislaus? Well, quite a bit. It shows that New Melones is not the only project opposed at the eleventh hour. But nobody had ever waged a campaign quite as late as this. To stop New Melones with its construction complete would be the toughest dam fight ever fought anywhere, and the prospects did not look good.

The dam was complete, but the reservoir need not be completely filled. "Parrotts Ferry is the Limit," the river people said. "We propose a compromise—fill New Melones to 300,000 acre-feet, three times the size of Old Melones. Go ahead and flood sixteen miles of river above the dam, but don't flood the last nine. Decision 1422 of the state can be satisfied while saving the canyon. We can have a working dam and a wild river."

How could they be serious? You mean to have a dam and not fill it? "I think it is just ridiculous to have spent $341 million on a dam and then let it sit there," says John Hertle. Milton Kramer, Al Sorrenti, Senator John Garamendi, Assemblyman Norman Waters, and just about every farmer between Redding and Bakersfield say the same thing. This alternative is variously "ridiculous" or "absurd," it "staggers the imagination," "blows the mind," or is "stupid." And so it would seem.

The Bureau of Reclamation, which would operate New Melones, estimated that it would need a pool of 595,000 acre-feet for the uses approved in Decision 1422. That would flood the canyon to elevation 903 feet, or roughly the lower third, up to the South Fork. During floods, a reservoir of 1,045,000 acre-feet would lap at the bottom pools of Rose Creek, two-thirds of the way up the nine-mile canyon. In keeping with Decision 1422, this assumed no storage for new irrigation water—only irrigation for prior rights (replacement of irrigation water that had come from Old Melones Dam).

Friends of the River countered with its own case for a moderate reservoir. First of all, they said, the dam would not just sit there. With a Parrotts Ferry limit, it would do most of its intended job. Tom

Burton, FOR researcher; Dick Roos-Collins, analyst and publicist; and Philip Williams, a consulting hydrologist (with help from Donald Kelley, a fisheries biologist), developed the rationale for partial filling. Later, in 1979–80, FOR researchers Rick Hardy and Betty Andrews would add to the calculations and update the case for the river. Roos-Collins always calls this a "moderate reservoir," not liking the half-effective sound of "partial filling."

Call it what you will, Friends of the River's arguments for no flooding above Parrotts Ferry went like this:

Hydroelectric power: Dr. Philip Williams concluded that about 140 million kilowatt-hours (kwh) could normally be supplied by a Parrotts Ferry reservoir, though turbine modifications would be needed to prevent damage at low water levels. Since 430 million kwh would be generated from a full reservoir, a decrease of about 290 million would result under the FOR plan. Yield could be increased another 50 to 100 million kwh if turbines were adjusted.

Even at full capacity, New Melones would produce power for only about two and a half hours per day, 265 days a year, and PG&E reported that its need for power of this dependability was "limited," and that the amount of time that the hydroelectric plant would operate was less than the utility considered acceptable. A moderate reservoir would not provide new water for irrigation (it would only meet the prior rights of farmers), and so it would not result in pumping demands of 50 to 100 million kwh. A full reservoir would therefore provide only 190 to 240 million kwh more than the moderate reservoir. FOR argued that energy and water conservation are better ways to gain energy.

Water quality: The Bureau of Reclamation, FOR, and the state all agreed that outdated water-quality data were used in the reservoir management plan. Much of the New Melones water-quality release was intended to dilute well salts that work their way down the Tuolumne and into the San Joaquin and Delta. Philip Williams reported that storage needs had been reduced by 30,000 and 60,000 acre-feet due to the capping of Tuolumne gas wells in 1977. Cleansing flows from New Don Pedro Dam were not considered either. Roos-Collins said that irrigation from New Melones would dump 20,000 to 50,000 acre-feet of polluted return flow from irrigated fields into the river, with the potential of offsetting much of the proposed water-quality release. A moderate reservoir would not provide new water for irrigation, and so it would not result in hot, salty return flows.

Fisheries: A state department of fish and game memo on February 5, 1976, said that a full reservoir could cause a 90 percent reduction in king salmon—a species that the dam was intended to restore. Holding back so much water, the river wouldn't have the high springtime flows needed to push smolts (young salmon) out to sea. Later the agency said that fishery needs might be met with a Parrotts Ferry limit, depending on water temperatures below the dam. Donald Kelley, FOR's fisheries consultant, reported that the proposed reservoir could be reduced by 150,000 acre-feet to the benefit of salmon by maintaining higher spring releases. The U.S. Fish and Wildlife Service estimated that a full reservoir would result in an average salmon run of 3,200 fish, and that a moderate reservoir would increase the run to 5,100 (the Fish and Wildlife Service listed a 600,000 to 800,000 acre-foot reservoir as optimal for downstream fish life).

Recreation: The U.S. Water Resources Council found that existing reservoirs (eleven within thirty miles) could accommodate the increase in flatwater recreation for fifty years. FOR pointed to Don Pedro Reservoir, which was used by 350,000 people in 1978, yet has capacity for 500,000. FOR questioned the Bureau of Reclamation's estimates of recreation use—ultimately three million visitor-days per year—by comparison with Shasta Reservoir, which is two times larger but receives only 2.1 million. The Resources Agency of California estimated that only 330,000 visitors would be registered at a full New Melones. FOR pointed out that flatwater activity is growing very slowly, while river recreation is booming.

As to jobs, a full reservoir would employ 37 people. A moderate reservoir would employ 25 to 30 workers, but river recreation would employ at least 150, as opposed to none if the canyon were flooded. Then FOR went through the values of the canyon: third most floated whitewater in the country (in 1979), the only river that combined accessibility, history, unique geology, exciting but not dangerous whitewater, and so forth.

Flood control: Williams reported that winter draw-down to 120,000 acre-feet could leave enough storage below Parrotts Ferry for most floods. For the highest floods, temporary filling above Parrotts Ferry would be possible. Flood control from a moderate reservoir would be even better than from a massive one, FOR argued, since there would be more empty reservoir space to hold back high water in emergencies.

Irrigation: FOR said that all prior users (irrigators who used water from Old Melones Reservoir) could be supplied with a Parrotts Ferry limit. Williams argued that the Bureau of Reclamation's estimate of prior rights allowed for 200,000 acres, instead of the 102,000 that Old Melones actually served (the difference represents the yield of Tulloch Dam, which the bureau proposed to supply from New Melones, thus allowing Tulloch to remain full). Even at full irrigation potential, which includes 200,000 acre-feet of new yield, the entire output of New Melones would equal only half of 1 percent of California's water needs. Roos-Collins even considered evaporation. The FOR-endorsed reservoir would lose 10,000 acre-feet per year to the Sierra sky, while a full reservoir would lose 40,000 acre-feet.

The recharging of overdrawn groundwater would not be possible with a Parrotts Ferry limit. But that would not be likely to happen anyway, FOR said, pointing to the past sixty years of water development in California: new water, even when intended to recharge groundwater, is usually used to irrigate new lands, because that is where the money is made. For solutions to the groundwater overdraft, FOR proposed water conservation. The group sought to make New Melones a symbol of waste and emphasized the need for water conservation and management programs.

All in all, FOR and its consultants concluded that requirements for prior irrigation rights could be reduced to 140,000 acre-feet below the Bureau of Reclamation's estimates; water quality needs could be reduced by 30,000 to 60,000 acre-feet; fisheries would be enhanced by a reduction of 150,000 acre-feet; and the "gross pool" for flood control could be cut by 120,000 to 220,000 acre-feet. All the requirements of State Decision 1422 could be met with a 270,000 acre-foot reservoir —30,000 less than the Parrotts Ferry level—with temporary inundation to 630,000 acre-feet (two miles above Parrotts Ferry) during extreme floods.

Most ways you look at it, a partly filled reservoir is better than a full one. Better for fish, water quality, recreation, and employment. Not quite so good for electricity and irrigation, but then a full reservoir isn't that great anyhow. Even moderate efforts at energy and water conservation can make up the difference.

Of course, that is what FOR says. We all know that they love the river, and while their analytical approach may be impressive, we had best be wary of their claims. To the Friends of the River, the Stanislaus is almost more than just a river. Amen to a prestigious member of the state legislature who said, "This river-religion is getting a little out of hand." Those of us who attach material and economic importance to a resource had best be on our guard against anyone who professes to see a metaphysical reality there. Of FOR's position, Milton Kramer said, "They just don't know enough about this thing. It's very involved and they just aren't as informed as they ought to be." Enough of these river friends.

And enough of the Army Corps of Engineers and the Bureau of Reclamation, clinging to the arthritic justifications cited in chapter 3: $3\frac{1}{8}$ percent interest rates; dilution of pollution; and the argument that motorboats are wonderful, but river rafting isn't worth a cent, because nobody was doing it when the rules were established for project justifications.

Enough of the Stanislaus River Flood Control Association, Californians Against Proposition 17, People of the River, and everything else the pro-dam people call themselves. It's as clear as a North Fork pool in August—the flood control association is a few farmers who cultivate rich bottomlands and want the government to flush out the cash to keep their crops from drowning. They've paid taxes all these years, they figure, and now they should have something coming for it. Other farmers salivate over irrigation water at $3.50 or $5.00 per acre-foot, which costs the government $50–100 per acre-foot to deliver. It makes sense that these people would support the dam. Money shouts.

Forget the FOR, Army Corps of Engineers, Bureau of Reclamation, and pro-dam people—let's take a totally different group and see what they say about this sticky subject of filling a reservoir.

The state of California is vested with a bundle of waterway duties bigger than a farmer's list of chores in May. The state can stop you from polluting. It licenses motorboats. It tests water and closes down restaurants if the customers are likely to get sick. The State Water Resources Control Board, as we have seen in connection with Decision 1422, must approve of the storage and withdrawal of water from rivers and reservoirs. The Department of Water Resources erects dams and carves out canals—the State Water Project. The Department of Fish and Game manages fish, and is responsible for a state wild and scenic rivers program. The secretary of the Resources Agency is directed to oversee the environment of California, which—like the Bureau of Reclamation's "multipurpose water development to meet diverse water needs of a maturing economy and an expanding population"—covers just about anything.

Here on the Stanislaus, we witnessed the role of the Reagan governorship's water board in denying the federal government a permit to fill New Melones, first losing in the lower courts, and finally winning in the Supreme Court.

The state took on an additional role after Jerry Brown appointed Huey Johnson as secretary of the Resources Agency in August 1977. Before Johnson, under Governor Ronald Reagan, Resources Secretary Ike Livermore had taken a concerned, but unaggressive, stance in the Stanislaus quagmire. He made some mud pies there, but wasn't about to venture into quicksand. Governor Brown's first resources secretary was Claire Dedrick, formerly vice-president of the Sierra Club. Immediately on taking office, she decided to require loggers to write environmental impact statements, resulting in a logging truck convoy to Sacramento, threats to cut the trees in Capitol Park, and the appearance in the governor's office of a bunch of loggers, wearing suspenders, fondling axes, and glowering. After that, Dedrick was not so assertive. Brown replaced her with Huey Johnson.

Johnson has done a good job of creating an earthy enclave in the institutional space of a sixteen-story germless office building where you can't open the windows. Of all the resources directors' offices in all the fifty states, I'll bet only his has a canvas chair that swings from the ceiling. The secretary's work is done on a desk of polished redwood burl that looks like a stump. In addition to the swing seat, visitors' chairs are woven like baskets from California oak and covered with leather. They surround a coffee table of a deep grain that I do not recognize. On one wall there is a personal note from Justice William O. Douglas, attached to an autographed exerpt from his acclaimed "trees have standing" decision. Another wall is dominated—it seems to me the whole office is dominated—by a five-foot surreal painting of a woman with a bird's nest and flowers growing from her hair. Wildflowers splash the foreground, zebras play in the middle, and another goddess rises into the background sun. I am already impressed, and the secretary has not even arrived. He doesn't arrive, so his receptionist schedules a lunch meeting at a modest restaurant for the next day.

A native of Michigan, Johnson looks like a resources secretary most anywhere. He wears a conservative suit, is partly bald, and moves quickly. His agency houses 13,000 employees and a budget of almost a billion dollars. He hardly conceals the fact that all the land, water, and air of California are his responsibility, and that we aren't treating these three elements right. Huey is a busy man what with trying to correct the oversights. He is thinking about smog inspection rules for cars; Yosemite Park's master plan; contracts for Oroville water; the gulls whose nesting grounds are being destroyed because Mono Lake is drying up; a Smith River management plan that may bring another convoy of loggers to town; whether or not to reinstate the Lake Tahoe Regional Planning Agency, which he earlier dumped in protest against Nevada's slipshod development; forest fires; a controversial campground proposal in Frank's Valley, tucked between Muir Woods and Muir Beach; and the population capacity of California—an issue that would get Johnson into a beehive of political trouble. Now here I am to bull about the Stanislaus.

People have warned me about a twenty-minute limit. The secretary gets uncomfortable after twenty minutes. "Make it quick and to the point," I have been coached. We talk, however, about the philosophy of resource management and the dynamics of change, and it is more than an hour before Huey signals the urgency of other state affairs.

"It's been twenty years since I left industry, and there has been a major transition happening," the secretary says. "We're struggling to leave an era of exploitation and enter an era of intensive management. California and the United States can remain very rich and comfortable if we just don't dump our resources into the dinosaurs of this age—doomed institutions. Look at the government's bailout of Chrysler. They don't have contemporary management. Corporations that do will survive. Some managers still believe in central technology. Finally, they'll be thrown out and we'll get a transition." Some legislative aides express bewilderment about Johnson. They say that he is out of his element in state politics.

"There is this desperate drive to supply more," he says. "It's difficult to get some people to listen to conservation appeals. We have never thought of resources as finite, but we live in a finite world. We can still have a healthy and vigorous economy if we recognize the limits of our resources. This is an era of limits."

Johnson developed a Renewable Resources Investment Fund—a program of state investment ("government investment is different from government spending") in resources that, if properly managed, will return wealth to Californians forever. Money from taxes and bond sales would be invested in resources that would result in commercial profits. Timber management, soil stabilization, and commercial fisheries would be stressed.

Richard Hammond, Johnson's deputy secretary, who was originally appointed by Claire Dedrick, is from Wisconsin. With medium-length hair, dark-rimmed glasses, khaki pants, a striped shirt, and a knit tie, he looks Ivy League-gone-Coast. Instead of a sports coat or suit coat, he has on a blue chamois shirt unbuttoned and untucked. Hammond once appeared wearing a bowtie at a Friends of the River conference where he was a speaker. He apologized for looking "preppy" (as he has been labeled by some hard-core Levi's wearers) and then disarmed his audience by saying that he grew up on the lakes of the upper Midwest and "that makes me a flatwater preppy." Next Hammond armed his audience with a speech that was nearly inspirational.

Hammond first heard of the Stanislaus and New Melones at an orientation meeting on his first day in office. He wasn't sure how to approach it, but money was one way. He and Johnson saw a need for hard economics in conjunction with the ecology and hydrology, forestry, biology, agronomy, limnology, landscape architecture, wildlife management, lawyers, park cops, PR, and politics that make up the concerns of a state resources agency. Johnson created the new position of assistant secretary for resources, and sought an economist to fill it.

He found Guy Phillips, also from Wisconsin, a PhD in environmental economics. Phillips had worked with the chairman of the Wisconsin State Legislature's Natural Resources Commission, was a founder and director of that state's most effective environmental lobbying group, and had unsuccessfully run for supervisor in a blue-collar county. The

University of Wisconsin hired him to conduct an economic analysis of LaFarge Dam on the Kickapoo River, a small southern Wisconsin stream that you have seen in bucolic water colors of green pastures, covered bridges, and rocky bluffs. A corps project to revamp the landscape was started, then stopped when Governor Patrick Lucey, Senators Gaylord Nelson and William Proxmire, and others scrutinized the benefits and costs exposed by Phillips (all these people had supported the project earlier). His analysis showed that only a select crowd would fatten from flood-control gravy. Flood-plain owners would be left dry, and so would the public, after footing the tab of a spendthrift. In spite of local outrage, the project was terminated, like Carter's Sprewell Bluff (at least until the politics change).

In 1976 Phillips accepted a position as chairman of the graduate program in Environmental Administration at the University of California at Riverside. While on a twelve-month leave of absence to direct the Public Interest Economics Foundation in San Francisco, he was hired as an assistant secretary by Huey Johnson in February 1979.

It is Johnson's style to expound a philosophy, as he did with me over lunch in a K Street restaurant, then allow his deputies enough slack to choose their issues, be creative, and set their own pace—enough to hang themselves if they don't know any better. He turned New Melones over to Guy Phillips, who saw a swamp of economic variables, oversights, and economists' fantasies—$3\frac{1}{8}$ percent interest, for example. He prepared a report in a modest blue cover titled *The New Melones Project: A Review of Current Economic and Environmental Issues.* The modern-day equivalent of the dynamite used on the Owens Valley aqueduct, it is the work of a qualified economist working for the agency that first proposed New Melones as part of a state water plan in the twenties, and that assumes more far-reaching responsibilities for the land and water of California than any other. We have seen what the Army Corps of Engineers says, what the Bureau of Reclamation says, what Friends of the River and the advocates of the dam say. Now here is what the California Resources Agency says about the intended purposes of New Melones:

Hydroelectric power: The annual difference between a Parrotts Ferry limit and a full reservoir would be equivalent to the energy Californians burn in oil every three hours. Sixty years of New Melones operation would equal the energy use of the nation for only one day. Hydroelectric output would occur only 10 percent of the time. When operated for maximum power output, power sales may not even cover operations, maintenance, and transmission costs. "The combination of relatively high capacity and low plant factor make New Melones power suitable for only specialized peaking purposes. . . . Operation for hydroelectric power would likely cause a $385 million fiscal drain on the already financially distressed CVP. By the year 2000, full hydroelectric potential of New Melones would equal only $1/10$ of 1% of California's electricity."

Water quality: Both a Parrotts Ferry limit and a maximum reservoir would yield up to 70,000 acre-feet in water-quality releases. A maximum reservoir would divert about 200,000 acre-feet per year from the Delta. To the extent that this irrigation water returns to the San Joaquin, it will aggravate water-quality problems in the Delta.

Fisheries: Both a moderate and a maximum reservoir would yield 98,000 acre-feet for fish life. Full operation for power and irrigation would conflict with fisheries.

Recreation: Flatwater with a Parrotts Ferry limit would amount to 3,320 acres; a maximum reservoir would provide 12,119 acres. The full reservoir would add only 8,800 acres of flatwater to the existing 45,000 acres within 25 miles. It would increase California's flatwater acreage by only 1 to 4 percent, but would result in the loss of nine miles of irreplaceable whitewater. Recreation benefits can be maximized with a 300,000 acre-foot reservoir (a Parrotts Ferry limit).

Flood Control: Both levels would allow for releases of 8,000 cubic feet per second—established by Congress in 1962 as the project floodway—and 450,000 acre-feet for flood storage.

Irrigation: Both reservoir sizes would satisfy prior rights. A maximum reservoir would provide up to 200,000 acre-feet of new water—enough to irrigate about 400 farms of 160 acres apiece. At a price of $10 per acre-foot (the Department of the Interior would probably charge much less), the maximum reservoir would result in a taxpayer subsidy to farmers of between $641 and $741 million over a fifty-year period. To recoup project costs, a charge of $17 to $27 per acre-foot would be needed. Income would still not cover operation, maintenance, and distribution of the water, thereby increasing the deficit of the CVP.

The report concludes that operation for full hydroelectric power and irrigation could result in subsidies far greater than Congress contemplated. "Current data do not justify increasing the reservoir elevation above Parrotts Ferry to meet conditions of Decision 1422 . . . a decision for a lower reservoir size is reversible while a higher reservoir is not." The Resources Agency asked for a New Melones review by the federal Office of Management and Budget, the General Accounting Office, the Water Resources Council, and the Department of the Interior's Office of Audit and Investigation.

While the report targeted New Melones, Phillips later pointed out that the findings are only symptoms. "The Central Valley Project is the main issue here. The economics of the CVP have been twisted for years, never exposed as they really are." The Bureau of Reclamation claimed a CVP surplus of $287,462,000, but in January 1978, the Department of the Interior's Office of Audit found a projected cumulative deficit of $10 billion by the year 2038. "Either things must change drastically or the taxpayer is going to be footing the bill," Phillips says.

All this, of course, did not pass unnoticed by the dam interests, which spewed acid outrage. The Western Area Power Administration (WAPA—formerly a part of the Bureau of Reclamation, later a part of the U. S. Department of Energy) attacked the Phillips report, saying, "We find the data existing in the report inadequate to support the conclusions drawn." Their main point was that the Resources Agency didn't recognize recent WAPA rate hikes that add to the power benefits of the dam. They argued that under the new rates, hydroelectric costs would be repaid, plus a $400 million subsidy to the dam's irrigation and fish and wildlife functions over a fifty-year period. Phillips countered by averring that the Resources Agency had used an energy charge of 5.7 mills [0.57 cents], where WAPA's new charge was only 5.1 mills. "Our estimates gave WAPA the benefit of the doubt," Phillips says.

Milton Kramer asserts that "The Phillips report is widely discredited, even by the U. S. Department of the Interior"—meaning the Bureau of Reclamation. "It boggles my mind that we would take a $320 million investment and let it stand there without returning a penny. If we don't fill the reservoir, all that loss of hydropower will be a subsidy to rafting," he says.

Joe Countryman of the Army Corps of Engineers calls the study "shoddy and nonprofessional," saying that there is absolutely no question that New Melones can pay for itself with hydropower alone." The way the dam is designed, he claims, the turbines will be ruined if power is generated when the reservoir is below Parrotts Ferry. Because of this, FOR recommended modifications to the turbines. Countryman thinks it doesn't make sense: "They say hydropower doesn't pay, then they say to spend money to modify the turbines."

The Bureau of Reclamation reports that use of New Melones could bring 31,000 acres under irrigation and reduce groundwater withdrawals from another 87,000 acres. New irrigation water would yield $52 million in annual personal income to Californians—the equivalent of 2,070 new jobs.

John Hertle does not agree that flood control would be adequate with a smaller reservoir: "Had New Melones been operated in 1980 as Congress intended, we wouldn't have had half a million dollars of crop and tree damage on the lower river. Now if that was your half a million dollars, you'd say how foolish it is to keep the water level nice and low so people can raft and to have hard-working farmers lose their crops when we interfered with the food production chain."

Roos-Collins says that during the 1980 flood, every major reservoir in the state was full and releasing heavy flows except New Melones. It was at a lower level before the rains, and could contain much more flood water when the emergency came.

Huey Johnson supported Phillips and then some. Calling the Phillips study a "post-Proposition 13 look at why taxes are so high," he said that New Melones was "a ripoff of the public to provide subsidies to farms and utilities"—a symbol of waste and the power of special interests. He cited Phillips's figures, and called the dam "New Lemones."

Johnson and Hammond had selected four water issues to pursue during the Jerry Brown administration: urban development around Lake Tahoe; the draining of Mono Lake; erosion and sedimentation of the Smith River, where loggers are harvesting headwater forests; and our river. Why the Stanislaus, the most difficult dam fight ever undertaken? "In order to create awareness," Johnson says. "Any one victory or defeat is only one step in a thousand-mile journey and 1,000 years of life. Through New Melones we've brought attention to the bizarre pricing of water that encourages its waste, that charges urban people for farmers' subsidies. New Melones water costs $70 per acre-foot and the Department of the Interior proposes to collect $3.50. If you're lucky enough to live in the city, you get to pay the difference. We're also working to save the Stanislaus because it's a wild and beautiful place."

Deputy Secretary Hammond said, "Even though the project is built, we decided it should be held up as an example of abuse in water planning, pricing, and benefit/cost ratios. It was so far down the line, but ultimately we decided to become involved because New Melones is such an important symbol of poor fiscal management. We needed an acute awareness of the kind of water development project we will accept in this state.

"I think it's rotten when there are laws on the books that are not enforced, and when you look behind the scenes at New Melones you see that the scope of the project was expanded after authorization, that the Historic Preservation Act was ignored, and that the federal government wants to ignore Decision 1422—they drag their feet even after the Supreme Court's decision. This is a classic case of how the special interests have always had access to the decisions. Agricultural interests want heavily subsidized water, but they are not willing to take the basic soft steps toward water conservation and groundwater management." Hammond became the driving force within the Resources Agency to save the Stanislaus Canyon.

A Friends of New Melones researcher went to the Resources Agency, asked a secretary for New Melones files, and gleaned letters to Friends of the River, internal memos, and draft reports. Friends of

New Melones then bound these into an inch-thick book, and held a press conference to charge "collusion" between Friends of the River and the Resources Agency. Huey Johnson had to hold his own press conference to defend his agency.

This didn't faze Huey. He, Hammond, and Phillips kept right on going. Johnson wrote to Michael Blumenfeld, deputy undersecretary of the Army Corps of Engineers: "I would like to suggest that there is need for a new philosophical base which can guide us in future decisions affecting the allocation and use of limited resources such as the Stanislaus River. The conflicts raised by the issues involved in the New Melones issue stem from the demand for unrestricted export of water for commercial use by special interests, and the often-conflicting need to preserve and manage resources and natural systems for the use and enjoyment of a broader part of present and future populations. . . . In this era of environmental awareness and growing need to manage resources on the basis of total public needs rather than narrow special interest benefits, I suggest that conservation be viewed as a resource management strategy equal in importance to that of building new projects."

Conservation. Saving water. It is a scarce commodity. About 97 percent is in salty oceans, 2.2 percent is solid icecaps, and 0.3 percent is too deep in the ground to extract, leaving less than 0.5 percent available for people's use. Of the globe total, the United States has about 4 percent (Canada and Russia each have about 20 percent). Water is especially scarce in the farming and urban regions of California. Central Valley agriculture and urban growth in Southern California are made possible only by diverting water from the Sierra.

In California, 15 percent of the water supply is for household, municipal, and industrial use. About 85 percent is for farming (nationwide, about 47 percent is used for farming). Of all water used in California, 60 percent comes from rivers, 40 percent from groundwater. About 150 gallons per day (gpd) are used per person at home, more than the national average. In the Central Valley in summer, the amount climbs to 660 gallons each. Only 2 gallons are for drinking and cooking. Total consumption of water per capita, including use in agriculture and industry, was 600 gpd in 1906, and is 1,800 gpd now. In 1978 Californians used about 37.5 million acre-feet (maf) per year. Estimates for the year 2000 call for 41–46 maf.

There is a bottom to the well. Huey Johnson said, "We live in a finite world. We have to quit this crazy thinking that resources will last forever no matter how we use them." Total California runoff is about 75 maf, but most of the reasonable sources have been tapped. Many of the unreasonable sources have been tapped. To store and transport more water will be exorbitantly expensive in dollars and social costs.

To tap more water would mean damming the wild rivers of the north coast, and using enormous quantities of energy to pump the water south. It would mean mining even more groundwater, which is due to run out at the rate it is now being pumped. It would mean a few final dams in the Sierra—Auburn on the American, Marysville on the Yuba, Hope Valley on the Carson, blocking every last canyon in every river that has a drop to yield. It would mean running New Melones Reservoir up to Camp Nine for the surrender of another 200,000 acre-feet of irrigation water.

To save water would not require the dams or the pumping or the filling. It would require that we be a little more careful. For example, at home, showers account for 30 percent of water use. Shower-head flow restrictors (washerlike devices) or valves that can shut off the water while you scrub can cut shower consumption by 35 to 75 percent. The state estimates that if everybody installed such inexpensive hardware, 4.3 million more people could come to California without increasing water demand. Ten million gallons per day are lost to dripping faucets that need only a ten cent washer. Half of the urban water used in summertime feeds lawns and plants. Use of drought-tolerant species can save 50 percent. Mulching of shrubbery can save 10 percent. Cisterns and use of laundry water can save 15 percent, while 10 to 18 percent can be saved by flushing less or installing low-flush-volume toilets. Montgomery County, Maryland, adopted a rate structure by which the less water used, the less people pay. Most water suppliers do the opposite, charging less if you consume more. The Water Resources Council predicts decreased industrial demand for water, however, because antipollution requirements are making it economical to recycle water rather than dump it.

We can all do our part at home, but domestic use totals less than 11 percent of the water used. Irrigation is where the water is spent. For one pound of cotton, we use 3,100 gallons of water. A pound of rice can take 500 gallons, and a pound of tomatoes, 125 gallons. For each gallon of milk, 932 gallons of water are used. A sixteen-ounce beefsteak represents 2,000 to 4,000 gallons of water. Of all the water used in California, one-half goes to livestock. This includes irrigated pasture, which used 7.1 million acre-feet in 1972—more than any other crop. Alfalfa is second, at 6 million acre-feet. Cotton is third.

The General Accounting Office reported in 1976 that "Irrigation practices have not changed appreciably in the past three decades even though irrigation science and technology have made substantial advances." In the GAO analysis, the two major causes of inefficiency are the cheapness of the water supplied by the Bureau of Reclamation and inaccurate estimates of farmers' needs. An irrigation efficiency of only 44 percent was found on farms supplied by the bureau. Eighty-five percent of the canals carrying bureau water are earthen, unlined, and leak. A 25 percent loss of water between reservoir and farm is typical, reports the California Department of Water Resources.

This does not have to be. The Department of Water Resources predicts that water conservation statewide could yield 3 million acre-feet. The National Water Commission's *Water Policies for the Future* concludes that in the year 2000, California agriculture could use 40 percent less water per acre than it does now, while raising the same amount of food. If California farmers conserved only two-thirds of 1 percent, the savings would equal the yield of New Melones Dam.

How can the water be saved? Government reports list many possibilities: lined or covered canals, more efficient weirs and gates, irrigation at night to cut evaporation, conversion to sprinkler and drip systems, and improved irrigation schedules based on water uptake, soil types, foliage, percentage of ground covered by plants, soil water content, and root density. In some cases, a solution is to simply irrigate less. The U. S. comptroller general reports that irrigators in the Westlands water district (where CVP water is most expensive) apply half an acre-foot more than is needed. Many other areas are worse. Studies have shown that crop production sometimes increases with a decrease in water use.

Location of crops makes a difference: studies show that in El Dorado County, farms on south-facing slopes use twice as much water as north-facing farms.

In the San Joaquin Valley, 15 to 25 percent of irrigation water returns to the river. The Bureau of Reclamation found that irrigation efficiency can be boosted 5 percent by installing runoff reuse systems at a cost of less than $10 per acre. One problem, however, is that reused water is higher in salts and pollutants than fresh water out of the canals.

Ninety percent of Valley crops are watered through flood irrigation, where the entire field is covered with water, or through furrow irrigation where water streams down furrows between rows of crops. Sprinklers can have three times the efficiency of flood or furrow irrigation, but require extra energy for pumps to shoot the water into the air. Drip irrigation, where tiny amounts of water seep from hoses into the plant's root zone, can be the most efficient method, three to ten times as efficient as sprinklers, though costly to install. The Irvine Ranch in Southern California reduced water use by 25–30 percent (enough for 10,000 families) through drip irrigation and wastewater reclamation.

Dr. Robert Hagan of the University of California at Davis lists other factors that can save water: use of short-season crops, changing planting dates, adjusting crop density, deficit irrigation that gives just enough water for the plants, reduction of the area to be irrigated, and growing crops that use less water.

These techniques need not require basic changes in habits or diet.

But suppose Californians did reduce beef consumption by one-seventh—eating something else one day a week? We would save the equivalent of ten New Melones reservoirs. Bob McBride, a river friend says, "Make Friday bean-tostada and save-the-river day."

Ultimately one comes to the question of which crops should be grown. Central Valley farmers have gone from dryland farming to growing almost whatever they want, regardless of water demands. If conservation of water becomes important, the type of crop becomes important too. Farmers use 8 acre-feet for an acre of rice. For pasture they use 5.2; for alfalfa 4.9; and for cotton 4. Avocados, garlic, dates, almonds, olives, and figs do uniquely well in California; but cattle, cotton, and rice do well in other places also. Should taxpayers be subsidizing water-hogging crops that can be grown in the South and the East, where it rains? Why are these crops grown in the Valley anyway?

They are grown because they bring good money, and the profit margin is great because water is subsidized to be cheap. The General Accounting Office, in 1981, found that farmers can afford to pay three to fifty times the amount that the Bureau of Reclamation intends to charge on five different projects. "The value of the repayments is less than 10%" of full costs, GAO says. In one project— Fryingpan–Arkansas in Colorado—the bureau figured farmers' "ability to pay" to be 27 cents an acre-foot, but GAO found it to be $14.91.

Standard charges to farmers in the State Water Project average about $27 an acre-foot, but for "surplus" water they pay only about $3.50. Because Southern California's urban needs were overestimated, an average of 300,000 acre-feet per year has been sold as surplus to Central Valley farmers. Much of this water goes to the southern reaches of the Valley, where large corporations farm huge tracts of tens of thousands of acres. Here lies a basic, but carefully concealed, incentive for new water projects—so long as there is surplus water, the big corporate farmers get $27 water for $3.50. John Hertle pays $2.50 per acre to the Modesto irrigation district, no matter how many acre-feet he uses (the district is not a part of the State Water Project or the Central Valley Project). Al Sorrenti pays for his pumping, which across the mid-Valley averages about $26 per acre-foot.

What is the real cost of providing the water? Philip LaVeen, professor of Agricultural Economics at Berkeley, says that water generally costs $50 to $70 per acre-foot to provide. For the proposed Auburn Dam, irrigation costs, including 7.5 percent interest, are $100 per acre-foot, the General Accounting Office reports. New water will cost four to five times as much as the existing supply. Guy Phillips reports that reimbursable costs (costs that farmers are supposed to repay to the government) from New Melones water would be $17 to

$27 per acre-foot. If actual taxpayer costs were to be repaid (total costs of providing the water), $68 per acre-foot would be charged. Yet the Bureau of Reclamation proposes to sell it for $3.50 or $5.00.

John Bryson, chairman of the State Water Resources Control Board in 1978 says, "It's obvious that with all the well-recognized subsidies in the bureau's projects, they're offering water at far less than it's worth. Does that discourage conservation? I believe it does."

A 1973 study by the Bureau of Reclamation paired a price of $4.25 to an irrigation efficiency of only about 40 percent, and a price of $7.50 to an efficiency of about 50 percent. At $10 the efficiency was over 60 percent. The higher the cost of water, the greater the efficiency.

Irrigation water comes cheap. In contrast, Los Angeles residents are paying the equivalent of $750 per acre-foot. Outlying areas of the Metropolitan Water District, such as San Diego, are charged $120. A power plant in Utah is paying $1,600 per acre-foot.

Richard Norgaard, an agricultural economist at Berkeley, says, "The cost of beef is really high, though we're not paying for it. It is included in subsidies and in the loss of wild rivers. If the cost of water went from $7.50 to $80 per acre-foot, the result is simple—we wouldn't grow much alfalfa in California. The agricultural economy of other, wetter regions would be revitalized."

While new water costs $50 to $80 per acre-foot to develop, and even more to deliver, the president's task force on water conservation has projected a cost of $5–$10 to conserve the same amount. The Interior and Agriculture Departments more conservatively estimate a cost of $10–$40 to save an acre-foot. These figures suggest that saving water is a better bargain than developing new sources. Our new source—New Melones Dam—is already developed, but resources agency figures show that operation, maintenance, and distribution costs exceed estimated costs of conservation.

If only conservation of water and the saving of tax dollars and wild rivers had the capitalist glamor and pork-barrel appeal of new construction. If only the water development lobby would line up behind it. But it is hard to imagine the New Melones contractors donating their Proposition 17 contribution of $200,000 to advertise water conservation devices instead of new cement. Likewise with the federal agencies. Phillip LaVeen says, "What the bureau does is simply subsidize its low prices for irrigation water so it can generate demand for its water and for more projects." Why would the U. S. Department of the Interior sell New Melones water dirt cheap at $3.50 or $5.00 per acre-foot? LaVeen says, "It has to. It's the only way it can get irrigators to go along with its project proposals and sign contracts to buy water."

Groundwater controls are viewed as another aspect of water conservation. Groundwater overdraft in California equals the yield of twelve New Melones dams. Even if all the new yield were used to recharge aquifers, which is very unlikely, New Melones would hardly touch the problem. Groundwater management programs have been proposed, but the slightest hint of regulation is hooted down by farmers. State Senator John Garamendi, a New Melones Dam supporter says, "We're going to have to have groundwater management in California sooner or later, but there are very difficult political issues. I don't know what the mechanism will be." Roos-Collins says that recharging groundwater with the miniscule yield of New Melones is just a token, stop-gap measure that distracts us from addressing the real solution—management.

Simple technical assistance is one way to promote water conservation. Even though water rates are low, many farmers still save what they can. If someone offered help, the way the Soil Conservation Service has been doing since the 1930s in fighting soil erosion, many farmers would listen. But who among the 3,700 public and private agencies that deal with California water is offering help?

Out of $28 million a year spent by the Bureau of Reclamation in California, how much is spent on conservation? Out of its 1,200 bureau employees in California, who is doing the soft sell on saving water? Six people are in the bureau's Irrigation Management Service, and four of them are part-time employees. Less than 1 percent of the water resources money spent by the Agriculture and Interior Departments is used to improve irrigation efficiency. In 1978 the Soil Conservation Service gave advice to farmers holding only 0.8 percent of the irrigated land. The Irrigation Management Service of the bureau helped farmers holding only 2 percent of the irrigated land. A general accounting office report indicates that federal water conservation efforts are inadequately coordinated, nominally funded, and minimally applied.

By contrast the California Department of Water Resources, with a staff of 2,400, employs 30 people full time on water conservation and many others part time. One year after Ron Robie became director of DWR, the *Sacramento Bee* identified a "philosophical change . . . for more efficient use of present water supplies instead of new water projects."

What do our Central Valley farmers think of water conservation? John Hertle says, "Sure, more can be done on conservation. It's gradually happening as the economy of agriculture changes. It just can't happen all of a sudden, and the answers are not simple. Sprinklers mean higher energy use. Drip irrigation is impractical for annual crops."

Al Sorrenti says, "Very little can be done unless the crops are changed. Night irrigation is hard to do, because you can't see where the water is going. There's very little drainage off the fields, very little waste. To cut back on water use, we would have to cut production.

There's hardly any money in dryland crops. The people screaming about costs are the ones who delayed New Melones and made it cost four or five times as much. Let them pay."

Cliff Humphrey comments, "After talking to farmers, the Farm Bureau, the University of California extension service, and others, I'd say we can't shoot beyond a 15 percent savings if we're to keep the present crop spectrum." But 15 percent of the water now used in California equals the irrigation yield of twenty-three New Melones dams.

Some people, including bureau of reclamation officials, argue that the waste of irrigation water is not nearly as bad as it seems, because much of the "wasted" water is recoverable—it is recirculated through lower fields, or sinks to the groundwater table, where it can be pumped out again. But the advocates of water conservation say that this analysis overlooks important points: much of the excess water cannot be recovered; water becomes polluted and is less usable the third or fourth time around; electricity must be used to pump the water back up from the groundwater table; excess irrigation results in more evaporation; and, finally, through water projects, the public pays to recharge groundwater that is available free to farmers who pump. Or, as Melinda Wright says of irrigation waste, "You aren't just wasting water, you're wasting stored, delivered water. Why put it in a dam, trash a canyon, hold it till summer, then send it down and put it in the water table instead of on the crops?"

Billy E. Martin, the mid-pacific regional director of the Bureau of Reclamation says, "In the future we have some tough decisions to make. We have to decide whether to cut down on the amount of irrigated agriculture we support, or to undertake the expensive projects needed to bring in more water." The bureau's options are to dam more or produce less, yet the National Water Commission reports that we could use 40 percent less water and grow the same amount of food.

What do Californians think about water conservation? A Mervin D. Field poll in 1980 showed that 69 percent of the people think it is very important to save water.

Water conservation is an inseparable part of the case for a moderate reservoir instead of a full one. What does Milton Kramer have to say on the subject? "That's one of the more ridiculous arguments made in this whole thing," he fumes. "Mark Dubois likes to show people that little thing you put in the shower to save water. Are you going to take one of those things and put it in the stem of a plant? People won't care until you go to the tap and nothing comes out. We're talking about small family farms—who would pay for the paving of ditches?"

Dick Roos-Collins argues for tax credits for farmers' investments in water saving similar to the energy-conservation tax credits that the federal government allows. Friends of the River have pushed energy conservation, saying that we don't have to save very much to make up for the hydroelectric power that will be lost if New Melones is not filled. Tying together the issues of water and energy conservation, the California Department of Water Resources found that a statewide program of residential and industrial water conservation alone would reduce electricity demand more than 6 billion kwh per year due to decreased pumping and heating. That would save the equivalent of thirteen New Melones dams—thirty of them if you count only the difference between a Parrotts Ferry limit and a full reservoir. Analysis of energy-conservation potential parallels that of water conservation. The Federal Energy Administration reports that better management of California generating plants could provide a 20 to 26 percent increase in power, compared to a .03 percent increase from New Melones. A 5 percent reduction in energy use by CVP customers would equal the hydroelectric power yield of the dam.

New Melones could provide the equivalent of .68 million barrels of oil a year; but the California Energy Commission found that 11.6 million barrels could be saved in California if tires were properly inflated, 7.5 million could be saved if car engines were tuned, and 10 million could be saved if people would slow down to fifty-five miles per hour. The energy commission concluded that 52 percent of California's energy is wasted.

The Joint Economics Committee of Congress and the Harvard Business School have said that by the year 2000, the nation's population can increase from 225 to 300 million, with proportionate growth in the economy, with only our present supply of energy. The committee estimates that conservation costs are only one-fifth of the costs of new power generation.

Conservation pays, and while the message hasn't trickled out to the federal offices in California, it was acknowledged by the government in Washington in 1978, when President Carter announced new national water policies with three main points: avoid wasteful projects, promote water conservation, and share costs with states. The policies favored non-structural solutions that would save money, water, and energy. For water supply, the policy recommended water-conserving devices, metering and price reform, outdoor water-use plans, and leak repair. For irrigation: more efficient use, irrigation scheduling, and pricing reform. For flood control: flood insurance, greenbelts along streams, floodproofing, zoning, evacuation of hazard areas, and warning systems. For hydroelectric power: insulation of attics and installation of storm windows, conservation, and peak power pricing (charging more during the hours of highest use). For recreation: use of natural river recreation, and development of recreation opportunities such as picnicking, hiking, camping, and biking, which do not require a reservoir.

Directives for agriculture were weak, but finally called for technical assistance and review of contracts for federal water every five years, instead of every forty (until 1979, irrigators faced no inflation on their water bills through the forty-year contract period). The policy also advocated federal-state cooperation, which has been an issue, to understate the matter, in the Stanislaus struggle.

Later in 1978, President Carter successfully vetoed a bloated public works appropriations bill that included dozens of proposals that flaunted the new policy and other environmental and economic concerns. It was the first public works veto since Eisenhower (whose similar action was overridden by Congress). A 1978 compromise also excluded 2,300 new employees for the Army Corps of Engineers and the Bureau of Reclamation and dropped eleven of twenty-seven new projects that Carter objected to.

Conservation and water policy reform were getting attention in Washington, but how lasting would it be? In 1979 the Army Corps of Engineers enjoyed its largest budget ever, under a president who had said that he would put the corps out of the dam-building business. The fill-it-up bill for Tellico Dam zipped through Congress (in spite of Interior Secretary Andrus's opposition) and on to the White House, where it was signed. In 1980 the budget for new water projects went up 21 percent, while overall government spending increased only 11 percent. Secretary Andrus recommended a token $5 million cut in the Bureau of Reclamation budget out of a total Department of the Interior cut of $292 million. Pork stayed in, parks got cut. The lone exception was irrigation projects on Indian reservations, which were slashed 50 percent. This was by an interior secretary who had said in 1977, "We are coming to the end of the dam-building era in America," and in April 1980 had declared, "This administration supports good water projects but opposes the boondoggles." The Carter administration remains the best in history for water-policy reform; but its concessions illustrated the power of pork-barrel politics.

Guy Phillips reports that, "Highly subsidized water is directly counter to state and federal water conservation policies." Unfortunately, however, a lot of policy has not been implemented. There was talk of price reform, but at New Melones, the Department of the Interior proposed $3.50 or $5 per acre-foot without any conservation requirements. There was talk of greenways, but in 1980, eighteen years after authorization, the corps had still not purchased all the flood easements along the Stanislaus. While Secretary Andrus said that the feds would voluntarily comply with the state's conditions as set out in Decision 1422 until a final court decision was made, his Bureau of Reclamation still did not concede that the state held authority.

Investigations requested by the Resources Agency were not carried out, and Secretary Andrus would eventually allow the raising of the reservoir above Parrotts Ferry in spite of a court order to fill no farther unless downstream damage was occurring, and in spite of a bill before Congress limiting the filling.

While the case for partial filling was being refined, many people turned their attention to the planned flooding. The Historic Preservation Act and other laws require that the government "mitigate" impacts on historic resources, and the entire canyon was considered by the Department of the Interior to be eligible for the National Register of Historic Places. State Historic Preservation Officer Knox Mellon and officials of the National Advisory Council on Historic Preservation, the Interagency Archaeological Service for the Department of the Interior, and the Society for California Archaeology stated that mitigation in the canyon was inadequate. Sixteen California congressmen thereupon wrote Andrus requesting "intervention on behalf of the archaeological resources on the Stanislaus River which are immediately threatened by the rising waters of New Melones Reservoir." Brad Welton and FOR attorneys prepared a lawsuit to stop the Army Corps of Engineers from filling the dam before archaeological work was done.

In spite of the case for partial filling, in spite of the delays sought for archaeological studies in 1979, the water was rising.

•

Tom Graff of the Environmental Defense Fund said, "If you would give the farmers a choice, they'd take the money, but they'll take water if that's all you're giving away."

•

A Sacramento neighbor offered to water the FOR lawn—the only brown one on the block. Dubois explained that they save water however they can. The neighbor looked at the ground seriously and said, "Oh."

•

Congressman Bob Edgar of Pennsylvania sent his constituents a tiny water-saving device that fits in the bathroom shower head. He had to stop—the shower insert was considered a gift, and the only gift a congressman is allowed to send is the American flag.

•

Alexander Gaguine said, "They're not just planning to fill a reservoir with water; they're planning to fill a canyon."

CHAPTER EIGHT

Risking Death

Friends of the River pioneered tactics against New Melones that are now standard in dam fighting: for example, appeals under the National Environmental Policy Act and the Historic Preservation Act. They nearly won our country's only statewide initiative to save a river, and they lobbied to put the Stanislaus in the California scenic rivers system. They held a walk for the river, a row for the river, and a roll for the river (on roller skates); they staged rallies, tree plantings, conferences, and concerts. The Supreme Court action on Decision 1422 was a boon to the state and the river, and could be significant across the country. A whole textbook of approaches was tried, but measured by the final question—would the canyon be flooded or not?—nothing worked well enough.

The water developers were tough, resistant, and devoted to the powerful common goal of money. They were influential with Central Valley congressmen. Past decisions had often been made by tenuous majorities, but the options had now been fused by the spending of $341 million. The reservoir supporters only needed to hold their ground.

Having lost on the dam, partial filling was now the objective of Friends of the River. So far, the river people had acted within the conventional realms of technical analysis, public information, politics, and the courts. They had played the game straight. Looking back at the commitment of the people involved, it seems inevitable that the New Melones opposition would go further.

In October 1978, the Army Corps of Engineers finished the dam, bringing to a close thirty-four years of authorization, twenty years of planning, ten years of hard opposition, and ten of construction. The next step was to fill it. Delayed by historic preservation laws, the corps's schedule called for impoundment in April 1979 to an elevation

of 808 feet above sea level—somewhere near the old Parrotts Ferry
Bridge. This would create a reservoir three times the size of Old
Melones, yet by design, this was the minimum needed to generate
hydroelectric power. Once the turbines could be tested, the corps's job
would be done and the Bureau of Reclamation would operate the dam.

On April 1 (an omen?), the huge gates slammed shut inside the
dam, and Sierra snowmelt began to flood the lower canyon. The new
reservoir drowned Old Melones Dam and kept rising. When it neared
the site of the Gold Rush town of Melones, FOR's rally man, Alexander
Gaguine, organized a gathering of 200 people there to witness and
publicize the destruction of the lower canyon. FOR intended to make
the Stanislaus the most publicized loss of wilderness in American
history, and they would. For two weeks, a few supporters remained
by the river, camping at the rising edge of the flatwater and moving
upstream as the impoundment swelled. The Indian petroglyphs at
Horseshoe Bend went under. Pendola Ranch, where Lorenzo Pendola
had raised food for miners in 1870, and where his grandson continued
to farm in recent years, went under. Kathy Hall from Weed, David
Wikander from Mt. Shasta, and a few others were the last to see the
lower river.

The rising water trapped wildlife on knolls and big rocks that
became islands. Susan Brooks, a fifteen-year-old high school student
from Marin, had first worked with animals as a humane society
volunteer when she was twelve. Encountering Friends of the River at a
San Francisco environmental fair, she learned about New Melones.
Now Susan ferried rabbits, pocket gophers, woodrats, lizards,
rattlesnakes, and even a tarantula to the shore in a canoe.

The flooding would belly out at elevation 808, wherever that was.
The corps said approximately Parrotts Ferry. Did that mean the ferry
site below the old bridge? Did it mean the river under the bridge?
Nobody knew exactly. And that wasn't the only source of doubt and
confusion. Later in April, the corps said that the test level for the
turbines could flood two miles beyond Parrotts Ferry. They qualified:
with high spring runoff, they might store flood water in New Melones
above 808. Wherever that was, it now seemed as if the water might go
higher, even though the historic and wildlife work, required by law,
had not been done. Mark Dubois didn't like the sound of this at all.

It was a secret, but nonetheless some people knew that if Parrotts
Ferry were to be drowned, Dubois would do something. His idea had
been jelling for months, maybe years, not in a deliberate, logical way,
but as an increasing commitment. Through early 1979, friends worried
about his emotional stability and the risks he might take when he saw
the inevitability of the flooding. Tom Burton calls the spring of 1979 the
most chaotic time ever for the river people, as they faced the closing of

the New Melones flood gates. People were split—some were ready to give up and turn to other streams—others wanted to stay with the Stanislaus, but didn't know what to do.

In mid-April, while slackwater was creeping up the walls of the lower canyon, Dubois went to Washington, D.C. to lobby and to attend a conference of the American Rivers Conservation Council—a nationwide group that works for river protection and for expansion of the national wild and scenic rivers system. With Gaguine, he showed slides of New Melones Dam and the bulging flatwater that now buried Miwok petroglyphs, Pendola Ranch, the Stanislaus rapids, hillside chaparral, and the Gold Rush town of Melones. "A full reservoir would go all the way to Camp Nine," Dubois explained in his even, seemingly unangered way. "This year they might try to go to the South Fork—far above Parrotts Ferry. But we don't intend to let them do that. We won't let them do that. There are already thirteen dams on the Stanislaus. We've given up the lower canyon. We feel we've compromised enough. Parrotts Ferry should be the limit." Parrotts Ferry would become the battleground.

This determination and confidence made people wonder what Dubois had in mind. "So what does he think *he's* going to do?" they asked. Many of these conservationists, farmers, and fishermen had lost dam fights themselves, and they knew the futility of struggling once construction was started, let alone completed. But they did not know the Stanislaus people. Dubois seemed to be talking about something besides another visit to a government official, FOR press release, or tedious lawsuit to delay destruction of archaeological sites. Dubois was onto something else. He shared his idea with only a handful of friends. Don Briggs was one.

Briggs was not about to give advice. That was one of the first vices he had given up. Neither did Briggs want anything missed, unconsidered. "Before you do this, there's a woman you should talk to," he told Dubois.

Marty Kent lives along Corte Madera Creek near Larkspur, Marin County. William Kent, her grandfather, was a friend of John Muir's and borrowed the money to buy Muir Woods in 1903, which he then gave to the government for a national monument. He also donated a good chunk of Mount Tamalpais, a landmark to the whole northern San Francisco Bay Area. Marty, mother of river guide Kent Erskine, had seen some of the things that Dubois would see: she had been arrested for trying to save Tamalpais Creek, which comes off the big mountain and winds down through the tides to San Francisco Bay.

Marty had tried everything to keep the Army Corps of Engineers from cutting the trees and ditching the creek into a concrete sluice. Finally, on April 28, 1969, when the woods were being ripped by chain saws, Marty and forty other people went down to the creek. Nothing was planned, but when she saw a workman slice into an alder in a blizzard of sawdust, Marty lunged for the tree, so close to the sharpened steel chain that the man's eyes flashed wide in fear and he let the trigger go and jerked back his saw. All the workers quit. The foreman called the sheriff, and soon forty-one people, including the celebrated landscape architect Lawrence Halprin, had been arrested. Marty Kent's creek is gone, but she says the effort cannot be considered a loss—risking her life changed her life for the better. Mark talked to Marty, who in a moment recognized Dubois's commitment and understood this was something he must do.

On May 17, Dubois sent a letter to Colonel Donald O'Shei, district engineer of the corps, the man directly responsible for New Melones.

Dear Col. O'Shei:

Part of my spirit dies as the reservoir fills and floods the lower Stanislaus Canyon. I have spent nearly half of my life getting to know the amazing Stanislaus River, its canyon and all its life and richness— and learning about the New Melones Dam. I am convinced that the minimal amount of power and water to be derived from the excessively giant 14th dam on the Stanislaus River cannot justify the flooding of this "unique asset to our state and the nation."

While the dam may have seemed a good idea in the 40's and 60's, when it was first authorized, we have acquired much new information since then. I believe we should have the courage and maturity to admit a mistake has been made and stop the blind momentum of this "public works" project which will cost us and future generations so much. All the life of this canyon, its wealth of archaeological and historical roots to our past, and its unique geological grandeur are enough reasons to protect this canyon just for itself. But in addition, all the spiritual values with which this canyon has filled tens of thousands of folks should prohibit us from committing the unconscionable act of wiping this place off the face of the earth.

The life of the 9 million year old Stanislaus Canyon is far more significant than my short tenure on this planet. While I and many other folks have spent the last decade working to correct the mistake made by Congress years ago, our efforts have been thus far to no avail. Upon learning of your intention to flood the canyon above Parrotts Ferry this year, I did some serious thinking.

While you have given vague promises to not flood the canyon too far above elevation 808, your staff has been unable to identify that location on the river. Knowing the annual snowmelt is about to flood the canyon and there is not much space in the reservoir to absorb that water without going above Parrotts Ferry, and direct experience with

*your overriding attention to construction schedules to the detriment
of the priceless resources behind the dam, I plan to have my feet
permanently anchored to a rock in the canyon at the elevation of
Parrotts Ferry the day the water reaches that elevation.*

*I urge you to do all in your power to prevent flooding of the canyon
above Parrotts Ferry.*

> *Sincerely*
> *For the River*
> *Mark Dubois*

Dubois warned that he would use his one remaining tool—his life.
He would be hidden near the rising waters, chained to a rock, with no
key to free himself. The corps could stop filling, or drown him.

The next night, FOR's Foothills Chapter met in the community room
of Sonora's El Capitan Bank. Don Briggs and Carol Nelson from the
Sacramento office arrived tired at 10:30 with 1,000 raffle tickets and
news of Mark's letter to O'Shei. Foothills leader Melinda Wright
numbered tickets, while Briggs and Nelson talked and Alexander
Gaguine listened. Nobody wanted Mark to chain himself. Gaguine
said that his first priority was that Mark shouldn't die. He considered
hunting for Mark, so that he could cut his chain if the water kept rising:
"Two kayakers and two hikers—there's only sixty miles of shoreline,"
he calculated. "He'll have to be in a three-foot band around the water's
edge." Then he remembered that Mark was Mark. If he said he was
hiding, he was going to be invisible. Briggs fell asleep. Melinda kept
numbering tickets.

Gaguine progressed to other plans. He'd follow Mark in. But Mark
could walk faster; he could swim the reservoir and lose anybody in
pursuit. "Mark could turn around and apologize and knock me cold."
He decided not to follow Dubois.

Briggs awoke with a start. Irritably he said, "Mark is making a
mistake. He doesn't have his electronic media lined up." Something
broke. Melinda and Carol sobbed with laughter. "It isn't funny,"
Briggs snapped. "It's serious. They're going to think he's a nut. What
good does it do to die out there if nobody understands what he's trying
to say?"

Meeting at Parrotts Ferry the next night, May 19, thirty-four people
wanted to dissuade Dubois, afraid he would drown, but they didn't
say anything. Mark's resolve was clear. Melinda had intended to
confront him, but Mark defused her planned lecture by picking her
up and lifting her two feet off the ground.

"So you're the one who's causing all the trouble," she said.

"You betcha," he said.

Dubois asked Gaguine to be the one person who knew his
whereabouts—the only one able to bring word to the hiding place.

Gaguine refused, flatly admitting that he would help in efforts to find and rescue Mark if he thought that his life were in danger. Mark thereupon recruited a secret contact for the job, and asked Don Briggs to be the official middleman—spokesman to the media. Briggs said, "Mark was skeptical of me [as a direct contact] because I was handling national publicity for the river, and he knew I'd want to max-out on coverage. He didn't want this to be a media event."

On Sunday night, Briggs drove the FOR leader and a small supply of fruit and nuts to Parrotts Ferry. In the darkness, Dubois began a lonely walk into the lower canyon. He knew this could end his life. Even if the corps wanted to dump water to lower the reservoir, they might not be able to in time. Something could always go wrong. New Melones was just being tested. The corps warned that surges up to five feet in height were beyond control. Briggs, on driving out, stopped at a high switchback on the road above, got out of his car, and shouted in a booming voice that shattered the night, "Parrotts Ferry is the limit!" Dubois smiled to himself; these were the last words he might ever hear, but he laughed with excitement. "It was amazing how strong I felt by then," he recalls.

Scrambling through the Stanislaus Canyon is no Malibu stroll, especially in the dark with the rip of spring floods and the rising reservoir covering sand and gravel bars, but Dubois knew the land well. He was barefoot, of course, and broke a toe—something he never mentioned and tried to hide, but an injury that would swell his leg to the knee while he was chained. Arriving at his chosen site, he hid the key to his padlock 100 feet away. Then he sank an irremovable expansion bolt into a crack in a boulder that stood two feet from the water at the Parrotts Ferry elevation. The stone sheltered a cavity where all six feet eight inches could hide from search boaters. Dubois's vigil, the ultimate New Melones protest, had begun.

This event may have drawn more media coverage than any other episode in dam-fighting history. Headlines fanned outward from California: "Chained Man Stops Dam Flow," "Protestor Hiding in Reservoir May Be Trapped as Water Rises," "Futile Search for Melones Protestor." Tongue-in-cheek, the New York *Times* called Dubois "an angry vegetarian. . . . It happened in California, of course." The Stanislaus had never been a national issue, and that was a shortcoming in the strategy of the fight. Now, the place was emblazoned across papers and television sets coast-to-coast. You couldn't avoid it, as Peter Behr once said. All this for Dubois, who shuns publicity. It embarrasses him. The Stanislaus has required him to deal with all kinds of people, but he remains shy. He refuses to cooperate with photographers. I know, because I've tried to take pictures of him, and they are mostly poor. The only way to catch him is when he's preoccupied, say kayaking through Bailey Falls.

Mystery blanketed the chaining from the beginning. That was one reason for the media's fascination. Not even Briggs knew where Mark was. Only the secret contact—nicknamed "Deep Paddle" after reporter Bob Woodward's Watergate contact "Deep Throat"—did. Only Briggs knew who Deep Paddle was. The secrecy was important: if Mark were found, he could be hauled out and the dam filled. His power depended on the mystery.

Briggs was the sole spokesman, and his telephone rang nonstop. "Once I went out for a paper, but otherwise, between Monday and Thursday, I didn't leave the house," Don says. For two full nights, he went without sleep. State Resources Secretary Huey Johnson called, concerned about Mark's life. Briggs said, "Mark wants to play this out. Things are okay"; but he didn't really know if things were okay or not. Scores of newspapers, radio, and TV stations wanted the story, and Briggs obliged. Scores of Mark's friends called, asked if Mark was safe, and offered to help. The Army Corps of Engineers never called to ask about Dubois or tried to get a message to him, except to answer his May 17 letter. Colonel O'Shei responded:

> . . . *The Friends of the River have been informed that, for operational reasons of our own, the Corps intends to limit the pool level to around elevation 808. You have been further advised that our control of filling is not precise and that it is possible that a warm spell or rain could cause runoff that we could not release without causing damaging flows downstream. This could result in a temporary rise of waters nominally above the 808 level. We do not plan for this to happen, but it could, and if it does the pool will be drawn down to 808 again for reasons involving execution of our own contracts. In the interim, however, anyone anchored to a rock at Parrotts Ferry would be in danger.*
>
> *I earlier agreed to the Friends of the River having access to Corps' controlled lands in the project area that are not, because of lack of sanitary facilities, yet open to the general public. This was done on your assurance that the area would be kept clean and that your group would be camping and picnicking in connection with a passive "farewell vigil" that you wished to conduct. Your threat to make your safety a hostage to our lawful prosecution of this project clearly falls outside the scope of those assurances. Accordingly, our agreement is void, and my consent to the presence of you or your group on those project lands under Corps jurisdiction and not open to the general public is hereby withdrawn. I will ask the appropriate agencies to enforce federal, state, and local laws as they pertain to future activities of you or your organization on such lands. A copy of this letter is being provided the Bureau of Land Management.*

The corps's position was softened on CBS-TV when a spokesman said that it wasn't about to drown Dubois. "We certainly don't want to hurt him or anybody else," said O'Shei.

"I did get one call from the corps," Briggs remembers. "Carl Greenstein in public information called about a film I borrowed a month before. He wondered when I'd be returning it."

The Army launched a twenty-man search party consisting of corps personnel, Bureau of Land Management rangers, sheriffs, and deputies. They used two helicopters and motorboats, but high technology would not work against this person. One boat was equipped with a bullhorn, and Don Moyer, an acquaintance of Mark, went along. "Mark, come out, there are other battles to fight. They've stopped filling the dam. You're needed. Shout if you can hear us," he called. Two guides from OARS hid in the brush and shouted back. Others in the search party were not so lucky—they had to walk the shore of the reservoir. Twice Dubois squirmed under his rock, while deputies ambled by above. They didn't find a trace, but the corps didn't doubt that Mark was in the lower canyon. "We really believe he's in there," said Lieutenant Colonel Hickman. "We have always felt that Mark has a lot of integrity, even if we march to a different set of drums."

Mark always said, "You get back what you give to people. If you give anger, you receive anger. I always trusted Colonel O'Shei, always respected him, even though I would get so frustrated I could just lash out. I tried to remember that he was an engineer and an attorney and he looks at things differently." Dubois got back the respect he had given. O'Shei believed that Mark was chained at elevation 808.

O'Shei said, "He's dedicated enough to do it."

Local authorities had a different opinion. "Our latest information is he is not chained," Tuolumne County Sheriff Wallace Berry said. "We've received information he is safe from the water. . . . I would say the threat of suicide is a hoax."

Meanwhile, FOR and government offices were in a frenzy.

Rich Hammond of the Resources Agency called Colonel O'Shei, who assured him that human life would not be risked. Huey Johnson and Hammond met for breakfast and drafted a telegram to President Carter, asking that the filling be stopped, stressing the values of the canyon, and pleading that the government not take action "needlessly precipitating the kind of strife too often associated in our lifetime with social conflict and change."

One hundred Stanislaus supporters converged on Wednesday on the steps of the state capitol, with signs reading, "Parrotts Ferry is the Limit" and "No Filling Past Parrotts Ferry." One held by forty-eight-year-old Cathy Duncan said, "No Filling Past Mark

Dubois." It was there that Governor Brown appeared unexpectedly for
a press conference on May 22. The river "is a priceless asset to the
people of California and to the people of this nation," Brown said,
echoing Decision 1422, and called for no filling above Parrotts Ferry in
1979. After the announcement, pro-Stanislaus people crowded in
on the governor to hug him.

In San Francisco, FOR volunteers stapled together flyers and
leafleted at both entrances to the Federal Building, bastion of the corps.
In the FOR office, Dick Roos-Collins finished a call and hustled over to
Tom Huntington. "Ready for this?" Roos-Collins asked. "A telegram
was just sent to the president from Governor Brown." Silence.
Everyone listened.

> I urge you to instruct the U.S. Army Corps of Engineers to halt the
> filling of the New Melones Dam at the Parrotts Ferry Bridge. The
> beauty of the Stanislaus Canyon and the life of Mark Dubois deserve
> your personal intervention.

Huntington gave a whoop. Dick said, "Since Prop 17 we've been
trying to get the governor to say 'don't fill.' Now he's done it. And he
says 'the beauty of the canyon.' That will still be there, even after Mark
comes out." There were no more skeptics about civil disobedience.

The corps pulled the plug, "stabilizing" the reservoir, but warning
that with spring floods, they might not be able to spill fast enough to
guarantee the existing level. "We feel we're doing exactly what
Governor Brown wants," said Lieutenant Colonel Hickman. "We're
doing better than he asks, in fact, at 803.5 since Monday." So
enthusiastic was the dumping that a head of water jettisoned out of
control, undermining the cliffside below the dam and devouring a road
that reportedly cost $250,000 to build. Dubois was blamed at first, a
reference that was later dropped. Colonel O'Shei told *Newsweek*, "We
will hold the level indefinitely. We are not prepared to flood the canyon
any further." Separate survey crews from the corps and the state set up
transits at Parrotts Ferry, calculated elevation from a bench mark near
the bridge, and pounded stakes in the ground at 808 feet above
sea level.

Everybody had an opinion about the chaining. At the San Francisco
Federal Building, FOR leafleters had never had it so easy. Many people
were sympathetic, but not all. "There's nothing there but a dried-up
valley," one red-faced man from Sonora said. Larry Wagner of
etcetera tried to talk to him, tried not to argue with him, but that was
impossible. The man and his wife walked away. Central Valley people
had mixed and confused responses. A young construction worker said,
"Guess there ain't gonna be a river there much longer. Lots of people
go raftin' down there, and they don't want to see it go. Me, I don't care
whether they fill it or not—they got a lot of dams everywhere anyway.

It'll make better water skiing. Construction workers and all I guess
wants it, but I can't really see it myself. One guy stoppin' these guys
with millions of dollars, that's all right."

Other reactions were hostile. A middle-aged rancher reflected:
"Guess there's lots who don't want the water back there, but look at
all the money they've spent. Everybody wants his own—not thinking
about anyone else, but we gotta' think about the future—the next
generation. What are they going to eat? What will they have for
energy? We gotta' think ahead. I say fill it. That guy isn't there. He'd
be a damn fool to be in there. What do they care about one person
down in there with all the money they've spent? Fill it up I say."

A second phase of the protest now began: Alexander Gaguine
decided to chain himself near the old Parrotts Ferry Bridge. Friends,
concerned that things would become too confused, tried to discourage
him. Gaguine maintained that it should be people—not just one man
—putting their lives on the line for the river, and he saw his action as
support for Mark. Like Dubois, Gaguine could not be turned aside. He
found an old chain and an open padlock with a missing key. Just right.

Gaguine would not be alone. David Lynch, a young, soft-spoken
river guide from Massachusetts saw an FOR meeting notice on the
door of the OARS boathouse. After hearing Gaguine speak, he joined
him. Expecting to be arrested within a few hours, the two activists took
no sleeping bags or food to Parrotts Ferry. They searched for a boulder
at the water's edge near the campground, intending to stay on Bureau
of Land Management property and to avoid the corps's land. Just
below the camping area, they found a waist-high undercut rock with
willows for shade, short on poison oak. A hundred yards from the
parking lot, they were accessible to the journalists and TV crews who
would tread a dusty path their way for a week. The pair looped half of
their chain around the boulder; with the other half, each man made a
tight loop around his ankle. Then they padlocked each loop shut.
No key.

In order to keep Friends of the River in the clear, a new name was
adopted—the Parrotts Ferry Non-Violent Action Coalition, otherwise
known as "the chain gang." As other people joined, they were called
the "Parrotts Ferry Five," "Parrotts Ferry Six," "Seven," and "Eight."
At noon on May 23, nineteen people met in support, and the coalition
of Gaguine and Lynch issued its first news release:

> People are taking part in this action of the Parrotts Ferry Non-Violent
> Action Coalition today by gathering at the border of the Stanislaus
> River and New Melones Reservoir. Some of us will be chained to
> rocks. We are doing this to stand in the way of further filling of New
> Melones Dam, and destruction of the Stanislaus River Canyon and the
> remaining rivers and wild lands in California.

> To many of us, Parrotts Ferry and the whole upper canyon are important parts of our lives. It is a part of our home, which we do not want taken away from us. There are many of us who feel this way.
>
> We recognize that this place links us with the natural and spiritual world. It is a part of our heritage and the heritage of our children. We intend to stay here with the river canyon and the rest of its life until the threat of flooding is over. . . ."

Sheriff's deputies put in an appearance, but said they were planning no arrests. At dusk on their first day, Gaguine and Lynch realized they would be left alone until Mark came out. The corps couldn't raise the water until then anyway. With friends' sleeping bags, the two men settled in for a long wait—days, weeks, maybe a month.

Lynch and the others (except Gaguine) who formed the Parrotts Ferry group had scarcely been involved in the New Melones fight. "This is direct action," Lynch explained. "I locked a chain around my ankle so they have to cut it or flood me if they're going to fill the reservoir. When you write letters to a congressman, you never know what happens. Letters probably don't even get read. This way, I feel more like I'm doing something, that it counts."

Like Gaguine, Lynch had followed a roundabout path to Parrotts Ferry. Just after high school, he took a student conservation association job in the Grand Canyon. Working for token wages, he cleaned johns at wilderness campsites, closed unwanted trails, and learned to row the rapids. In the canyon and its life, he found a new home. He also met people from OARS, who encouraged him to move to the foothills and work as a Stanislaus guide. That was how, in 1979, he came to sit chained to the bed of the Stanislaus, a long way from suburban Philadelphia and Boston, where he had grown up. "I'm amazed at the harmony of nature in this canyon," David told a reporter during the chaining. "Everything works out. Where else do you see perfection? If only we could get along with this instead of killing it. A reservoir is dead, nothing like a river. I look at this as a civic responsibility. I guess we all try to take a stand somewhere, and this is it for me." Soon the pair of activists were joined by Doris Grimm, Laurie Pavey, Matthew Lawson, and Debbie Baker.

Doris Grimm was twenty-seven, a blonde native of Long Beach. After studying anthropology and archaeology at Humboldt College on the north coast, she had settled into the slow pace of the Sierra foothills. She thought she was getting away from urban pressures, but wasn't. "Up north, they're cutting the redwoods," she says. Here, they're damming the rivers. You can't get away from people using up the earth." Working nine months a year as an archaeologist for the Forest Service, Doris had an archaeologist's sense of timelessness. "Nine million years of creation destroyed in three months. For what? There were people who lived with this river for ages, and now it's one of our few remaining wild canyons. We need farming and electricity, but today, a place like this is rare. We need it, not to eat, not to turn turbines, but to restore our spirits. That's where we're having the worst drought of all."

Laurie Pavey and Debbie Baker worked as river guides for Zephyr. Matthew Lawson was a boatman for OARS. Late on Thursday, Pavey and Baker were to leave, but two more people would come on Saturday—Marjene Olsen, a boatwoman for the American River Touring Association, and Ron Pickup. At forty-one, with a grizzly dark beard, Pickup was the oldest chainer. Having grown up in Sonora, he is a local. Pickup dropped out of nuclear power, resigning his job at an experimental plant near San Francisco in the late sixties when he saw the inadequacy of the safety regulations, and subsequently taught English, first at a community college, then at a Northern California prison. He has written a book of poetry about the Stanislaus. Of all these people, only Lynch and Lawson were well acquainted before they chained themselves together. This would be a social experiment as well as environmental activism.

The New Melones protest was now fully set, with Dubois hidden in the lower canyon, his safety a "hostage to our lawful prosecution of this project," as Colonel O'Shei put it. Five people were chained at Parrotts Ferry, available to newspeople and to the sheriff, if his design included jail, always a possibility with civil disobedience. (My *Funk & Wagnalls'* calls it a "refusal to comply with certain civil laws, usually done as a matter of conviction and by means of passive resistance.") The river people may have been trespassing, since the corps had revoked permission to camp, and Gaguine and crew were inadvertently on corps property, having gone beyond the BLM sanctuary to find a stout boulder for their chain. More to the point of disobedience, the protestors were thwarting the activities of the corps.

Picture yourself, for a moment, on a slope of sand, five feet wide, twelve feet long, studded with sharp rocks, partly shaded by scruffy willows, fringed with poison oak. The river streams by, lapping at the big boulder at your feet. A chain is fastened around your ankle by a padlock. You can move maybe ten feet, but that depends on the person next to you moving part of the distance, because you are shackled together. You can't get up and leave. You can't walk. Privacy is only inside your head. What about calls of nature? "You know, that's the first thing people would ask," Lynch says. You go behind the boulder, where two chained friends hold a poncho as outhouse wall, and you use an army ammo can, the kind used on commercial river trips. At any time, you could be busted by a sheriff's deputy with a hacksaw. You never know what the water will do. You listen for its rise through the night.

I hitchhike to Parrotts Ferry on Thursday afternoon, the fourth day of Mark's chaining, and the second day for Gaguine and the others. Just past the camp sites, I see a group near the water. Right next to it. The men are shirtless, and everybody sports a fresh tan. In the middle of six people, I spot Gaguine. He holds out his hands in welcome. "Who's chained here?" I ask, and when everybody rattles their ankles, it sounds like a gang from Folsom.

Earlier in the day, the beach was packed with reporters and TV crews, but now it is quiet. Doris massages Matthew's back. Everybody massages everybody's back sooner or later; you get stiff when you're chained to a rock. Your back aches and your butt aches and you get headaches, maybe from slow blood circulation. Maybe from the sun. Maybe from newspeople. Laurie sits on the boulder, staring miles away. David listens while Alexander and I talk about the protest and rehash the day we met in the Atchafalaya Swamp of Louisiana. Toward dark, the group shares some food—a salad, cheese, and crackers—leftovers from one of the commercial trips that afternoon.

Through a solid week on this beach, everybody got along. There was no bickering. But individuals had problems; "I can't believe I'm burned out already," I heard Matthew say on Thursday afternoon. He claimed a long novel donated by Melinda Wright, and retired to seventeenth-century Japan. Doris said she faced a crisis every day, but she did not show it.

Gaguine fuels the event, galvanizes and spurs on the group. Late at night, when everyone is lethargic, he is lavish with enthusiasm. "I'm going to stay here," he says. "Why should I leave? If I leave, the corps'll just raise the water. Why should I leave? I'm comfortable. I could stay here for two months. They'll just flood Parrotts Ferry if I leave. Let 'em come down with cable cutters and arrest me first. Why should I leave?" Nobody answers.

Gaguine can't help thinking of the past, the chapters of the Stanislaus battle he and others had been through. "Years of work to save the river, and now here's the dam, and we're in its way. Right now we're winning. It's never been this good." Everybody is high on the fact that they are doing something and it is being noticed. Gaguine grabs his guitar and wakes up the evening with songs. Later the Stanislaus takes over, and a few of the faces are lost to the dark and the steady hiss of the river.

David Lynch talks of being a river guide. "I really get a good feeling, showing this place to people," he says. "You get men and women who start out in a hurry, and by the second day they've slowed down, they're looking at the canyon." Lynch might go to college. "Maybe this winter for a few courses. In three weeks we're going to run the Selway in Idaho if I can get $200 together." That says much about a boatman's life—a few dollars here and there. No commitments. Rivers and a loose style of life. Yet Lynch is different just by virtue of being here. A lot of guides don't even show a commitment to the river that feeds them. I wonder why the guides aren't more active in the New Melones fight, and the answer is that many of them don't want to be bothered. Most are young people who aren't attached and don't want to be. The politics of resources are not for them, even if the resources are.

At night, the Parrotts Ferry residents are heaped in sleeping bags of many colors, the whole mass inadvertently inching downhill like a slow mudslide in the Santa Monica Hills. Debbie, at the bottom end, woke up with wet feet.

Through the following days, newspaper and TV reporters came in shifts. "There isn't even time to take a piss between cameramen," Matt Lawson groused. Gaguine usually starred in the interviews. He was the only one fluent on the issues. "We know an investment has been made in New Melones Dam and we feel it should be used. But with a Parrotts Ferry limit we've stored three times the volume of the Old Melones Dam. It's enough to satisfy our needs for a long time. We recognize that downstream people want flood protection; they can have it with a Parrotts Ferry limit if the dam is managed right." Then he would cite figures and embellish his argument.

One newsman complained of the heat. Debbie Baker advised, "You ought to roll your pants up and stand in the river. It feels real good." He smiled and continued to sweat. A local TV newscaster showed up in a tie and wing-tip shoes that he couldn't keep the sand out of. The camera flashed from him to the shirtless Gaguine in the willows. Not all reporters were so formal. One newswoman from Sonora arrived in shorts and shower thongs. She used to be a river guide.

Then there were visitors. Dozens of them. Old friends, new friends, complete strangers, the crowd that swims at Parrotts Ferry, and the crowd that watches fires in downtown Sacramento. Picnickers and curiosity seekers. Doris would welcome visitors and talk to them about the river. Half of a high school class from Angels Camp landed together after a river-trip with OARS. Doris gave them notepaper, and a half dozen young people sat in the sand and wrote to Congressman Shumway—as though they had a chance of changing his mind. "I saw the river. I think Parrotts Ferry should be the limit. Please don't let them drown the Stanislaus."

Days were twice warmed by the media: talking to reporters, then reading what they wrote. Reporters could easily have styled the event a fantasy or a nuisance perpetrated by radicals, but the protesters were respected.

Dubois remained a mystery. People who knew the man didn't doubt that he was chained to a rock, but rumors proliferated from

Alexander Gaguine, chained at Parrotts Ferry

Doris Grimm

Alexander Gaguine and Mark Dubois after the chaining, Parrott's Ferry

Mark Dubois at Stanislaus River Rally, June 2, 1979

Old Parrotts Ferry Bridge

Chained to the rock at Parrotts Ferry

Stanislaus Rally ends, June 2, 1979
(Parrotts Ferry Bridge)

other sources. He was at a friend's home. He was in Washington, D.C. Somebody called the Tuolumne County sheriff's office and said that Mark was eating ice cream at the Sonora Frosty. This was funny, because everyone knew that Dubois was an ice cream addict. He avoids drugs, beer, even caffeine. No grass, coffee, not even tea or cola. But quarts of ice cream are not too large. Friends knew the Sonora Frosty rumor was a fake, because Mark would have gone to Foster's Freeze in Angels Camp. To be so close to Foster's—the river guide's favorite—and go someplace else for ice cream just wouldn't be Mark.

The fantasy of Dubois being everywhere at once had some basis in experience. Mark and other guides had once rowed a group down the river from Camp Nine to Duck Bar, where he hiked out in the evening and sped off to Sacramento via motorcycle for a TV interview. The next morning he was back at ARTA headquarters in Vallecito by the time the river trip was finished.

Dubois could be everywhere, it seemed, even against the odds. On another occasion, he was driving the FOR struggle-buggy (an old Datsun with a camper shell on the back) from San Andreas, where he had met with county supervisors, to San Francisco for a radio show. The truck, donated by an association of outfitters, broke down in the suburban outskirts of Stockton. Dubois hitchhiked to the San Francisco radio station, split like a blur for the Greyhound terminal, and landed by bus in Sacramento fifteen minutes before a TV interview. He arrived sweaty, but the other TV participants—John Hertle and Billy Martin—quickly caught up in the ninety-degree studio. The truck, plastered with "Parrotts Ferry is the Limit" signs, did not do so well. Its windshield was smashed and the camper shell stolen. Stockton is no place for Friends of the River.

When New Melones Dam was dedicated, it was rumored that Dubois would hang-glide from the overlook to the dedication site. Like a crop duster at a county fair, he would be towing a "Parrotts Ferry is the Limit" banner behind him.

But now, with rumors suggesting that Dubois was not really chained to the riverbed at all, Don Briggs felt it was time to arrange an interview.

In the dark of the night, Deep Paddle slips his raft into the river, then loads camera gear. Tom Harris of the San Jose *Mercury* and Bill Rood of the Los Angeles *Times* climb on. Without a sound, the three drift from Parrotts Ferry through the only remaining rapid of the lower canyon and into the mirrored stillness of the reservoir. The boatman rows with hardly a ripple, while beavers—flooded from their riverbank homes—slap their tails on the water and scuttle under. Surreptitiously the guide aims for shore, and the raft crunches against flooded chaparral. From behind a boulder where water laps in the shadows of midnight, a tall figure folds back a tattered Columbian poncho, thrusts out a beanstalk arm, and clutches the calloused hand of the guide, then his shoulders. So much for rumors.

Starlight barely gleams on the site. Mark's bearded face seems white in the incongruous explosion of a flash bulb. A thick old sock protects his right foot and ankle from the steel chain. Poison oak, rooted among the rocks where Dubois sleeps, has left a rash on his legs. A bag of dried fruit and nuts sits beside the rock. Resting comfortably on the ledge, Dubois says to the reporters, "I came here to guarantee Parrotts Ferry for this year, so that people can stand on the bridge and look downstream to a nice reservoir and upstream to a wild river. We've compromised enough.

"Frustrations with the bureaucracies are what finally drove me to do it," he explains. "We watched the corps flood the Miwok sites of the lower canyon against the position of the State Historic Preservation Office and the Department of the Interior. We saw the chance of flooding above Parrotts Ferry, but the required mitigation hasn't been done—downstream, 4,700 acres were to be bought to replace 12,500 flooded acres upstream, and the corps hasn't done it. We did everything else we could do. I just couldn't think of any other way to make the agencies more responsive. And I had to make a personal statement."

How long would this action be effective? "There are no victories in the environmental movement, only delays," Dubois says. "Maybe this will delay flooding for a year. And that can give time for longer-term protection.

"I never felt fear or hesitation. Something felt right inside; I didn't feel I'd drown." A flowering buckeye tree casts a soft shadow on Dubois, who seems comfortable and serene, staked out, his body separating the land that is lost from the land that remains. "The corps seems to value human life more than it values the life of this canyon." One reporter asks about Colonel O'Shei. "Mostly, I know he's doing what he thinks is right. He just has different values."

There is a long silence in the dark, awkward to the reporters, not to Dubois. "I didn't feel I'd drown," he repeats. "But at the same time, I was very much ready to accept the fact that if that's what happens, that's what happens. At least I would be sharing the same fate with all of my friends in the lower canyon. I keep seeing all of the life going out of the canyon, and it really hurts. It's very painful, and I've shed a lot of tears." He fights back emotions that are rising close to the surface again. "We've done a pretty good job of severing ourselves from these beautiful places." The toughest part of the decision to chain himself, he adds, was knowing the effect it would have on the people he is close to.

The next night a CBS crew is rafted in, and Roger Mudd talks about Dubois on the national news. Then, on Friday morning, in the hazy light of dawn, the same raft carries Thorne Gray of the Modesto *Bee* and Theresa Baggot of the Sonora *Daily Union Democrat* to the scene. These papers publish stories on Friday night, prompting a statement from O'Shei. "It's almost getting to be a silly situation. Pretty soon we'll be able to follow the empty film rolls to him." Then the colonel adds, "The responsibility for Mark's safety is no longer one hundred percent mine."

Half a dozen people arrive at Parrotts Ferry on Friday afternoon. Melinda Wright and friends. A middle-aged man walks up quickly with an intense gleam in his eye.

"We've saved the river," he says, but he looks as though he needs saving himself. "We've saved the river—we're seeing Jimmy Carter on Tuesday—me and Mark. The airplane tickets are bought. Who can take me to see Mark?" Slightly balding, sweat beaded on his forehead, he stares at the group.

"Who is this?" I ask David, Doris, then Alexander.

"Who's going to take me to Mark?" the stranger says. He's impatient. "All I need is a boatman."

Marty Booth, who arrived with Melinda says, "Mark wanted everybody to go through Don Briggs. That's what you have to do, just like everybody else."

"Hey, don't lay any of that heavy shit on me!" Sweat begins to drip from the man's face. "I got an appointment with Carter. Now who's taking me to get Mark?"

Gaguine introduces our guest, since nobody else knows him. Gaguine tries to say more, "He was involved in Proposition 17 . . ."

"Since 1973 I've been involved. Longer than most people. Where were you in 1973?"

"We don't know where Mark is," Gaguine says. "We can't take you to him."

"Look, all I need is a boatman."

"We don't know where he is," Marty says.

"I'll find him anyway," and the man takes out a bullhorn and demonstrates, blasting at us point blank. "Mark, the river is saved," he shouts. "We have a meeting with the president. Tell me where you are."

This is absurd. Now everyone knows they are dealing with a madman. He could get violent, and I am the only person between him and the chained people. No one knows what will happen next. No one has the vaguest idea what to do.

"No one here knows where Mark is," someone else answers. The man fumes. "Christ, are you people just going to sit here?" Then he stomps off toward the rafters take-out area. We never see him again.

It was sometime during that same afternoon—the fourth one of the chaining—that the most hopeful news arrived: FOR's Washington lobbyist, Patricia Schifferle, had persuaded Don Edwards and seven other California congressmen to introduce a Stanislaus national wild river bill. In the hype of the protest against the dam, it took a while to see the importance of this. National wild river status would keep the flatwater at 808. It was the best way—maybe the only way—to get long-term protection. Through 1980 FOR's efforts would be directed at getting this bill passed. The same congressmen sent a letter to the president, urging a Parrotts Ferry limit through 1980 while Miwok and Gold Rush sites were studied.

Saturday was slow; most newsmen didn't work weekends. In the evening, Charles Bloodgood came and introduced himself: "I'm your lawyer." No one had known they needed a lawyer, but now farmers were threatening to sue the coalition, Dubois, and the corps. This spiced things up for a while. Gaguine had talked to Bloodgood in Sacramento when civil disobedience was first discussed. If anyone got into trouble, the lawyer said, he would represent them. They talked for two hours.

Sunday night was intense. Things started happening quickly. Arriving from Melinda's house with another man, David Boyd announced, "We'd like to have only a few people to talk about this." He asked if I was Mike somebody, a suspected informer, who works for the corps. This was beginning to sound like an Irish revolution. Gaguine spoke up and said that everybody was okay, just talk.

"Mark might come out real soon," Boyd said. "The corps is really pissed about this, and as soon as Mark is unchained, they're going to bring the water up and float you people straight out of here." Someone raised the possibility that Gaguine might go in and hide the same way Mark had done.

The group's feelings came slowly out of a strained silence. Suppose Gaguine didn't want to risk his life? After all, he hadn't wanted Mark to go in the first place. "Whatever anyone does, they should volunteer," said Craig Rieser, an old river guide and Stanislaus supporter. To run the whole escapade again seemed like overkill. Besides, why would Mark come out if he didn't think Parrotts Ferry would be safe? No, Gaguine would not go in.

Through the day, the water's rise had been ominous, creeping up inch by inch on the big rock. It got spooky that night as the chained people sat at the edge, picturing all those miles of the North Fork, Middle Fork, and South Fork above, each fed by a snowpack that was melting by the yard in eighty-degree heat. Here they were, on that critical edge, chained at the boundary of a flood being dumped from above and impounded from below. The lowest of the group had to put their feet up on rocks to keep them from being soaked. Later four river guides arrived with a pile of old boards from a scrap lumber pile at ARTA. "Everybody move up as far as you can, we're building you a platform to keep you out of the water," they announced.

The group thought about staying chained, even if Mark came out. They could make statements about the turbines: "Since the state's position is to not fill the dam, there's no need to test the high head turbines, therefore no need to flood elevation 808." Then they remembered that the Department of the Interior would assume operation as soon as the turbines were tested. Interior Secretary Cecil Andrus might be better to deal with than the generals and colonels. Then again, he might not.

The coalition could say, "No more flooding, period." Ron Pickup wanted to do this. He had come to keep water off Parrotts Ferry, and he planned to be arrested. But Friends of the River had already conceded that the river elevation beneath the bridge—half a mile upstream—was their compromise for 1979. One member said, "I think I'm ready to leave tomorrow."

Once the platform was built, Gar Dubois, Mark's soft-spoken younger brother, asked for people to listen. They stood still around the chained group. In the dark, you could see only the silhouettes of a dozen visitors. Gar read a letter taken down in longhand over the phone from the governor's office, asking the corps to stop filling at 808. The chief threat to the 808 limit had been the chance of high runoff that the corps would have to hold above Parrotts Ferry to avoid flooding farmers' fields down below. The state's new position included California officials in decisions to determine if "flooding" was occurring. The last paragraph warned that California would sue the corps if it didn't meet the 808 request.

Jerry Meral had written the first draft of the letter. Richard Hammond, Gray Davis (Governor Brown's chief of staff), and Ron Robie then met with Colonel O'Shei. They had some harsh words. The final letter had been written by Hammond and sent to the corps by Davis.

Gar folded the letter, snapped off the flashlight, and faced the silhouettes. "That's about as strong as it's going to get," he concluded, and it seemed clear that Mark was coming out. Maybe he was already out.

It is just after dawn, long before the sun will rise over the eastern hills. A car door closes—too early for a newsman. Over the sandy rise that separates the campsite from the parking lot come Mark Dubois and Gracielle Rossi. "Deep Paddle" had unlocked Mark during the night, and Gracielle met him at the ARTA house.

The Parrotts Ferry Six sleep, with dreams of swimming. And drowning. They are discernible only by the color on their sleeping bags. Mark asks, "Which is Alexander?" and sneaks up to give him a bear hug, a Dubois hug. Gaguine is drunk with sleep, but he smiles and says, "All right, this is not to be a media event," quoting Dubois and poking him in the ribs. They laugh, and the others wake up. "Mark!" Doris cries, and the group hug in one big bundle.

"The farmers are talking about getting chained up, too," Dubois announces with the mischievous grin of an instigator. The farmers threatened to stake themselves out on their flood plains, forcing the corps either to hold back the water and flood Dubois and the Parrotts Ferry group, or release water and flood the farmers. I can see why the corps, after thirty-four years, is anxious to dump this project onto the Department of the Interior and get out. John Hertle jokingly threatened to chain his wife down in the oat field.

"What did you think of the search parties?" David asks Mark.

"They made a nice try," Dubois answers. "But those motorboats go really fast." He mimics them, "Varoom! Well, I guess he's not anywhere around here." They speculate about a dam-fighter's national monument at Mark's rock, or inclusion on the National Register of Historic Places, a designation that would protect the site from "adverse impacts" of federal projects.

"We didn't know you played basketball," Marjene says, remembering a biographical sketch in the San Francisco *Chronicle*.

"Well, I tripped a lot."

"Ha! We didn't know you were the Rotary Club's boy-of-the-year either," Gaguine teases. Mark has to leave for a strategy session in San Francisco. What will the Parrotts Ferry people do now? Last night, one of them proposed leaving. Now everybody but Ron agrees. Finally, they all reason that to stay would be anticlimactic, since Mark is out.

A final statement is needed—one that takes advantage of this last opportunity. Gaguine and Ron Pickup draft a press release that says that the conditions of the coalition have been met: Mark is out and reasonable assurances have been given of an 808 limit. The group is leaving because a turning point has been reached—Parrotts Ferry is safe for 1979. "Now is the time to work toward long-term protection, to lobby for House Bill 4223 which would include the upper Canyon in the National Wild and Scenic Rivers System," it reads. The group decides to leave at noon.

Since the beginning, everybody had wondered when the corps would warn them of high water. They thought that the Army or sheriff's department would come with cable cutters and snap the chains if the water was going to rise. The corps comes at 10:00. Major Keller warns that the river will rise another half foot or so due to natural runoff. Then at noon, May 28, the chaining is over. Gaguine hacksaws through his chain and holds an interview for Modesto's Channel 3.

Gray Davis of the governor's office called the settlement "a great victory for environmentalists." Colonel O'Shei said that the only thing that the protestors had won was a pledge by the corps to consult with the state before flooding above Parrotts Ferry. "I think this guy marched everybody up the hill and down again," O'Shei asserted.

The editors of the San Jose *Mercury* answered, "Maybe so—but even the Colonel would have to admit Dubois did it with consummate skill. For a man who professes to dislike media attention, the young environmentalist has an uncanny knack for staging a media event."

The Army's Joe Countryman says, "O'Shei saved the project. He could have lost it right then. I think Dubois' action caused total political unity among the people who want the reservoir filled. The symbolism of that act may have pulled the river interests together, but it did more for the dam supporters. Before, it was just the Army Corps. Friends of the River had the political edge. Now the locals and the politicians are up in arms. Now they say, 'Fill it!'"

John Hertle says, "I disagree with that kind of protest. It hurts other people who had to give up time and safety. It was costly. It solidified public opinion for the dam.

"It's not a good example for others, particularly young people," Hertle continues. "The average citizen is not going to flout the law. It antagonizes people when they see someone else do it and get away with it. There are less dramatic ways of accomplishing the same thing. There are a number of other things that they could have done."

Milton Kramer calls the episode, "Mark's stunt up there." He too, feels that the chaining solidified local support for the dam and against the Friends of the River. He thinks that without the alarm that civil disobedience triggered, Johnson, Hammond, Meral, Robie, Burns (assistant secretary for resources), and "that whole gang in Sacramento" would have been successful in keeping the water down for a long time. Kramer, the publicity expert, says, "It was a good publicity stunt, but I find it hard to believe someone would risk their life that way."

In the country's long history of dam fighting and river protection, this was the first time civil disobedience had been used to save a river (tiny Tamalpais Creek excluded). There may have been cases where people wouldn't move from homes that were to be flooded, but never before had people risked their lives at the water's edge.

Countryman, Hertle, and Kramer raise an important point, however. How much did the action mobilize the dam supporters? And would the chaining jeopardize FOR's future efforts in working through legal channels? The pro-dam people had been against FOR before, but now they were infuriated, ready to mobilize their Valley politicians. Was stopping the 1979 flood—which wouldn't have gone much above Parrotts Ferry anyway—worth it? Was the national news coverage worth it? Probably. Because the only chance at long-term protection was through the national wild and scenic rivers system. To gain inclusion in the system, nationwide awareness and support was essential. John Garamendi, pro-dam state senator from Stockton, thinks the chaining was a "brilliant" public-relations stroke, and that the river movement may not have survived without it. But to do it again might be a different matter.

On June 2, five days after Dubois, Gaguine, and the other people unchained, a Stanislaus River Rally was celebrated at Parrotts Ferry. Visitors began to arrive in the morning, swelling to a crowd of 500 in the heat of the foothills' afternoon. Friends of the River sponsored guided walks to see plant life and archaeological ruins that would be flooded, and kayak tours were taken into the reservoir to see the flooding. Everybody swam or waded in the river, cool refuge from the 100-degree heat. Don Harriman and Steve Menicucci kept a raft filled with water as a wading pool for kids, and a Sonora restaurant supplied vegetarian sandwiches and fruit juice. Folk singers performed half a dozen songs about the Stanislaus River, with lyrics less than complimentary to the Army Corps of Engineers. John Amodio of the Sierra Club and Patricia Schifferle spoke. Susan Brooks talked about the flooding of the lower canyon and how she had rescued animals. Knox Mellon, state historic preservation officer under Governor Brown, said that Parrotts Ferry was enough flooding. "I'm with you all the way," he assured the crowd, referring to the wealth of threatened archaeological and historic resources.

Dubois drew applause. "I had to act when I realized that nine million years of evolution in the canyon were far more valuable than my short life on this planet," he said. "The bulldozers are fast, but together we have more strength than any bulldozer, more strength than a thousand of them."

Meanwhile, in Stockton, Congressman Norman Shumway was announcing a new organization, Friends of the Dam. "I intend to fight water with water if that becomes necessary," he said. "There comes a time when we must recognize the facts, take a responsible, balanced approach and stop catering to the whims of a selfish minority. The purpose of Friends of the Dam can be stated very simply—to make known the facts that New Melones must be filled right now." He pointed to the wild and scenic river legislation of Don Edwards as a threat and as a reason for forming the new group. "Obviously the silent majority which supports New Melones has been silent for too long," Shumway concluded.

At the rally, a motorboat roared past the swimming beach, sounding like half a dozen chain saws. The New Melones floodwaters were approaching the Parrotts Ferry limit, introducing a new style of recreation. The boat lurched and strained against the rapids and failed to penetrate any farther.

Then people gathered under placards for the different California congressional districts and the various organized lobbying efforts. As a human chain, a quarter of a mile long, the crowd went hand-in-hand to the old Parrotts Ferry Bridge. Shoulder-to-shoulder, they formed a circle of friends covering the bridge in silent dedication to a wild upper river. There were many familiar faces from the long Stanislaus struggle: Mary Regan, Dennis Fantin, and other disabled people; Gracielle Rossi, Larry Wagner, Roger Newman, and others from etcetera; Catherine Fox and Tom Huntington from FOR in San Francisco; Don Briggs and Nancy Magneson; environmentalists from Chico, the north coast, and San Diego; Gaguine and the Parrotts Ferry Eight; Richard Close, who had sculptured a memorial to the lower canyon; young foothills residents; and a crowd of Bay Area people who had rafted that day—200 altogether. They celebrated and sang songs with a sense that they might yet save this wild place of the Sierra.

Once again there was hope.

CHAPTER NINE

A National River

There are still good rivers in this country: the legendary Salmon and Snake of Idaho and the Pacific northwest; the boundary-making Rio Grande; the Deep South's Suwanee; the northwoods Allagash of Maine; and the most floated whitewater—Pennsylvania's Youghiogheny. Washington's Middle Fork Snoqualmie in the craggy North Cascades. The canoe waters of the Current and Jacks Fork in the Ozarks. The upper Hudson and the lower Rogue. Outside Alaska, Idaho's Selway may be our wildest, and Montana's Yellowstone is our longest, undammed river. There are 50,000 large dams in the country, but we can still find wild, free-flowing streams, or sections of them, including the best nine miles of the Stanislaus.

In 1968 Congress created the national wild and scenic rivers system to save the best free-flowing waterways. On a national river, dams, canals, or other federal water projects are not allowed. Designation also encourages local land-use regulations, and usually results in recreation management and some public land buying for open space, access, or camping. Eight rivers were designated at first, including the Middle Fork of the Feather in California, and twenty-seven others were to be studied. By 1980 the list of designated rivers had grown to thirty (including the North Fork of the American in California), and fifty-four were in the study category (including the Tuolumne, just south of the Stanislaus).

During the chaining of May 1979, Patricia Schifferle, the Friends of the River lobbyist in Washington, persuaded the staff of Congressman Don Edwards, who then sponsored a bill to designate the canyon of the Stanislaus.

Schifferle's grandparents—wheat farmers near Marysville—were born in California. Patricia herself—nicknamed "Shortcutt"—grew up in Lafayette, near Walnut Creek, in the Bay Area. As a guide for the

American River Touring Association, who had rowed some of the West's toughest water in Cataract Canyon on the Colorado, she knew the Sierra rivers. She had been on the fringe of the Stanislaus campaign, working with Bruce Simballa during Proposition 17, helping with the Behr bill, and testifying at an Angels Camp hearing on archaeological studies. In the fall of 1978, she was traveling to Washington, D. C. to see friends, and asked Mark Dubois if there was anything she could do. "Sure, go see the California delegation about the archaeology and historic work," he said. "Let them know why the reservoir should not be filled above Parrotts Ferry." In September 1980, Schifferle was still there.

"What she has done by herself in Washington is incredible," Alexander Gaguine says; but Schifferle works best alone. A strong, tough woman, with a big smile and an attractive face, she is the most volatile of all the river people. She becomes embroiled, outraged; she dances on success, but with failure she plunges into despair. Some think she is bossy, arrogant, unorganized, independent, and not at all humble, but she has taken on Washington, and no one else from FOR could have survived there for so long.

First working from the office of the American Rivers Conservation Council in the Capitol Hill neighborhood, then from the Environmental Policy Center next door, Schifferle drafted two pages of Stanislaus legislation with the help of Howard Brown of ARCC and Brent Blackwelder of EPC. San Jose Congressman Don Edwards then introduced the bill.

Edwards is a senior Democrat. As chairman of the Civil and Constitutional Rights Subcommittee, he led a sensitive and careful investigation of the FBI, for which he used to work as an agent. One of the most liberal members of the House, and a leader of the liberal establishment, he was an early opponent of the Vietnam War, onetime chairman of Americans for Democratic Action, and, in 1979, floor manager for the time extension for the Equal Rights Amendment ratification. On a staff member's wastebasket is a bumper sticker that says "ERA Yes." On the wall is a poster that says "La tierra pertenece al que la trabaja . . . The land belongs to those who work it." Edwards's League of Conservation Voters' record has been 100 percent. Other sponsors of the bill were Peter Stark, Pete McCloskey, George Miller, Anthony Bielenson, Edward Roybal, Lionel Van Deerlin, and Ronald Dellums—all Californians. Robert Weaver of Oregon and Peter Carr of Michigan joined as co-sponsors a month later. From the beginning, Edwards was clear, "You'll need Phillip Burton for this."

Talk about the eleventh hour. Most rivers are not considered for the national rivers system unless they are non-controversial—i.e., no dams are proposed. An authorized reservoir site is anathema. But here was New Melones Dam, built and partly filled, and the Edwards bill would require that the unfilled remainder—the wilderness canyon—stay wild. Two other rivers offered precedents for last-minute protection. In the case of the New River of North Carolina, federal power commission licenses had been issued for the Blue Ridge project of the American Electric Power Company. After a struggle by locals, the American Rivers Conservation Council, and the state against the power company and the Federal Power Commission, the river was added to the national rivers system in 1976. Likewise, all of the plans were ready for Tocks Island Dam on the Delaware when that section of river was approved for protection in 1978. However, neither of those dams had been built, and New Melones was.

Because of the chaining, the Edwards bill hit front page. This was not civil disobedience, not Mark Dubois, not a temporary fix or a one-year delay for the digging up of antiquity. This was a congressional bill to establish a national river, and it alarmed the dam people. Stockton Congressman Norman Shumway announced formation of Friends of the Dam, a coalition of foothills people who were angry about the chaining and Valley people who had been involved all along. The effort was headed by John Hertle and Nancy Whittle, a Calaveras County supervisor from Angels Camp. The Whittles had been required to sell part of their cattle ranch for New Melones Dam, and now, because of Friends of the River, the reservoir was not being filled. For the third time, Milton Kramer was hired.

The financial records of the group are not available, but during the next fifteen months, "over $100,000" would be spent in fighting the national river legislation. John Hertle estimates that half of the money came from business and half from individuals. About 20 percent, he says, came from agricultural interests to the south, clear through Kern County.

"Friends of the Dam" soon disappeared and "Friends of New Melones" emerged. One might speculate that the name would seem more politically appealing. Who wants to be the friend of a dam costing the taxpayers $341 million—sixteen million cubic yards of dirt and rock dug up by the Guy F. Atkinson Company and dumped in the river to make a 62-story pile? It is better to be a friend of New Melones.

While Schifferle began knocking on congressional doors in Washington to solicit support for the Edwards bill that could forever protect the canyon, the dam that could forever flood the canyon was being dedicated with a pledge of allegiance, prayer, and plaque. Air-conditioned buses shuttled Central Valley guests, many wearing "Fill Er Up" T-shirts, from corps headquarters to the dam overlook at 10:00 A.M., July 14. Local bands played festive music. The master of ceremonies was the same as at the groundbreaking event, fifteen years before—John Hertle, who played back some of his experiences during Stanislaus floods for the audience. From a podium framed by the giant pile of stone—320,000 of Atkinson's truckloads plugging what used to be Iron Canyon—the dairy farmer said, "Our well-being depends on our land, labor, and water. We are going to fight like the dickens to keep what is ours."

Assemblyman John Thurman of Modesto said, "The war of Melones is over. . . . Anyone who would go up that canyon and chain himself to a rock has to be nuts," and the applause was powerful.

Lieutenant General John W. Morris, chief of engineers in Washington, D. C. said, "I didn't know New Melones had so many friends. All I get back there are complaints. I will have to bring back some T-shirts. . . . New Melones has been a test bed for the Army Corps. I don't think any agency of the federal government has been asked to do its business more differently overnight than the Corps of Engineers. The project came at a time of change in national attitude. It is a better project for our being put to the test. I wish we could have got this to you sooner and cheaper, but at least it's here. I believe this is the greatest project ever constructed by the Army Corps of Engineers."

Congressman Harold T. "Bizz" Johnson said, "God knows we need water."

Then the dam people went home and sent letters to Washington—to the congressmen Schifferle was visiting. Caustic mail bombarded the desks of Edwards and other California representatives. "You mean you're going to let a $341 million dam sit there and not earn a cent?" was the typical demand. To many people, this seemed the ultimate in government folly.

Questions were fired at Schifferle by congressional aides. Under congressional guidelines, did the river qualify for the national wild and scenic rivers system? Why should it be protected? What would the results of designation be? Do you mean to tell me the dam is *already built?*

Normal procedure is for Congress first to authorize a study of a candidate for the national rivers system. Then, with information and alternatives compiled by the Park Service or Forest Service, Congress decides whether to designate the river or not. By this time my own experiences on the river had led me to become involved with the Stanislaus, writing magazine articles and lending support as a board member of the American Rivers Conservation Council. At the time, I was a planner in northern Pennsylvania, where I had worked for years doing environmental, land-use, and natural-resources work, including wild and scenic river reports. I recognized part of Schifferle's problem: no wild and scenic river study had ever been issued for the Stanislaus.

With my offer to serve as volunteer project director, Friends of the River and the ARCC decided to do their own river report. They would answer the questions that were being asked; they would avoid accusations that no study had been done and that the river didn't qualify. The report would further galvanize interest and focus attention on the proposal. A good-looking report would help Congress take it more seriously.

It would be a big job—one that normally takes government agencies two to five years—and impossible without the help of many people who knew the river. Dubois contacted Melinda Wright, FOR foothills coordinator at Columbia, just up the hill from Parrotts Ferry, and half a dozen people met in her trellised garden to map strategy. Melinda's mother grew up along the lower Stanislaus at Riverbank, then moved to the Monterey Peninsula, where Melinda was raised. At nineteen, Melinda moved to Knights Ferry, below Old Melones Dam, and in the late seventies she moved to Columbia, where she taught math at the junior college.

After taking a raft trip down the river in 1972, blonde, blue-eyed Melinda heard about the dam, but "just tried to forget about it." Then, after Proposition 17, she said, "Come on, this is ridiculous!" When she was in Sacramento she did some research, and discovered the contractors' $175,000 contribution. "It was scandalous. Then I found a Friends of the River newsletter and called them up. I got involved. I had letter-writing parties and set up a table at the river, and helped to organize foothills people." Melinda had formed the Mother Lode chapter of FOR.

Now, from dozens of names, a special team of people who had critical skills was assembled. The report would describe the river, documenting features that made it eligible for the national rivers system. It would list alternatives for protection, such as different lengths to be designated. The report would forecast environmental impacts, it would weigh the trade-offs between protection and development, and it would suggest a management plan. The deadline was set at three months so that the report would be available to Congress in the fall.

Kirk Ford would do a fish and wildlife section. A senior in wildlife management at Humboldt State College, he was anxious to put his school skills to use. Lorraine Vogt would do population, transportation, and land use. Marty Blake, history and archaeology. Doris Grimm would collect data on hydrology. Jan Harper, one of the first women river guides, had crawled through Stanislaus caves for ten years, and would write a chapter about them. Craig Rieser, an artist and a guide for ARTA, would sketch maps and river scenes. Terry Wright, Sonoma State University professor, would report on geology. Mark Zaller, airplane pilot and river guide for Zephyr, would document plant life and prepare a South Fork description, since that tributary was included in the bill. Dick Roos-Collins of FOR, San Francisco, would cover New Melones Dam, and Mike Zischke, a retired aide to Congressman Peter Carr of Michigan, would probe legislative history. This was the study team for the background chapter. Each person would collect information and write a draft report of a few pages. I wrote other chapters, and edited the report.

It was important to let the government agencies know what FOR was doing, so meetings were held with the Bureau of Land Management, the Forest Service, the Park Service, the Heritage, Conservation and Recreation Service, and later with the Bureau of Reclamation and the Army Corps of Engineers. One of the first meetings was with Jim Burns of the California Resources Agency.

Burns was middle-aged, trim, and clean-cut, with an open, honest air about him. His background was in fisheries. I had no trouble getting an appointment with him; he even offered to meet at 5:30 in the afternoon. For a few minutes, I explained the wild river study. I summarized our findings: the river was eligible. It had most of the qualities listed in the Wild River Act. It was the first or second most-floated whitewater in the West; it had caves that rivaled those of any other riverscape, unique vegetation including a fig tree that may be the country's largest, a rare species of harvestman spider, and hundreds of historic and archaeological sites. I summarized for only one minute because it was unnecessary. Burns already knew.

"We'll give information and whatever help we can," he said. "Volunteerism is something we like to encourage. This is one more step, one more piece of evidence. It's worth documenting. Even if we lose the river, it will have been one hell of a fight, and everybody will be able to see what happened, what was lost. We will have made people look at our water demands. We'll show that we're tough fighters. Even now when I hear something about water development that I know isn't true, I say, 'Don't pull another New Melones on me.'" You might say that the assistant secretary was encouraging. "We'll be real interested in the study. Sometimes we learn more from FOR than from our own departments." Burns offered to schedule a meeting with resources officials when the study neared completion.

Next was a meeting at the regional office of the Bureau of Land Management in Folsom, twenty miles from Sacramento. I talked with Steve Howard and Kevin Clark there.

Howard's views were mixed and his positions obscure. He criticized both the corps and FOR: "The army corps's Environmental Impact Statement ignored that the river exists, that the canyon is there. FOR is loose-knit to say the least, very young, and they made one mistake after another.

"As for the Wild River bill, the Senate will never vote for it. Edwards in the House won't even vote for it." I didn't know where Howard got this information. It was not true. "There's only one way for the bill to pass and that's for the eastern delegation to push it."

"One thing for sure," Howard said, "it can't be a wild river. It can't even be a scenic river. With all the use up there, recreation is the only thing it could be." He was talking about three classifications in the system—wild, scenic, and recreational. Undeveloped rivers qualify as wild. The more developed ones are recreational. I explained that the wild and scenic classifications of the act are not defined by the amount of recreational use, but by the amount of development on the shores. The act and guidelines are very clear on this.

We talked about BLM's position, which had recently been conveyed to Interior Secretary Andrus (BLM is within the Department of the Interior): "The Bureau of Land Management recommends that consideration be given to not filling in the reservoir above Parrotts Ferry and that the Bureau be allowed to develop this stretch of the river to its full potential . . ."

Kevin Clark said, "The draft report stated that the canyon should be protected, straight and simple, but that got taken out in Washington. Instead, it now says that the canyon should be considered for protection."

BLM had always been known as a weak member of the Interior Department. Now, in a report prepared because the secretary was considering not filling the reservoir, they said that he should consider not filling the reservoir. Did anyone above Kevin Clark's field-office echelon have one-tenth the chutzpah of Schifferle?

Assistant Interior Secretary Guy Martin had said that he had to make decisions on conflicts between the Bureau of Reclamation and the Bureau of Land Management, both under his direction, and that BLM didn't offer him the strong position he needed. Was BLM passing the buck up, or was Martin passing it down? Whichever it was, BLM lost. The canyon land was transferred to the Bureau of Reclamation in the fall of 1979. Martin said, "It was always assumed Reclamation would get the land. That had been the intention for years."

Just two years before, Secretary Andrus had said, "We intend to break up the little fiefdoms which have divided Interior for years. For too long, each of the interests—grazing, mining, timber and so forth—has had its own domain. The place was like a centipede with each little pair of feet scuttling off in its own direction. That is going to change." On the Stanislaus, the change seemed to be that all would scuttle in the direction of the Bureau of Reclamation.

Joe Nagel, special emissary for Secretary Andrus in California, thinks that Interior is the most fascinating of all federal departments because of the built-in conflicts. "I've never heard an argument from outside the department that I didn't first hear inside," he says. "On the Stanislaus, the Heritage, Conservation and Recreation Service was strong in pushing for protection, especially from their urban-recreation perspective. From the Fish and Wildlife Service [standpoint], it was almost a wash—a full reservoir would hurt spring spawning runs, a low-level reservoir might hurt fall runs. The Bureau of Reclamation had their position. BLM had a relatively minor stake in the thing— they were in charge of the recreation, a routine function. The major institutional conflict was between the bureau and HCRS." According to Nagel, only the Bureau of Reclamation pushed for a full reservoir. He also calls BLM's function (owning and managing the canyon) a "routine" one, yet it seemed that it, if any agency, was the steward of this place. It was BLM land. If BLM's role was small, that struck me as a clue that "stewardship" may not mean much. The decision makers were all policy people, who dealt strictly in utilization of resources, squabbling from their offices over whether the BLM farm should be subdivided for a power plant on the one hand or an amusement park on the other.

One purpose in my meeting with BLM was to collect information about river recreation, and I did: in 1978 there were 90,000 visitor-days on the Stanislaus. If the reservoir was not filled, BLM would improve facilities at the put-in and take-out. How about the one-lane road to Camp Nine? "It shouldn't be widened or changed," Steve Howard said. "It's now safe because peope drive slowly."

Kevin Clark, powerfully built, bearded, and wearing the thongs typical of his generation of Californians, walked me out to the door. We talked about a canyon wilderness recommendation that the regional BLM office had backed, but the state BLM office cut. "If there's a groundswell of public support, I think the recommendation could change," Clark said. "And about FOR, there's a difference of opinion about their effectiveness. We got more support for the Stanislaus wilderness than for any other in California." Assistant Secretary Martin would say, "The wilderness argument was not strong. The wild rivers system was a more appropriate way to go." That system was not under Martin's responsibility. It was under the other assistant secretary, Robert Herbst. If it seems as though the canyon was a pinball bouncing off the bumpers of bureaucracy, it's because it was.

The Forest Service office for the Stanislaus is a neo-rustic building on the sprawling fringe of Sonora. Carl Rust, who worked on the Tuolumne national river study and was recognized as a knowledgeable riverman, was away for a few days, so I met with Edward Tonneson, who headed up wilderness evaluations under the Roadless Area Review and Evaluation (RARE II) program and was familiar with recreational use. When I arrived, he welcomed me with a list of a dozen Stanislaus dams. "The Stanislaus isn't a wild river. There are already dams built on it." I had heard this argument before. My job was to get information, not to sell this man on wild rivers, but I had to say something since it was implied that I was wasting my time and that of the Forest Service.

I said, "The Wild and Scenic Rivers Act specifies that no dams can be in the section to be designated, but upstream or downstream is okay. In fact, lots of the national rivers have reservoirs above them." I changed the subject. "I wonder if you have some information about recreation along the South Fork." That opened another trap. Tonneson didn't know the South Fork was in the Edwards bill. Suddenly this Stanislaus thing involved *his* agency.

"There's timber scheduled for cutting on the South Fork," he said. We looked at the locations, all on high slopes above the stream. I said that timber management is allowed along protected rivers, that it's more a matter of technique to avoid siltation, road scars, and obvious clear-cutting. "You talk to people from the state about that," Tonneson said skeptically. Logging, with its muddy erosion and stormwater runoff, was a hot issue along the state-designated scenic rivers of California's north coast. I was getting nowhere in this meeting.

I dug in and pursued the information I needed. Pinecrest, near the South Fork headwaters, is the second most used Forest Service area in the Sierra Nevada. Lake Tahoe is first. We checked on commercial timber along the lower South Fork—a limestone canyon—and found that saleable trees were nonexistent below Italian Bar (seven miles above the Stanislaus). The South Fork headwaters are partly in the congressionally designated Emigrant Wilderness, which prohibits logging, dams, and roads. I asked about the RARE II findings in the rest of the area above Pinecrest—a stunning section of white granite, waterfalls, and small stands of ancient fir and cedar. "We didn't recommend wilderness," Tonneson said. "There's commercial timber on higher slopes and we couldn't see having such a thin corridor of wilderness. And the area gets a lot of hikers from Pinecrest Lake. We didn't have very much public support for wilderness in that area either."

The national rivers system has no equivalent to this section of upper river, and it seemed clear to me that this, of all the South Fork, should be protected.

Reports were completed by Ford, Harper, Wright, Blake, Zaller, Roos-Collins, Grimm, Vogt, and others. This crew of local experts, river guides, and California river zealots put together a $50,000 study flat free for the congressmen. No wonder Jim Burns says that the Resources Agency encourages volunteerism.

The time came to make decisions. How much of the Stanislaus Canyon, Rose Creek, and the South Fork should really be designated? Schifferle wanted at least twenty-five miles, since federal guidelines suggested that as a minimum. Because of logging and development, Zaller said, forget the South Fork between Pinecrest and Lyons Reservoir and forget Rose Creek above American Fork Bridge (four miles above the Stanislaus). We all knew that the main thing was Camp Nine to Parrotts Ferry. I called the Washington office of the National Park Service and talked to Bob Eastman—the most knowledgeable person on river protection policy. He said twenty-five miles was only a guideline; don't worry about it, and don't compromise quality for length. Howard Brown, director of the American Rivers Conservation Council, told us to make it long because compromises were inevitable. The report finally recommended the Stanislaus, lower Rose Creek, the South Fork above Pinecrest, and the lower South Fork from Lyons down, excepting the scrabble of gold mining scars at Italian Bar.

Jim Burns set up a meeting with twenty resources officials and our findings were presented. Questions and support came from Guy Phillips, Jonus Minton of the Department of Water Resources, Rich Hammond, and Burns. The Fish and Game people were silent, for their position had been uncertain. They had opposed the Parrotts Ferry limit, though they found that salmon would be hurt by a full dam.

"The Stanislaus has none of the complications typical of national river proposals," I said. "No private landowners, no new agencies to become involved, no land acquisition, and recreation management is already in force."

Phillips smiled, and said, "But you'd trade New Melones Dam for every typical problem in the book, wouldn't you?"

The report was written, refined, edited, and reviewed by a dozen people, rewritten, typed four times, and shipped off for printing in Sacramento. Only a month late. Total costs were $2,500, including $1,800 for printing. The report documented the specialties of the Stanislaus Canyon in a way that had never been done. The case for national river qualification and designation was clarified, and the New Melones trade-offs were addressed. In the spring of 1980, Congressman Phillip Burton sent a copy of the study to Secretary Andrus, asking for an official Interior position on eligibility as a national river. Andrus's department did a Stanislaus wild river evaluation using the ARCC and FORF study, and reached many of the same conclusions. It, too, found that the nine-mile canyon and lower reaches of Rose Creek and the South Fork qualified as national wild rivers. The Heritage, Conservation and Recreation Service would become the most vocal lobbyist for the Stanislaus within the Department of the Interior. Assistant Secretary Robert Herbst worked hard to persuade Secretary Cecil Andrus that the river should be protected, but he was betting against the Bureau of Reclamation, which can strong-arm Interior with pork-barrel politics.

Meanwhile other events were breaking in Washington, Sacramento, and at the river. Prompted by a letter from sixteen California congressmen, and supported by Assistant Secretary Guy Martin, Secretary Andrus decided in October 1979 that unless Goodwin Dam (below New Melones) releases hit 5,000 cubic feet per second, the reservoir should not be filled past Parrotts Ferry in 1980 so that historical and archaeological sites could be investigated under the Historic Preservation Act. This decision bought time to get the wild river bill moving.

Regarding the delay, the *Los Angeles Times* said, "We think it is a wise decision. New Melones Dam has become a central symbol of the disarray in water policy for this state, and there are many unanswered questions about consequences of full-scale operation of the dam and hydroelectric plant."

In submitting Guy Phillips's economic report to Secretary Andrus in October 1979, Huey Johnson pushed for water price reform. "Realization of true costs," Johnson maintained, "is the key to conserving water and saving rivers." The resources secretary was taking bolder and bolder stands on water policy reform.

New Melones and dam interests shouted for his dismissal. Johnson couldn't have cared less. He wrote Andrus asking for federal reviews of New Melones:

> While the value of some of our natural resources cannot be measured in economic terms, water and energy, among others, are of such great importance to our economy that we must learn to use them in ways that will return the greatest overall benefit for each commitment we make.
>
> As an initial step in that direction, when such water and energy resources are to be developed with the public's dollars, I think it is also critical that the consumers of the resource pay the full cost of it. Payment of less than full price devalues the resource, encourages wasteful use that is counter to the water and energy conservation ethics we should be fostering, and leads only to still further demands for development projects.

Andrus replied:

> Although I agree that a review of the New Melones Project by Congress is appropriate, I do not agree that a review by WRC or this

Department's Office of Inspector General is necessary. In my opinion, New Melones will receive adequate review through Congress' action on HR 4223 and this Department's consideration as to the question whether the Stanislaus River should be included in the Wild and Scenic Rivers System. Although I cannot speak for GAO or OMB, in my opinion, review by these agencies is also unnecessary.

Joe Nagel, Andrus's special assistant in California said, "There was a lot of excitement when the secretary announced the delay in filling, but a lot of people didn't look closely at what he really said—that the archaeological work needs to be finished, a basin for the use of the water needs to be defined, and a supplemental EIS needs to be completed. Then we will fill the reservoir."

In Sacramento, the State Water Resources Control Board held hearings in October about Decision 1422 and the operation plan for the reservoir. After months of preparation by FOR researchers Tom Burton and Rick Hardy, and with reports from hydrologist Dr. Phillip Williams and fisheries biologist Donald Kelley, FOR presented its case for a moderate-sized reservoir. About 270,000 acre-feet (just below Parrotts Ferry) would be adequate, FOR said, to accommodate state-approved uses of the dam.

Nancy Whittle, co-chairperson with John Hertle for Friends of New Melones, presented testimony calling for a full reservoir. Guy Phillips of the Resources Agency testified that available data were insufficient to warrant increased storage behind the reservoir. Ed Roberts, head of the Department of Rehabilitation for the state, spoke on behalf of the disabled people, including himself, who used the Stanislaus:

> It's an experience that I have seen day to day with so many of our people with disabilities who don't recognize their own strength and power and ability, and who see themselves as much more limited than they really are. This canyon has been a place for the past four years where people with disabilities have been experiencing this kind of change, this kind of growth, and now it's mushroomed into something of a legend, and more and more people with disabilities are asking to go. It has become kind of a magical place for an awful lot of people.

Since Interior Secretary Andrus had decided to not fill the reservoir in 1980 anyway, the board delayed action until fall 1980. It seemed that Parrotts Ferry would not be flooded for at least one more year.

Things were looking good, and then, once again, the rains came. They began on January 8 under dark skies, and it rained through the day. It rained through the night, and the next morning it rained some more. Heavy rains, light rains, torrential rains, two inches in one hour. It poured for eleven days, a deluge straight out of the Old Testament. Warm rains, Hawaiian storms—seven, eight, nine of them. Then came the flood.

The river people had been assailed by pork-barrel politics, mass media, slick ad men, a cult of engineering, the U.S. Army, Central Valley agribusiness, and now the weather. One said, "God ought to have more respect for what we're doing. Nature will be nature, disasters and all, but why couldn't she have given us an earthquake at New Melones instead of this?"

Hertle and son employed the ever-present bulldozer and pushed up a dike around the house. The Stanislaus boiled up into the oat field, reducing the Hertles's crop to a bed of mud. The San Joaquin rose like a boiling brown soup. It was sixteen years after John Hertle founded the Stanislaus River Flood Control Association, thirty-six years after Hertle's father had said, "When they build that dam, we won't have any more floods." They were having another flood. But not because the government was saving the canyon. It wasn't.

Interior Secretary Andrus had announced in October that 5,000 cubic feet per second would be released from New Melones to hold the reservoir below Parrotts Ferry. Why 5,000 cfs? Partly because Friends of the River advocated 8,000, a volume that the congressionally authorized flood channel would contain, and partly because the Stanislaus River Flood Control Association said that farmers began to incur damage at 3,500 cfs. Five thousand was a compromise. Moreover, the Bureau of Reclamation computer calculated that if you released 5,000, the odds of running the reservoir up above Parrotts Ferry were slim, about 50:1.

The odds on a flood taking place were slim, but the winter of 1980 would be the third wettest on record. From the Sierra and the hills and the Valley itself, January floodwaters surged up the banks of every river, stream, and wash. Up the breast of every dam. Joe Nagel says, "The American River usually runs about 15,000 cfs through Sacramento in winter. Well, we were running it at 95,000."

Nagel doesn't say the river was "running"; he says, "we were running it," meaning that the people in charge of the dams all over California were turning valves and adjusting gates to control the water as best they could. "There were tense days in January and February," Nagel recalls. "Very tense."

Let me say something about Nagel. Probably in his early forties, he has an Idaho accent, is stocky and muscular, and wears a trimmed black beard with gray spots in it. I have written that he was the interior secretary's emissary and special assistant in California. It was an important position. Nagel's receptionist answered the phone, "Secretary Andrus's office, can I help you?" Nagel is from Idaho, where he ran manpower and social service programs under Governor Cecil Andrus in the mid-seventies. When Andrus moved to Washington, he took Nagel along as a special assistant. After a few years there, Nagel was moved to the West Coast, a hotbed of Interior debates. His job was to oversee certain day-to-day operations and to advise the secretary about controversial issues: reauthorization of the Central Valley Project, the Westlands "problem," Auburn Dam, the Trinity River fishery, water-quality standards in the Delta, and Mono Lake. Nagel ranked the Stanislaus, "near the bottom of the list." He says, "The issue was pretty much decided. There were parameters and laws in place. Some technical things needed completing, but they were odds and ends. Our options were limited and didn't require the imagination needed in the other issues. Wild river designation is an option, but not ours. It is Congress's option." When the floodwaters of January came flushing down the canyon, Joe Nagel was a busy man, and the Stanislaus was near the top of his list.

While rivers were rising, the moon was pulling nine-foot tides landward and up San Francisco Bay. The Delta—some of its islands being man-made enclaves twenty feet below sea level—was flooding, and flooding badly. More storms were coming. Reservoirs were filling up. Releases could not be cut any further without risking burst dams. Levees were in danger of being ruptured. The upper Stanislaus jettisoned only 1 percent of the Delta flood, but 1 percent could make a difference. Because its reservoir was below the Parrotts Ferry level, New Melones offered flood retention that was essentially unlimited. New Melones was the one link in the vast and intricate web of California water management where something could be done. New Melones was the only dam that could be shut off, the only one where the gates could be kept closed.

Nagel consulted with Huey Johnson, Rich Hammond, and Ronald Robie, head of the state Department of Water Resources. "We could lose the Delta," Robie said. "Cut releases from New Melones." So the gates of New Melones were shut and the flatwater climbed quickly upward behind the dam.

When the Bureau of Reclamation closed the gates, it reduced the lower river to 2,090 cfs. Then it was reduced further. On January 14, 43,500 cfs were flowing in, and almost nothing was flowing out, but, because of tributaries below the dam, the lower river still peaked at 7,500 cfs. On January 18, the reservoir flooded Parrotts Ferry and kept on rising to 846 feet—above Chinese Dogleg, one and a half miles beyond Parrotts Ferry. This time Dubois didn't chain himself to the riverbank. This was different from May 1979. People were really getting flooded downriver. Three islands went under in the Delta. If the previous year's chaining had caused hard feelings, a protest now would cause war. Friends impressed another point on Dubois: only so much water could be let out of the dam. Even if the Bureau of Reclamation wanted to dump water, they could not do it fast enough to stabilize the reservoir when 45,000 cfs was flowing in.

The water eventually receded. Then, in February, a second set of storms hit. California weather maps showed them stacked nine deep the whole way to Japan. After a San Joaquin levee broke, Nagel again cut New Melones releases to a minimum, and the reservoir again spread beyond Parrotts Ferry.

We have seen what floods do to politicians. The 1964 flood tipped public opinion for the dam, galvanized water development forces, and delivered an appropriation of $1.5 million to begin New Melones. The 1980 flood was similarly embraced by state politicians, especially foothills Asemblyman Norman Waters and Senator John Garamendi, who demanded that the hedging and delaying be stopped and the dam be filled up. Friends of the River countered that the dam provided the ultimate in flood control—no water had to be released during the peak of the flooding because there was so much space in the reservoir. While all the other dams filled up and discharged floodwater downstream, New Melones alone was able to hold more. Their point was lost on the people of the Valley and the California legislature, as we shall see shortly.

Back in Washington, D. C., Schifferle was her hyperactive self, trying to pry the Stanislaus wild river bill loose in a national capital scene that was at first baffling to her, and even more so to the Californians who stayed home under the sycamores at 401 San Miguel Way or at the Fort Mason office, where the gulls and cormorants of San Francisco Bay keep you company. The bill's passage depended on Phillip Burton, a congressman who was not even an official sponsor.

Burton represents most of San Francisco, from downtown to fringe subdivisions, Chinatown to Sunset, Telegraph Hill to Nob Hill, St. Francis Wood to the Hunters Point ghetto, the Mission to the docks. It is probably the most polyglot district in America: 12 percent black, 18 percent Spanish-speaking, 8 percent Chinese. Only one-fourth are white, English-speaking, third-generation Americans. Burton is a classic California liberal, a champion of the poor, labor, and minorities. He is also a hard-nosed, wheeling-and-dealing, scheming politician. Journalists Doug Underwood and David Shapiro say that he is a "throwback of the old days of Congress when power was wielded by manipulating House rules and employing a relentless mix of flattery, arm-twisting, backroom dealing and outright intimidation."

In 1974 Burton beat Bernie Sisk, a New Melones Dam pusher, for the House Steering Committee chair. In 1976 he surpassed John McFall, father of the dam, for the position of majority leader, but then lost by one vote to Public Works Chairman Jim Wright—pork barrel personified. (During the Tocks Island Dam debate, Wright said, "We cannot keep people from intruding upon the earth. And the interests of the people must come first. Nature sometimes, as in this case, needs the corrective surgery of intelligent man.")

Burton is a champion of the environment, applying power politics to the preservation of landscape. He chaired the Subcommittee on National Parks and Insular Affairs, where, in 1978, he piloted the most massive expansion of the wild and scenic rivers system and the national parks system ever. Eight new national rivers were designated (including the threatened Tocks Island Dam reach of the Delaware and the wild North Fork of the American in California), and seventeen new national river candidates were named. Burton's strategy: collect votes from all over the country by offering a piece for everyone. It was the first great parks-barrel bill. In recognition, the American Rivers Conservation Council named Burton Distinguished River Conservationist for 1978. He was named the Sierra Club's Conservationist of the Year. In May 1980, the San Francisco congressman rammed a follow-up appropriation of $90 million through Congress only two days after it cleared the Interior Committee, before members even had a printed report to explain what they were voting on. Burton pushed a Big Sur coastline protection bill through the House in two minutes, leaving opponents agape. It seemed that this politician's support for the Stanislaus just might help.

In late June 1979, Schifferle talked to a Burton staff member who said, "He's with you, but his name won't go on the bill. That would alarm the anti-Burton faction." Schifferle later saw the congressman outside his office and told him about the bill. Burton said he would look into it and do what he could to help her out. That wasn't enough. She needed to talk to this master of seemingly hopeless causes. Shortcutt got Marion Edey, director of the League of Conservation Voters, to arrange another meeting (Burton had a league voting record of 100 percent). Schifferle, Edey, Howard Brown of the American Rivers Conservation Council, and Mark Dubois—in town to lobby—sat down with Burton.

Schifferle recalls, "He listens, grunts, and asks questions. Lots of questions. He sorts through all the information. He gets the FOR position, then he wants to hear the other side. He remembers everything with an amazing grasp of detail once he's focused. He's amazing to work with, but he leaves you in the dark; you never know which way he's going to turn."

Why was Burton interested? He never saw the river and didn't particularly want to. It may have been a challenge to him. He was impressed by people who worked against heavy odds for something they thought was right. An aide said, "We saw a lot of dedicated, honest people who really wanted it. We wanted to do the best we could for them." Another said, "Phil wanted to get this done because it was right." They considered it a long shot, but there was just a chance that they could make it. Schifferle called the FOR office and told them to prepare for hearings.

No hearings were schedulec.. Schifferle met with Burton again. He said that he'd take a run with the bill. He'd give it everything he had. She reported back that if it could be done, he would do it, and really sounded the alarm this time. "Hearings in late January for sure. Everybody get ready." Gaguine dashed off an action alert that was mailed first class to Stanislaus supporters, asking them to prepare testimony. But no hearings were scheduled, and people wondered why. "Burton doesn't like hearings," Schifferle said. She speculated, "Burton knows what everyone is going to say. He doesn't want to go through all those motions. He doesn't want to give the other side an audience."

Time passed. The winter rains of 1980 came, the reservoir swallowed Parrotts Ferry, then the water dropped, rose, and dropped again. Burton's staff said, "When the bill is ready to move, Burton will move it." He was planning another omnibus bill, chock-full of streams from any district where there was political support for wild and scenic river status. Burton intended to grease the legislative machine and slide the Stanislaus through on support for other rivers.

Then the May primary season was upon Congress, and nothing but campaigning happens during election time. "After the primary, the bill will move," Schifferle advised FOR headquarters. Having no other choice, the river people trusted Burton. They believed that if the bill could be passed, he would do it, but they realized that other congressmen, too, were interested in the Stanislaus.

Bizz Johnson was interested. Bizz (Harold) represented District 1, the largest in California, 22 percent of the state, from Oregon to Sacramento, from the coastal mountains to Nevada. Inside its boundaries are Oroville Dam, Shasta Dam, the Middle Fork of the Feather, the North Fork of the American, the Klamath River, Lake Tahoe, and Lassen National Park—a veritable empire of land and water, dotted with only 2 percent of the state's population. Bizz had been a supervisor of the Pacific Fruit Express Company, mayor of Roseville, California state senator, then U. S. congressman since 1958. Patriarch to a magnificent chunk of American landscape, he received only a 44 percent rating from the League of Conservation Voters. During the authorization of New Melones, Johnson's district bordered the Stanislaus River, side by side with the territory of Congressman John McFall. These two men are mainly responsible for the dam.

In 1978 Bernie Sisk, another dam supporter, and a member of the powerful Central Valley clique, retired, and John McFall lost his seat after a House Ethics Committee reprimand in the indecorous wake of the Koreagate scandal. Bizz remained as the lone Central Valley oldtimer, aged seventy-three. (Not that new Valley congressmen are

all that much different.) The *Almanac of American Politics* called him
"a Democrat of the old school." Another congressman had said that
Johnson's district might sink any day—not from another Oroville
earthquake, but from the sheer weight of public works projects.
During 1979–80, Bizz chaired the House Public Works Committee, one
of the most powerful, doling out projects. It is a wonderful position for
dealing, as it offers superior leverage for the twisting of arms. Nobody
in Congress wanted to be Johnson's enemy. Even though he was an
old codger, other congressmen needed his support; or else, as with
Burton, they had to gun their way around him.

Before the struggle for the Stanislaus was over, some congressmen
would find themselves caught between Phillip Burton and Bizz
Johnson, not a pleasant place to be.

In April 1980, Dubois, Huntington, Fox, Doug Linney, who was the
Los Angeles coordinator, and I joined Patricia Schifferle in Washington
to lobby and attend the annual rivers and dams conference of the
American Rivers Conservation Council and the Environmental Policy
Center. A meeting was scheduled with Congressman Johnson.

We slop four blocks from the Environmental Policy Center
headquarters through the chill spring rain to see Bizz in the Rayburn
Office Building. "This is hopeless," Linney says. Shortcutt, so often
one degree below kindling temperature, retorts, "You don't just back
off when you run into opposition. What do you want to do, roll over
and play dead? That's not the way you do things around here." Oh.
There is nothing to say. We walk another half-block in utter silence
except for splattering rain and splattering traffic.

"This is hopeless," Shortcutt says. Dubois smiles down, and puts a
hand on Schifferle's shoulder. Shortcutt smiles. Everybody feels okay,
even if this is hopeless. Who knows? Maybe Johnson had Scrooge's
dream last night. Maybe Bizz has mellowed with old age. Maybe he
will decide to leave a legacy of the real California instead of cement and
reinforcing bars. No sense being defeatist. All enter on an upbeat note.
Let's give it a try. The receptionist, along with everybody else in
Washington, knows Schifferle, and smiles and offers us seats.
Schifferle taps her foot. Dubois must be as comfortable as an Oakland
longshoreman at the opera, but looks peaceful. Linney remains cool.
Catherine Fox and Tom Huntington arrive. Catherine is tense;
Washington is starting to bug her already. On the subway, a woman
had tripped in front of her, then blamed her, threatening to sue her.
"When is the next flight back to San Francisco?" Fox asks. Her tension
is contagious.

In a few minutes the weighty door of Bizz's office swings open. The
suspense is broken. This is it. We shall have our chance at Johnson. But

the older man in the brown suit, starched white shirt, shiny brown shoes, marketing grin, and bushy eyebrows is not Bizz. Yes, it is Milton Kramer. A greeting committee for Friends of the River. To make them feel welcome.

"Hi."

"Hi."

"Well, California in Washington. Ha ha," Kramer says. I can read Schifferle's thoughts but will not convey them here. Kramer goes over to Mark. "Friends of New Melones have a press conference scheduled tomorrow. We have to get some things straightened out," Kramer says. What kind of things? "The Phillips economics study—we have some answers, some challenges."

Bizz calls out from his office in his gruff Godfather voice, "Come right in." The tone is flat. We say goodbye to Milton and shuffle in, as far as one can shuffle on an inch-thick carpet. Bizz's style is elderly congressman. If you are unfamiliar with that, it is the same as elderly banker. White receding hair is slicked back, where it stays, even should the wind blow up. His glasses add a certain erudite touch; sagging jowls suggest grandfatherly benevolence. Three scenic photos are on the wall. Almost every congressman has three photos on the wall. Barry Goldwater, Jr. has two of the Stanislaus Canyon. A model of a rocket—maybe the Apollo—sits on a shelf behind Bizz's ponderous congressional desk, which supports a model jet airplane and a statue of Smokey the Bear. What, how did Smokey get in here? On the desk is a small sculpture with United Airlines' name on it. In front of the desk lies a small, hand-hooked rug with white and green letters that say "Bizz." Story goes that Harold, a tyke of five, was playing with friends near the Roseville front porch where his uncle and aunt sat watching in 1912. His uncle said, "Why, he's a regular little Bismarck, leading everybody around." Since then, they had called him Bizz.

The inevitable congressman's bookshelf is behind him. *Beef, Living on a Few Acres* (Johnson fought the 160-acre limitation of the federal reclamation laws), *The Water Crisis, This Is the American Earth* (a gift from the Sierra Club?), and a hundred other titles.

Silence becalms the place. Bizz does not ask us what we'd like to talk about, nor what he can do for us. These are young Californians, 3,000 miles from home, first trip East for some. Bizz does not say, "Welcome to Washington, kids." Bizz says nothing, but waits. "Using the most current data, we've made this chart," Schifferle says, holding it up for just an instant. "We support the use of New Melones Reservoir and this information shows that its benefits can be optimized without filling it the whole way up. It's now Congress's dam, and . . ."

Bizz interrupts, "It's the people's dam. We didn't put much into it here."

Schifferle: "Okay, the people. We feel it should benefit the largest number of people."

"I think it does," Bizz glowers.

Schifferle: "This chart shows that a moderate size can . . ."

Bizz: "Now it's just about useless for power."

Schifferle: "We can show you that it's not."

"More figures and data," Johnson says with ennui. "The engineers have already figured this all out."

Schifferle: "The dam was only for 150 megawatts when you authorized it."

Bizz: "Now there is new technology and we should use it."

Schifferle: "We might not be able to use it. I brought you comments from Pacific Gas and Electric. Would you read this?" She takes the PG&E letterhead over to Bizz, and kneels next to him. Johnson smiles ever so slightly. He cannot help it. She is charming for an instant. While she is there she wings the chart on him also. Figures, figures.

Bizz's jowls return to normal. "I'm no engineer," he says.

If you have a chart that the audience won't look at, you have to try something else. Mark says, "Let me point something out. They wouldn't have been able to stop the floods this spring if the dam were completely filled." Mark details the amount of water released in recent floods versus what he thinks ought to be released. He says that a release of 8,000 cubic feet per second is authorized. More figures. Mark's argument takes a circuitous twist and he loses Bizz.

Bizz: "Well, that's all calculated."

Mark: "Yes, and turns out there's more flood control without the reservoir being filled."

Bizz: "Oh, I don't know about that."

Mark: "They were able to hold back all the water when the floods were the worst and when the San Joaquin levee broke. Again, most major reservoirs in the state were releasing maximum amounts, but New Melones wasn't, because it had enough empty space."

Linney thinks that Kramer was just in here pitching hydroelectric power. Non-Arab electricity is to the eighties what flood control was to the sixties—a reason to build dams. To fill dams. "Peaking power is the only kind we can get from New Melones," Linney says. "It won't give us much energy."

Linney is not finished, but Bizz changes the focus. "We have two wet years out of seven. That's why the cyclical storage," he says.

"But there are thirteen dams already. On the Stanislaus, I mean," Schifferle answers. "You can't get blood out of a turnip. You can't get more water out of the river."

Bizz: "Oh, I don't think so." Pause. "I think that New Melones should operate as a full partner in the Central Valley Project."

Schifferle: "We do too."

Bizz: "But full. We've had more floods on the Stanislaus than on the American River. If it were not built it would be a different thing. [Note: Johnson just said that if the dam were not built it would be a different thing.] It should have been built by 1972, before all this came up. I didn't know what air conditioning was until the last ten or twenty years. Now that I have it, I'm not giving it up. We need the power." Power, power, power. Kramer has advised Friends of New Melones well.

Tom: "You say if the dam were not built. But we have a national treasure. Should we flood it just because the dam is built?"

It is difficult to see where Bizz's eyes are focusing when he listens. I decide it is either his glasses or a habit from playing poker so long on the Public Works Committee.

Bizz: "On the Eel and Klamath there is more of a problem with the fishery than if you put a dam there. The Indians are killing the fishery in the river. This dam will repay the government."

Schifferle: "We dispute that."

Bizz: "I know that. The average project built under reclamation pays back 80–85 percent. There will be a lot of people who will use that lake when it's done."

Catherine: "There are twelve other reservoirs within thirty miles —not even fully developed for recreation, because they don't have the people. The state says there'll be more recreation with a reservoir *and* a river in the canyon."

Bizz: "Well, that's your case. I think this was engineered differently than what you say. You people think differently, and you have every right to."

There is other discussion, but that's how it went. We parade out of Bizz's office. Schifferle heads straight for a telephone to call Guy Phillips and tell him Friends of the Dam is preparing to blast him in a press conference, so that Phillips can have a press release the same night. The other river people head for the House of Representatives' snack bar, since the cafeteria is open only to card carriers during the lunch rush. No seats, so we all sit on the floor of a small tributary corridor. Dubois produces nuts and bean sprouts from his daypack. Others buy food, though the selection is not what these vegetable-eaters consider good. They do not sell avocado and sprout sandwiches in the Rayburn Building basement. Nobody wants to talk about the Johnson meeting. Of all things, we talk about the parents of the friends of the river.

Tom says that his father does not show much interest in the river stuff, but gets into FOR public relations or management. "He's a corporate business type. He says, 'Here's how you ought to present this.' Mom kind of wonders when I'll quit this 'volunteer' job. She sends away for business school catalogues."

Doug says, "My father hates pork barrel. 'Keep on that part of it,' he says."

"My father is an executive for Alcoa in Ohio," Catherine says. "He and my mother live in a huge house and don't understand us doing this. They see us in tiny apartments with hardly any money and they say, 'What for?'"

"Your folks are pretty much with you, aren't they Mark?" somebody asks.

"Well," Mark says and smiles, "it took about four years."

Enough chatter. The nuts and sprouts, and the cheese on Wonder bread sandwiches from the House snack bar are devoured. Off to work. Mark asks Doug, "Could you find Peter at Friends of the Earth—he's supposed to have a letter from David Brower to Congressman Siberling." Linney is off. Catherine and Tom fly in different directions to see House Interior Committee members.

Mark goes to the office of Abraham Kazen, Jr. of Texas, whose League of Conservation Voters rating is 20 percent. One in five times, he voted for the environment. He has consistently wielded influence on behalf of the Trinity River Barge Canal, which would bore and dam a 300-mile ditch up the beautiful Trinity River to make Dallas–Fort Worth a seaport. Dubois talks to Bob Fleming, an aide. Fleming says, "Well, I've heard about this dam—those people were in here." He means, of course, Friends of New Melones. Mark says that we've made a major investment and we can use it. He stresses compromise. Fleming says that he makes no decisions; he will pass on the information.

Next Dubois stops at the office of Lionel Van Deerlin, one of the wild river bill sponsors. Mona Knight, the receptionist, is a friend of Mark's. They talk and schedule a picnic lunch for tomorrow. They discuss political strategy: the need for a strong Stanislaus spokesman, the need to ameliorate Bizz's influence. Good luck. "Bizz seems to recognize this is a symbol," Mark says.

"Pride, that's why New Melones will be filled," I remember Alexander Gaguine saying.

Mark visits Pete McCloskey's office, and talks to Donna Williams, one of many women who work there. "Power is going to be the key this year," she says.

"With twenty-four times the water of Old Melones, you'd expect twenty-four times the power, right?" Mark asks.

"Right."

"Wrong. Three times the power." He tries to explain the equation of hydroelectric power to barrels of OPEC oil. "Sorry, I'm just learning this too. I didn't get into this for kilowatts," he adds. McCloskey's aide asks about Mark's optimism right now. "Our hearts tell us to keep going, that this river stands for every threatened river in the country." Donna nods at "hearts."

"You can't back down now," she says. "May as well fight it to the end like Tellico." But that flooded valley, holy to the Cherokee, is not the end Dubois has in mind.

Dubois and Schifferle then rendezvous for a meeting with John F. Siberling, who has one of the best environmental records in Congress. Siberling was a leader in the fight for Alaska. He led the campaign for a Cuyahoga River national recreation area near Cleveland. This meeting should be easy. Schifferle gives the congressman a copy of the wild and scenic river study. Siberling asks if Razorback Rapid, the scene on the cover, will be flooded by New Melones Reservoir. Its marble-cobbled bars would be 100 feet under.

Siberling has a Friends of New Melones photo showing dead fish. It's the Simpson-Lee paper plant dead-fish photo that was touted by Californians Against Proposition 17. The picture has been recalled from retirement, like an old baseball manager with a winning record. Siberling does not know the fish were killed by chemicals from a paper plant. "What about the argument that fish need the water downstream?"

Schifferle answers, "The downstream reaches are heavily polluted by agricultural runoff, making it difficult for fish. Salmon need certain amounts of water early in the year and then later on in the fall. It's hard to tell what the effects will be, since temperature and volume and a lot of things are involved . . ." She says more than she needs to, but finishes eventually. Siberling is supportive, but wants lucid answers to counter the opposition. Siberling says, "The photo looks like it was taken in a dried-up farm pond somewhere." He asks, "What is the status of the bill? Is Burton going to take it up?"

"We were at a fund raiser of his a few weeks ago," Dubois answers. (FOR received special donations from board members to attend.) "He said there would be no problem getting the bill out of committee, but the floor fight is another question. The floor fight will be tough."

"Well, I will probably follow his lead," the Ohio congressman says.

Don Clausen is the congressman for California's northwest reaches, from Marin to Oregon. He represents San Rafael, Eureka, and the north coast, where most of the remaining wild rivers of the state rip down to sea. This region is the least-spoiled part of the state; it is to California what Alaska is to the nation. The north coast contains the exquisite Smith, the prodigious Klamath, the cool forests of Redwood Creek, and the variable Eel. Clausen worked in the Navy, banking, insurance, aviation, then ran for Congress against incumbent Clement Miller in 1962. Miller died in an airplane crash just before the election, but won anyway. A new election was held, Clausen won, and has been there ever since. His League of Conservation Voters' record is 7 percent. He is now the ranking Republican on the House Interior Committee—first hurdle for the Stanislaus wild river bill—and third-ranking Republican on Bizz's Public Works Committee.

Clausen is fifty-seven. His gray hair is streaked with black and recedes halfway. He is strongly built, but running to fat. It strikes me that his younger years could have been spent as an athlete. He seems tough, loaded like a spring, macho, eyes squinting a bit. His dark, bushy eyebrows alternately rise and fall to punctuate his feelings. He conveys a feeling of no-nonsense, but politically, that can mean only certain types; the best of politics is full of nonsense. We shall see where the Stanislaus fits in.

Schifferle starts by handing Clausen a copy of the Stanislaus wild and scenic river study. "We put this together as a citizen study to help Congress consider HR 4223."

"Oh," the congressman says and sets it on a table. Joan Tunney, a staff member, picks it up and peruses it.

Schifferle begins by talking about north coast rivers, especially the Smith, where the development and acceptance of a state scenic rivers management plan has been a red-hot controversy. Eileen Bartholomew from the American League of Anglers is with us, and she helps to make a Smith River pitch. The approach dwells too much on procedural details and the complexities of the plan's adoption, and not enough on the leadership desired of Clausen. It remains unclear what he has to do with a state-prepared plan, since his responsibilities are in Washington. Discussion turns to the importance of the fisheries on the Mattole River. "You don't have to worry about dams on those rivers," Clausen says. This is in reference to the old state water plan, a catalogue of north coast reservoirs whose water could be pumped to the Central Valley and Southern California (bleeding the north to transfuse the south; the "vampire scheme," as northerners call it). "No program will go forward unless state and local areas agree on it." Mark asks if Clausen feels the northern rivers are really safe. "You ask what confidence I have; I sit on the committee that will consider them." This sounds good, but nobody is really being fooled. We all know that hundreds of dams are built over local objections. Southern California could out-vote Northern California at any time.

Then, with a lightness unprecedented in this meeting, the

congressman says, "Of course, if they (the south) give us too much trouble, we'll form our own state. I've even got a plan for it." This is a raised-eyebrow statement.

The discussion ranges back to its marginal focus on river management plans. "I see two kinds of rivers," Clausen says, "managed and natural rivers. The Mad, Russian, and Eel are managed. We need to address flood problems, erosion, low flows. Many of the others are natural. I tell people we have to work on the three F's: farming, fisheries, forestry. They're interdependent." Clausen smiles very slightly. He, too, is a conservationist.

Schifferle has waited to broach the matter of the Stanislaus. Perhaps too obviously, she pitches to Clausen's local issues and his fishing interest. She says, "We're vitally concerned with the Stanislaus as a symbol. The fisheries there are important." The big congressman lowers his eyebrows. "We have a lot of members on the north coast and they feel they haven't really heard from you on this question." This takes us beyond the realm of furrowed eyebrows to the scratching of an eight-hour-old beard. Clausen does not smile.

"What do they mean?" he asks, but allows no time for answers. "The way I operate is I don't make a decision until all the information is in, until I get closer to the time to make the decision. In the salesman's field, don't push too hard. I'll evaluate all the information on both sides. When I have everything I need, I'll make a decision. If you have new information, fine. But it's pretty clear to me you are just pushing. Don't push."

Well, I think, Clausen is showing an openness and capacity for critical thought. He talks about reviewing costs and benefits. It seems he will look at the issue's merits. He shuns pressure. Dubois has always said that if the people of California had all of the true information about New Melones in front of them with no nonsense, they would choose not to fill the dam. Clausen goes back to the north coast rivers. It is clear he has spoken his limit about the Stanislaus, eight sentences.

The congressman says, "You don't have to worry much about new dams anywhere."

Schifferle's jaw drops. "Mr. Clausen, do I need to remind you about the public works appropriations bill?" Earlier in 1980, this same congressman pounded on his peers to authorize the largest budget ever for dams. Clausen was a leader in moving a $4 billion bill for cement and ditches. Not only that. He argued for more lenient criteria, so that even more projects—ones that the Army Corps of Engineers says are economic losers—would be eligible. During the debate, he said, "The fact of the matter is that in addressing the methodology for evaluating projects, the project purposes, in our judgment, have been too limited in scope."

The *Almanac of American Politics* says this about Clausen: "Like Johnson, Clausen tends to favor substantial public works projects, even when environmental objections are raised, and has worked to make sure that his local area is favored with its share of projects."

Marty Kent recalls Clausen saying, "If you're going to dig into the federal honey pots, you may as well do it with both hands."

Schifferle has called Clausen to a standstill. He gives her a poker-faced stare. His eyebrows do nothing. He neither smiles nor frowns. He doesn't scratch his beard or fidget. Aide Joan Tunney says, "Mr. Clausen, she's done her homework." It is one of those we-know-you-know-we-know moments.

There is no more to say. The river people have no specific request about the Smith River management plan. Clausen will not discuss the Stanislaus. Schifferle has called him on duplicity. There is nothing else to do, so everyone smiles. Mark offers that the Stanislaus wild and scenic river study may contain some of that new information Clausen was talking about.

We leave, exit into the canyon court of the Longworth Office Building, where cars, mostly big black ones, pull up and drop off people. We are surrounded on three sides by the building, which echoes back a vibrant wild whoop of a laugh from Schifferle. "He had the gall to say 'No more dams,' and we called him on it." But a tiny victory in a word battle inside Clausen's office is no victory at all. We laugh at what has happened, but our lightness barely covers the pain, the realization that Clausen is needed, but Friends of the River does not have him.

It has been a busy day. Schifferle still has testimony to prepare for a House Appropriations Committee hearing tomorrow. She has press releases to deliver around town, but her arm is twisted, and the FOR group makes a rare trip to a restaurant, a dark Greek place on Capitol Hill. They cut up about the appointments and conversations they have had. Huntington is a real fun lover and is loud, so Schifferle admonishes him by tugging on his arm to get him to shut up. At first she is uncharacteristically subtle, then resorts to gagging him with her hand, because a congressman from the House Interior Committee has just walked in. We censor ourselves. After dinner, everybody is still wired and talking. The group decides that grassroots support in critical areas is needed. "Grassroots!" has become a battle cry around the FOR offices and is properly said by raising both arms and striking the air twice with your fists as you say it. A basket of rolls is passed, emptied, and left next to a candle. A big paper napkin, lining the basket, hangs over one side.

The river people get into a heavy discussion. Just how important is grassroots, anyway? Probably the best way to influence congressmen is through congressmen. They make deals. Next best might be influential friends of congressmen—fishing buddies, campaign contributors, brothers-in-law. Then the media, the hometown editor. Finally your grassroot, who sends a mailgram. But Friends of the River does not have much access to congressmen, their contributors, or brothers-in-law. Roos-Collins, back at Fort Mason, does what he can with editors. "Grassroots is the one thing that we . . ."

"Look out!" The napkin from the roll basket is bursting into flame. Tom strikes at a burning piece of paper that falls on the table. Catherine dumps a water glass on it, but she has already drunk her water and only ice hits the lengthening yellow flames. The fire grows. Catherine grabs another glass, a full one, and floods the blaze. When the smoke has cleared, there is a pall of silence. Doug Linney says, "Yeah, Friends of the River goes to Washington."

Friends of New Melones had not been idle. We saw Milton Kramer in the office of Congressman Johnson, but the power of the Valley farmers was even more evident in Sacramento. They had been organizing at the state capitol ever since they had passed a law forbidding hydraulic mining in the 1800s.

Politically speaking, most actions breed an opposite reaction, and backlash is almost always immoderate. While the river people sought national river status, the pro-dam people lobbied to rescind state Decision 1422 and fill the dam. Why fill it now? Friends of New Melones argued for generation of power. Pro-dam people were also concerned that if the coming years were dry ones, the irrigation water would be needed. "The New Melones Dam should be filled," they said. "The people of California voted to do so in 1974. The will of the people should not be set aside by administrative edict." They boosted "family-oriented recreation." They asserted that fish kills would be stopped, and that "the groundwater table overdraft would be stopped and the water table recharged." Bill Lyons, a Valley farmer testified, "Rafting is enjoyable, but how do you compare a good time and scenic view with the business of food production? As a farmer, I don't want to depend on energy from a foreign country and I don't want to depend on energy from polluting sources. Society needs energy and food supply, not river raft rides."

Mainly Friends of New Melones argued for the power. Milton Kramer said that even if the energy were not used locally, these people were still concerned. He said that energy was everybody's business, and that the Valley people still held old-fashioned values. "They are concerned about others and the welfare of this country. They are willing to share."

Joe Nagel says, "The irrigation water is a pittance. The dam would never be built if it were being considered today." I ask him why people want it filled. "Because it's there," Nagel says.

California Assemblyman Norman Waters, representing Stanislaus River counties, introduced a bill to immediately begin filling the reservoir to its "maximum operating capacity." As with the Tellico Dam amendment, all conflicting laws could be forgotten. Just fill it up. The most important provision of State Water Resources Control Board Decision 1422, for which California had so tediously and effectively fought through the Supreme Court, would be rescinded. All of that effort for nothing.

Waters said, "It is irritating as a representative of the district in which the dam is located to see a project's progress—a $341 million investment paid for by the taxpayers—continually being delayed by the emotional demands of a small special interest group."

In listing reasons for filling, Waters seemed to be oblivious to lockers full of research and documentation by the state water board that concluded there was little reason to fill New Melones now. Waters is a politician. How did his constituents from Stockton and Oakdale and Angels Camp feel? People in Oakdale said this in the spring of 1980:

"I think they ought to fill it. We need the water. Some don't think it's true, but we do. There are places down here where it hurts."

"Fill it. There are other places they can come down in rafts. We spent all that money, we ought to fill it."

"Why stop it because of those jerks having a good time. It's stupid. There isn't one Californian in 10,000 that's even seen it up there."

"I think they should fill it, but I'm not a river rafter."

"Last year there was a water crisis and we could have another one. We need it for crops and all."

"It's hindsight now. It's built and we've spent the money."

Joe Nagel says that most people don't look at the intricacies of an issue, that in any crisis you deal with two different things: reality and the perception of it. During the 1980 winter floods, TV cameras juxtaposed scenes of the flooding Delta with scenes of the unfilled New Melones. They didn't say that New Melones Dam was holding back almost all of the Stanislaus flow. They didn't say New Melones was able to hold back more water than it could if it had been filled. "Reality and the perception of it are two different things to deal with," Nagel said. He added, "Politicians do two things: follow and lead."

Norman Waters followed his people, who wanted the dam filled because it was there. He did not lead them through the intricacies of the issue. Instead, he helped polarize people and led the California Assembly toward a decision.

Waters garnered 44 fill-it-up votes on April 10. The opposition, prepped by Megan Eymann, who had lobbied for FOR since August 1979, and David Dickson, an ARTA guide who took off work to lobby, got 32 votes—enough to sustain a veto, thanks to the leadership of Assemblyman Mike Gage of San Rafael. Gage was introduced to rivers by Mark Dubois, and now rows his own raft on the Tuolumne, Stanislaus, and American.

The Waters fill-it-up bill moved on to the state senate agriculture and water committee, where a hearing was held in May 1980. "We'll begin with the bill by Mr. Waters," announced Senator Rubin Ayala, chairman of the committee. It was Ayala who had been showered with 1,500 letters from river supporters during the last two days of the Behr bill campaign in 1976. Though he sometimes voted pro-environment, he would not support the Stanislaus. In April 1977, Ayala tried to abolish Peter Behr's state wild and scenic rivers system.

Norman Waters stood up to summarize his bill, and, in his easy-going style, addressed Senators Ray Johnson of Oroville, Robert Presley of Riverside, Kenneth Maddey of Fresno, Rose Ann Vuich from Cutler (near Fresno), William Craven of Oceanside (near San Diego), Alex Garcia of Los Angeles, and John Garamendi of Stockton. Waters reminded the committee that $341 million of the taxpayers' money had been spent and that voters had approved the project under Proposition 17 of 1974. "I just think it is incredible to me to have a facility and not fill it." He documented his case by adding, "New Melones has a power capacity of 455 million kilowatt hours, equivalent to 780,000 barrels of oil. To not follow through on this I cannot understand. We need the energy. We have serious flooding. During the winter floods the Resources Agency was going to require that the New Melones flood gates be left open to cause even more flooding. Without the reservoir, low water levels could endanger the king salmon. As for irrigation, some of the finest farmlands in our state could be served, not to mention cities that need the water. We could have a drought, and right now there is 800,000 acre-feet of snowpack in the mountains that could be salvaged, could be saved."

An important question of water rights was raised by the Waters bill. It would withdraw authority from the State Water Resources Control Board. Waters said, "When a board makes a decision that is wrong, we need to change it. When they screw up, we need to change it."

Senator Presley asked, "How did they screw up? I'm not that

familiar with the case." Waters answered that D-1422 allowed only one-third filling of the reservoir.

Chairman Ayala says, "This is a federal facility. If they decide to not fill, what the state says will not matter." Ayala gets himself off the hook—it is still a federal decision. The implication is that the committee can follow its constituents' plea to fill and still not be responsible for what happens.

Mr. Waters has witnesses. Robert McKee, an elderly, crew-cut member of a Tuolumne County tourist group supports the bill, and for ten minutes talks about flatwater recreation. "The federal government is offering us a park for free. A lake, landscaping, equipment, fishing, boating, wildlife study. Yet people are saying we don't need or want it. Warm water fishes are just as plentiful as cold water in California and it's because of these great reservoirs along the Sierra. Mountain sailing is energy-cheap and will be popular at the lake, and there will be sixty miles of trails. I'd like to talk about mountain sailing for a minute . . . "

Dick Roos-Collins for Friends of the River sits at the front table with McKee, John Hertle, Milton Kramer, and other fill-it-uppers. Behind him are eight senators. The fate of the Stanislaus, a national river candidate, is viewed here as a local issue. Six senators are from the Central Valley. Two are from the south. Nearly every member of this committee votes for water development at every chance he/she gets. In front of Roos-Collins sits the audience, all but two of whom are for water development. Roos-Collins is deep in a den of hostility.

Dick Collins grew up in Nashville, then went to school at Princeton, where he met his wife, Marget Roos. In 1979 the pair decided to move to San Francisco, sight unseen, job prospects unknown. Within a week, they were toiling as paralegals in law offices. One day Alexander Gaguine called Dick, whose name appeared on a Sierra Club list. "Want to do some volunteer work?" Off and on, Roos-Collins helped in the San Francisco office; then, on a river trip, Brad Welton suggested that he work full time, $150 a month. The Tennesseean wasn't sure. Dubois sneaked up behind Roos-Collins and playfully tossed him in an arc that ended with a splash. "Are you going to work for us or not?" they asked as Dick spat Stanislaus and swam back to land.

Now he sits with eight water developers behind him and thirty in front of him, John Hertle on one side, Milton Kramer on the other. Roos-Collins is not here to take guff, but to offer testimony. He waits and waits and seems to have the patience of a Tennessee hillbilly in a deer blind, but, truth be known, he gnashes his teeth, and his blood pressure climbs at what he hears.

McKee continues. "We can have whitewater for the few or general recreation for the many. A raft trip costs $45. That shows you how

affluent the whitewater people are." He does not say a motorboat costs
$10,000 or more.

Darrell McConnell from the State Association of Marinas testifies.
He is for a full dam. "We should use this dam for the good of all instead
of the pleasure of a few. Where were these whitewater people during
the floods last winter? Where were they when the Webb Tract in the
Delta went under? They weren't filling sandbags."

John Hertle is next. Big John, as some people, including Bureau of
Reclamation officials, call him, does not screech, attack, or accuse.
That is not his style, and he knows it is unnecessary. These senators
are in the bag. Hertle is cool, concise, taking one minute. "There is
legislation in Congress and it is very important that we have a clear
directive from California so our representatives in Washington
will know."

Senator Garamendi, having the prerogative to speak at any time,
does. "In 1974, the people very clearly stated what they wanted. In the
four-county area [Stanislaus, San Joaquin, Calaveras, and Tuolumne],
we know there is need for more than this amount of water. We cannot
deliver it immediately because the works are not there, but the water
will never be delivered if the reservoir is not filled."

Garamendi represents the Stanislaus basin. He is tall and handsome
and sports a flashy smile whenever he talks to friends. He reminds me
of Bob Mathias, the old Olympic decathlon champion who served as a
Central Valley congressman in Washington a few years back.
Garamendi is your all-star politician: Berkeley and Harvard graduate,
Peace Corps veteran, rancher. He even has four kids. Another on the
way. His environmental record is good. He has led in efforts to protect
Lake Tahoe, Mono Lake, and prime farmlands, but he wants to fill
New Melones now. When I interviewed Garamendi, he said a full New
Melones was needed because of groundwater overdraft, water quality
in lower sections of the river, and energy demands. He said that, in the
long run, filling the dam would do much for the environment of the
Central Valley Stanislaus and for agriculture and economic activity. I
asked Garamendi if it would be political suicide to oppose filling. The
senator said, "The prevalent local opinion is certainly for filling
the reservoir."

With a few other supplements, the fill-it-up testimony is concluded.
All those who testified stand up, bantering about. Milton Kramer is
jovial. The witnesses gradually filter back through the room. It seems
as though the hearing is over. Amid this jocular, unannounced recess,
Roos-Collins sits like a statue.

Eventually, Senator Ayala calls the session back together. B. J. Miller
of the State Water Resources Control Board takes the podium. "The

water board is opposed to the bill," he says. Clear enough. That is the only really clear thing. Miller says that the bill would restrict the water board, but not necessarily the Resources Agency. A senator makes a muffled remark, something about the agency or Huey Johnson, and there is widespread laughter. Miller clarifies that the water board's position really isn't that bad. "We contemplate ultimate filling of the reservoir."

Ayala interjects, "The lack of contracts for irrigation water seems a poor excuse for not filling. Couldn't a full reservoir be used for water quality in the Delta until there are contracts for irrigation?" Miller does not say no, which is what Decision 1422 says. He says maybe, but points out that adequate releases for water quality were provided under D-1422. It is very unclear.

Senator Ray Johnson, tall and grey, has been reading something, but now offers his best analogy to the board's action postponing the filling: "Your board is like me—you know you'll be leaving this earth but you're trying to put it off." He asks, "If the dam is not for power and irrigation, then what is it for?"

Miller answers, "Indirectly the decision addressed uses that . . . "

Johnson: "Some of my people might have a little more gasoline to run a motorboat if we had the power from that dam."

All too procedurally, Miller says, "We're here against this bill with a procedural argument, we admit that. I know that procedures may not stack up against your frustrations. The board's issue is not if the reservoir should be filled but if the procedure should be changed." The water board is concerned because its authority is being stripped away.

Johnson accuses the board of changing the law. Miller says this would be the first time the legislature changed a board decision. Senator Maddey asks Miller not to take this grilling badly. "You are doing your best and should not take the senators' blasts personally. It's not you, it's the whole administration." Laughter is widespread from the front of the room and through the gallery. "Remember, this is very political," the senator consoles him.

Miller adds one parting comment—that under law, the board really does have the authority to make Decision 1422. One of the senators oozes sarcasm as he says, "Do you really mean that?"

It seems to me that Miller has the choice of laughing or crying, so he steps down and laughs. "It's been a pleasure." Everyone else laughs too.

It is in this climate that Dick Roos-Collins takes the stand. He begins speaking while Assemblyman Waters is talking to Senator Johnson. "It is not a question whether the dam should be used, but *how* it should be used," Roos-Collins says. He begins to itemize the half dozen uses, and the case for compromise, or, as Dick says, a "moderate reservoir instead of the massive reservoir."

"For flood control the dam was very effective. No more than 3,000 cfs went out during the floods, and while San Joaquin levees were endangered, almost nothing went out, even though releases of 8,000 cfs had been planned in the project's design." He says that prior irrigation rights have been provided for and that already this year, and it is only May, the dam has generated one-third the power that was expected of a full reservoir. "The reservoir is now being used for flatwater recreation while the river is also being used."

He is asked about Decision 1422.

"We agree with the provisions of the water board. They have done a responsible job in looking at California's needs and making sure that money and resources are not wasted. We do not agree that the reservoir should eventually be filled."

Somehow Roos-Collins begins talking about the federally required environmental impact statement. He says the reservoir should not be filled until the EIS is done. Ayala asks, "Why do an EIS if the project is built?" Roos-Collins becomes mired. He says it is a legal requirement, but it is clear these senators are not enamored of the letter of the National Environmental Policy Act.

Johnson has another analogy and interrupts. "We could have another drought. Not saving water now is as stupid as not putting money in a savings account until you know what you're going to spend it on." There is laughter, especially from a family that sits on the left side of the audience. They have been laughing right along.

Roos-Collins begins to retrieve a point that he intended to make before he was cut off. "This is difficult . . . "

Johnson interrupts, "Maybe to you, not to me. Water is a necessity of life."

This goes on for another few minutes, but Roos-Collins cannot recover order from an unwilling committee. He is not willing to force his position, not able to make these people listen. Pacifism, a part of the FOR philosophy, is cousin to non-aggression, part of the FOR style. We see it here. It is intentional. Most of the river people (with exceptions such as Jennings and Schifferle) don't scrap or argue. They do not interrupt, even when they are being interrupted, even when interruption is the only way they can fit a word in. This comes in part from their philosophy of peace and human respect, and part is just a matter of the personalities drawn to save this river. Most of the river people do not pursue points that nail down their opposition. They do not rebut insults; they are slow to answer challenges. They are peaceful people and they are not good at put-downs. Is this a strength or a weakness? Who knows?

Maybe Roos-Collins can rejoin, refute, counterstate, and smash through some of the stone wall he has hit, but he cannot see much point in continuing. He steps down. Senator Presley leaves the meeting. The committee votes 7–0 to forward the bill to the senate floor, where it will pass handily, 26 to 6.

To lobby the governor, Friends of New Melones scheduled a rally at the state capitol on May 28, predicting hundreds of supporters. Thirty-four showed up. John Hertle said, "Most people have never done this kind of thing before; they feel uncomfortable at rallies or meetings. They don't get out with the general public. They don't like to go to Sacramento." Hertle seems to enjoy it. "To me, going to the capitol is a day off."

The fill-it-uppers listened to pep talks by Waters, Hertle, and Garamendi. Waters said, "There are needs far greater than rafting that have to be met. We no longer have the luxury of debate over these things."

John Hertle said, "We are trying to get Governor Brown to realize that he must help come to grips with very real problems in our area."

Then they unrolled part of a 15,000-signature petition—800 feet of papers taped together—and carried it into the governor's office. They couldn't unroll it all, because there weren't enough people to carry it.

Meanwhile, Kevin Wolf, FOR Davis coordinator, had scheduled a press conference to announce a new organization called Best Friends of New Melones. "The reservoir will function best at the Parrotts Ferry level," Wolf said. He had scheduled a meeting with the governor's chief of staff for the very moment that Friends of New Melones would be congregating in Brown's office. While the pro-dam people milled about the lobby with their 800-foot roll of signatures, thirty river people with signs trooped past in their finest cotton dresses, pressed Levis, and even a few sports coats dug from seldom-opened trunks, for a long meeting with Gray Davis, Brown's chief of staff.

In politics, good people do bad things and bad people do good things, sometimes even for good reasons. For all their shortcomings, President Nixon signed the National Environmental Policy Act and Governor Reagan signed the California Environmental Quality and Scenic Rivers Acts. Jimmy Carter, for all his strengths in conservation, signed the Tellico Dam bill to drown the Little Tennessee. Politics delivers a mixed bag. So does Jerry Brown, but few governors or presidential candidates, if any, have his record of environmental stands and accomplishments.

Brown's presidential campaign slogan was "Protect the earth, serve the people, explore the universe." He has waved his copy of E. F. Schumacher's *Small Is Beautiful* ("Economics as if People Mattered") in the air during speeches and hammered home a philosophy that recognized scarce resources in a state that has been growth-crazed and guzzling energy, land, and water since 1849. With strong appointees in environmental, energy, water, and planning positions, the Brown administration led the nation in environmental protection. Nothing less would dent the consumption and ravages of a perennially red-hot Coast economy.

The Renewable Resources Investment Fund, a Huey Johnson/Jerry Brown creation, offers innovative potential for water quality, fisheries, timber management, and soil conservation. Brown's stands against nuclear power and for solar energy and conservation have been dramatic. He has supported protection of Lake Tahoe and more wilderness than the U.S. Forest Service wants. He has been a champion of mass transit, calling for a fourfold increase in its funding. The League of Conservation Voters called his air quality and toxic waste records superb, and he strengthened a good water-quality program established by Ronald Robie under Governor Reagan.

But Brown first supported reform of the 1902 Reclamation Act and a modest acreage limit on farmers receiving federally subsidized water, and then backed down. He gave good speeches about resource recovery (bottle bills) and agricultural land protection, but did little.

In water development, his record includes some of the best and some that is not so good. Auburn Dam, considered by many people to be one of the most ill-conceived projects anywhere, received support, but later Brown allowed heavy criticism of the project by the Resources Agency. When Huey Johnson tried to attach stringent environmental conditions to Warm Springs Dam, the governor did not back him up. The peripheral canal—one of the costliest water projects in the history of the United States—has consistently been pushed by Brown. The canal would divert part of the Sacramento River around the Delta for pumping to the south. Opponents fear that protection for Delta water quality and northern rivers will be scuttled as soon as the ditch and valves and pumps are in place to deliver the river south. Brown accepted peripheral canal legislation without all the environmental safeguards he had advocated.

Then he did something bold and clever. He asked Interior Secretary Andrus to include all the designated state scenic rivers in the national wild and scenic rivers system. The law allows for Andrus to do this without legislative action if the governor requests it. Lawsuits by southern water developers, timber companies, and northern counties held Andrus at bay until nineteen hours and fifteen minutes before Ronald Reagan's inauguration, but lawyers finally had a lower court's ruling overturned, and Andrus signed the paper to protect the Smith, Klamath, Trinity, Eel, and American rivers—1,246 miles of river, which doubled the national system, not counting Alaska. While some environmentalists may be lukewarm about Brown's water policies, the water lobby and farm interests think he is a wild-eyed radical.

With the Stanislaus, as we have seen, Jerry Brown has been off and on. During Proposition 17, he ended up a strong supporter. After the election, he could not be jarred loose from inaction; he was not willing to buck the vote of the people. Then, when Mark Dubois chained himself to the rock, Brown telegraphed President Carter, "The beauty of the Stanislaus Canyon and the life of Mark Dubois deserve your personal intervention."

In early June 1980, the Waters fill-it-up bill flew through the legislature and landed on Brown's desk. Brown would make his choice, but he would not make it a big deal or a splashy show. He vetoed the Waters bill on June 11, signing a letter to that effect in Frank Fats Chinese Restaurant, while an aide delivered the message to Norman Waters, who happened to be eating there at the same time. For the press, a spokesman said that eventually the reservoir would be filled. Brown supported the water board and Decision 1422, but not really the river. His support for long-term protection through the national wild river bill would come with approval for Huey Johnson to testify in Washington, but Brown himself would not surface on the issue.

Back in Washington and at the river, things were not going well. Secretary Andrus challenged the Stanislaus wild river bill sponsors: "I do not want to inundate a whitewater canyon if there is a serious chance that new Stanislaus River legislation will emerge from this Congress, but if there is not, I must follow the mandate of existing law."

To hear the California congressmen, Andrus attended a meeting called by Representative Tony Coelho of Fresno, headquarters of the giant Westlands water district. This is the region of John Steinbeck's *Grapes of Wrath,* where Mexican-Americans today share much of the same plight that other immigrants did in the 1930s. The district had been represented by Congressman Bernie Sisk, one of the most powerful Central Valley advocates of water development. On his retirement in 1978, Sisk hand-picked Coelho, who had been Sisk's administrative assistant for many years, to succeed him. Coelho vehemently opposed the 160-acre limitation, federal reclamation reform, and the wild river proposal. So Coelho was the man to call together the California delegation for Andrus. Several of the wild river bill sponsors, including Don Edwards and Pete Stark, didn't find out the meeting was being held until the last minute. Burton did not attend.

Secretary Andrus told the congressmen that if it were his choice, the Stanislaus would be a wild river, but the choice was not his. Jennifer

Jennings, then an attorney for the Federal Trade Commission in Washington, went to the meeting and asked the secretary, "Why didn't you meet with the Alaska delegation before you designated national monuments there? Why didn't you meet with the Colorado delegation when you considered public lands there?"

Andrus responded that this California water issue was different. "I know what you're getting at," he said. Jennings was getting at an old Stanislaus bugaboo: in Washington the river was regarded as a state issue, even though Andrus's department clearly documented national significance, and even though federal taxpayers would pay for the dam. In the California legislature, too, the Stanislaus was regarded as a local issue. Coelho, Shumway, Johnson, Waters, and Garamendi ran the show, and they were run by agribusiness and local farmers. California Assemblyman Mike Gage said, "When local legislators support a dam, just about everybody else goes along. Most legislators don't look at the overall matter, but see it as a district decision." Dale Crane of Phillip Burton's committee staff would say, "It never had the image of national concern."

At the Coelho meeting, Andrus released his Heritage, Conservation and Recreation Service's wild river study of the Stanislaus, documenting the river's eligibility for the national wild and scenic rivers system. Though the report was available, Andrus did not push for the designation. He didn't get the president to twist any arms. The secretary was tugged both ways by the competing views in his department. Congressmen Edwards, Stark, and McCloskey were angry with Andrus for not being more positive and supporting them as sponsors of the bill.

Robert Herbst, assistant interior secretary for parks and wildlife (including the Heritage, Conservation and Recreation Service), advocated river protection. As Minnesota's resources secretary, Herbst had overseen one of the best state scenic river programs. The Heritage, Conservation and Recreation Service report toed a conservative line, however, finding only geological and recreational qualifications. They didn't even say that scenic values were outstanding. "They could have done a better job," a high Interior official said. Guy Martin, assistant interior secretary for land and water resources, also wanted protection. As Alaska's resources secretary, Martin had almost single-handedly instigated the state's repurchase of oil leases to save Kachemak Bay. "My position was that the Stanislaus should have been designated, but I knew we would not be able to submit a formal position to Congress," he says. The Office of Management and Budget would never go along with it. I devoted my efforts to keep Interior neutral, to give FOR the best opportunity with Congress." The Bureau of Reclamation, presumably under Martin's direction, also held power of its own. It was somewhat of a stalemate in Washington, which gave Joe Nagel a better chance to influence decisions.

Nagel, Andrus's fellow Idahoan, transplanted from a Salmon River ranch and Boise to the federal building in the booming, car-choked suburbia of north Sacramento, said this: "The river doesn't qualify for the national wild and scenic rivers system. Fourteen dams up above are okay, but I looked at New Melones, and if it were operated as authorized, it would affect the section we were considering." Nagel said the river was not free-flowing. The important thing, he said, was not the river—which he had not floated, not walked, not really seen, field man though he was. The important thing, Nagel said, was the congressional authorization that said the Stanislaus was to be dammed. I am puzzled by Nagel the way I was puzzled by Kramer, because I went up to Camp Nine and saw a free-flowing river. With my own two eyes. Nagel's views on this point did not prevail. Herbst prevailed—the Interior report said the river qualified.

More importantly, however, Nagel believed the reservoir should be filled to repay itself. He said, "It is an economic question. How do you recoup $346 million of sunk cost? If you don't make it on the water supply, which is admittedly a pittance and subsidized, you make it on power, and New Melones is a hell of a money-maker on power.

"If we were discussing building the dam today, I doubt if Congress would authorize it," Nagel said. "No doubt this administration would pursue protection very aggressively. But the dam is there, and so the department didn't push hard one way or another. The secretary said the river qualifies, but did not recommend for or against.

"If the secretary were king and had the choice, he would not fill the dam. He would put it in the wild river system tomorrow, no doubt, but the action is not with him. The ball is not in his court. It is Congress's decision," Nagel concluded.

On May 29, Congressman Burton announced that he planned on passing the bill through subcommittee and committee. FOR expected the long-awaited hearings within the month.

On June 6, Interior Secretary Andrus ordered that the water be allowed to rise to at least 818 feet—ten feet above Parrotts Ferry. This time there was no flood emergency. The secretary said, "The archaeologists have done the necessary mitigation work well above that mark," and argued that the higher level could protect California against possible electricity shortages in August.

Just two years earlier Andrus had said, "As a westerner, I grew up with the ideology that dam building was good per se. But somewhere along the line we lost sight of what reclamation is all about. It is improving life, not destroying it. . . . Streams and rivers have other values than just for electric power generation and irrigation and transportation. We need free-flowing water left in the nation for many reasons—including the protection of certain forms of life, for recreation, for scenic values, for maintenance of the tenuous link between modern man and his natural world." Now, in spite of his earlier decision to hold the water at 808 through 1980, despite the wild river bill, Andrus was beginning to fill the canyon with a reservoir.

Assistant Secretary Guy Martin said, "Reform in water resources has been the most frustrating effort of this administration. We've made advances in land and energy, but water . . . ?" He added, "The New Melones Dam colors the issue with the secretary. Because the dam is there, this is not the most important fight in his life."

FOR waged yet another campaign. "Write Andrus and ask him to hold the water level at 808," Dubois told dozens and dozens of people over his telephone in the garage. FOR staff alerted the grassroots. River guides provided their passengers with paper and envelopes for letters to Andrus. John Bryson, chairman of the California Public Utilities Commission, sent a letter to Andrus saying that the state's summer power reserve was about 6.3 percent, not 1.8 percent as Andrus stated during the Coelho meeting with the California delegation. State Energy Commission Chairman Rusty Schweickart telegrammed California congressmen saying that the electricity to be produced by New Melones was "insignificant." But Andrus had decided to raise the water and he was not changing his mind. It was time, once again, for a slugfest in court.

Brad Welton prepared the case with FOR attorneys Robert Thum and Brian Smith. On June 13, FOR, the Environmental Defense Fund, the Sierra Club, the Society for Californian Archaeology, etcetera, and Californians for Preservation Action requested a temporary restraining order against raising the reservoir. They argued that the supplemental environmental impact statement was not finished, that historic and archaeological mitigation was not adequate (a position supported by the president's Advisory Council on Historic Preservation and the California state historic preservation officer), and that the State Water Resources Control Board had not approved the operation plan of the Bureau of Reclamation. The U.S. district judge in Fresno smartly responded that the Historic Preservation Act does not require, "the mapping and/or exploration of every acorn-grinding site, the examination of every square meter of midden or the recovery of every scrap of bone lying within the basin." He did not issue the restraining order. The circuit court of appeals refused to intervene. The water continued to rise. Andrus approved flooding to 860 feet—two and a half miles above Parrotts Ferry—almost to the South Fork. The Bureau of Reclamation cut releases from New Melones to 1,000 cfs for irrigation diversion, and reduced the in-stream release to a trickle of 10 cfs. For the canyon, it had never looked so bad.

The water kept rising above Parrotts Ferry, and some people, especially a group of the disabled who had first encountered wilderness on the Stanislaus, planned civil disobedience. They would go into the canyon and chain themselves. Brad Welton told them that a backlash would result and the lawsuit and the wild river bill could be jeopardized by civil disobedience. One night before the planned chaining, the people called it off.

The Environmental Defense Fund appeal was finally heard in San Francisco on June 26. A three-judge panel ordered the Bureau of Reclamation to limit inundation to minor variations needed for flood control. The court ordered that the bureau was, "restrained from impounding water in the Service's New Melones Reservoir to a reservoir pool level greater than attained as of 12 noon, Pacific Daylight Time, Friday, June 27, 1980. Provided, however, that nothing in this order will cause property damage below Goodwin Dam on the Stanislaus River." Details were left to the Department of the Interior. This issue clearly fell into the controversial category, and that meant that Andrus's own emissary would handle it—Joe Nagel. As directed by the court, Nagel considered what flood control ought to be. It was his responsibility.

"Nobody had decided with precision the flow that would cause flood damage downstream," Nagel says. "Everybody danced around it: farmers said they begin to suffer some damage at 3,500 cfs; the corps used 3,500; we used 5,000 in late 1979; and the bureau's operation study didn't say. Friends of the River thought 8,000 was the level."

Was FOR right? "Yes, *but.* If the corps had done what they were supposed to do over the last eighteen years and gotten off their ass and bought the flood easements we would have had the 8,000 cfs channel. But the corps never said that 8,000 would provide absolute flood control. Because the flood plain is not urbanized, they said absolute flood control is not needed."

Joe Countryman of the corps says, "We saw no sense of urgency for the easements. Under full operation, without court fights, it would be four to twelve years before the reservoir would fill up anyway. By then we would have the easements." The corps accelerated the program, and by the end of 1980 it intended to have claims on the entire 8,000 cfs channel.

"Anyhow," Nagel says, "the court said to stop raising the reservoir, but don't cause flood damage. At what level does flood damage occur? Walnut orchards were on the flood plain, so we contacted some guys at

Davis who did walnut research: 50 percent of the trees could die after their roots are flooded for nine days. We located the orchards, estimated their elevation, depth of their roots, and depth of groundwater." They used the lowest walnut trees there were.

We know the project was authorized for flood releases up to 8,000 cfs. Since 1962 downstream landowners have known that, even with the dam, water would get that high. During an average year, flooding hits about 6,000 cfs. In June, flows often exceed 4,800 cfs. But Joe Nagel said that flood damage would occur at 1,000 cfs. The Stanislaus River Flood Control Association, testifying before Judge Price in Fresno, had also advocated 1,000 cfs.

"I disagreed strongly with 1,000 cfs," says Assistant Interior Secretary Guy Martin. "And the Interior solicitor, Clyde Martz, also disagreed, but Joe convinced the secretary that the decision should be made 'in the field.'"

FOR and EDF won the court appeal, but because of Nagel's decision, the water kept rising. "Nagel doesn't only intend to protect almond trees that farmers planted on the flood plain; he intends to keep willow trees dry too," said Jim Kenrick, a FOR spokesman at Parrotts Ferry.

So the water kept rising. While a small river of 1,000 cfs meandered through the Central Valley, past the new shopping center hard by the river in Oakdale, past Riverbank and Ripon, past walnut trees with dry roots, past John Hertle's dairy farm, past crops growing on the rich soil kept dry by Joe Nagel, a large reservoir crept up through the willows, then the oaks, then the buckeyes and pines. "Here is where the flood is really killing trees," Jim Kenrick said. New Melones swallowed Parrotts Ferry, the campground, and the access road, and crept upriver past the beaches and flat river rocks. It buried Fred's beach, where Fred Dennis, Mark Dubois, and Ron Coldwell had lived, where they had met Brad Welton. The reservoir flooded Chicken Falls, and swamped the pool below Chinese Dogleg.

After five years, Gaguine had still not exhausted his ideas for rallies. He organized a protest of "human water markers." People would stand in the river at the 820 elevation—the limit of the reservoir when the judge ruled that the canyon should not be flooded any further. First the people stood, then they leaned on inner tubes as the water swelled to 827. On their seventh day, a drunken motorboater buzzed three times within five feet of Sally Kenrick. A person could get killed doing this, so the swimmers called it off and concentrated on their land-based operations. At a Parrotts Ferry letter-writing table Gina Cuculis—the "sweetheart of Parrotts Ferry," Gaguine called her—in one day collected 297 letters asking congressmen for wild river status.

While the water markers were still swimming, the president came to town. Jimmy Carter spoke to 5,000 people in Merced on July 4th, six years after he had spoken to a mere dozen people in Los Angeles and derided New Melones Dam during the Proposition 17 campaign. A woman raised her hand and asked a question, "I'm a farmer's wife and I'd like to know what you will do if Congress passes a law to make the Stanislaus a national river."

The president answered, "If the bill gets to my desk and is otherwise acceptable, I would sign it. I believe in the wild river concept, and I think the Stanislaus River is one of the most beautiful in the world."

"Carter: Save Stanislaus," screamed the front-page headlines of the *Stockton Record*. It fueled the spirits of the river people, but that was as far as it went. Guy Martin says, "In three and a half years I was never able to find *any* support in the White House for saving the river, and I did everything but talk to the president." It seems that Carter managed to alienate the Valley voters while still not taking the wild river initiative. Of course, he may have felt the positions coming up from Interior were not strong enough.

Two days later, the *Los Angeles Times* editorialized against filling the dam. "We think a case can be made that the rapids of the Stanislaus belong under the protection of the Wild and Scenic Rivers Act, and we hope Congress will agree." This, of course, was a turnaround for the *Times*, which had editorialized in favor of building the dam in 1974. In spite of the flooding of Parrotts Ferry and delays with the wild river bill, Friends of the River's hopes rose with the endorsements of Carter and the *Times*. Guy Phillips flew to Washington to lobby congressmen, and he returned saying, "I think we have a 50–50 chance."

Don Edwards decided it was time to push the bill. For publicity and also to get acquainted with the place, he scheduled a river trip. On July 17, Dubois and Briggs guided Edwards, Pete Stark, Huey Johnson, and Ed Roberts—director of the state Department of Rehabilitation—down the Stanislaus, along with reporters from the *New York Times, Newsweek,* and *U.S. News and World Report.* The Stanislaus had made its impression by the time the group reached the still waters of the reservoir, half a mile above Parrotts Ferry. They rowed through the flatwater and over the tops of trees that could be seen under five feet of water, and when they reached Parrotts Ferry, Melinda Wright and fifty members of FOR's Mother Lode chapter were on the bridge singing the Stanislaus River song with signs that said "Thank you Don Edwards," "Thank you Pete Stark," and "Thank you Huey." "It was enough to make a believer out of you," says Bob Wiekowski, Edward's aide. At the take-out, the congressmen and river people planted a tree where the higher waters of the winter flood had killed a young digger pine. Congressman Edwards said that they could get the votes to save the river.

Sierra runoff peaked, and soon the reservoir subsided, returning to the Parrotts Ferry elevation in late July, but the message was very clear to everybody: the fall of 1980 might be the final chance to save the river. It had run for nine million years, but this could be the last. Time was running out in the struggle for the Stanislaus.

At the river, tensions between foothills residents and river people were strung tight. Relations had been difficult for a long time. When Dubois talked to a group in Modesto after his chaining, some people said they would have let him drown. One man said he would hunt Dubois with a shotgun. Then a fire-bomb was thrown from a car passing the OARS boathouse near Angels Camp. Bumper stickers said "Fill Melones," "Fill the Dam," "Eat a Sierra Clubber," and "Drown the Parrotts Fairies." A second-generation bumper sticker asked, "Who is Fill Melones?"

On July 25, local roughnecks blocked rafters from using the Camp Nine road. The sheriff's department dispersed the locals and kept a tenuous balance of law and order. The same week, Skeeter, a driver for OARS, was lumbering his empty bus up the Camp Nine road when twenty local toughs—mostly teenagers—stood in his way forcing him to stop. One waved a pistol in the air. Skeeter inched the bus forward and past them. A pickup truck peeled out in front of him and then crept at five miles per hour in front of the bus. "I managed to slip alongside the pickup on a bend," the river guide said, "then with that big sixty-passenger bus, it was easy to force the truck off the road and keep going."

Local pro-dam people scheduled pancake breakfasts at Camp Nine on Saturday mornings in August, trying to congest the put-in area. The Calaveras County sheriff and fourteen deputies were there at a cost of $1,000 per weekend, along with Bureau of Land Management staff from all over the district. It was mostly peaceful. Kevin Wolf of FOR spent an hour talking to the pro-dam people. "We agreed on most things when I would talk to just one person, but it was a stone wall when they were in groups." Why did these people want the dam filled? They wouldn't get the flood control, irrigation, or downstream water quality. They might get some motorboating, that's all.

"It's culture shock," Wolf says. "These people see the dam as the way to get rid of the rafters, who look like hippies, who dress differently, who act differently. Men and women guides live at the same place. Local people don't like it. They don't want their kids to see it. One older man complained of young people driving past his house and yelling, 'get outta here old man.' Another said they had to take care of all the rafters' garbage." Two local men parked a pickup on the new Camp Nine bridge and dumped something liquid on rafters as they went under. Where was this all heading? Where would it end?

Richard Roos-Collins

Tom Huntington

Patricia "Shortcut" Schifferle,
June 2 rally

John Garamendi, John Hertle, and Milton Kramer at the State Capitol

Melinda Wright

Gina Cuculis at Parrotts Ferry letter-writing table

Dam supporters at Camp Nine,
August 1980

Dam supporters debate with
river supporters, 1980

On August 23, Tim Riedell, a guide for etcetera, arrived at Camp Nine late in the night and passed fourteen to twenty young locals partying there. They jeered Riedell, but he kept going. He was scheduled to guide a trip the next morning, and he rolled out his sleeping bag near the parking lot, the way he had done many times before. The local boys boozed and joked and "goddam-hippied" the rafters, until the cussing grew to dares. Soon there was nothing left to say; it was their duty to do something. Tim Riedell became that other world that didn't suit the cowboys of the foothills. A drunken gang of kids cannot change much, but they can make someone pay.

While asleep, Riedell was kicked in the head, immediately knocked unconscious, and kicked again. Eventually he woke up bleeding from the ears, nose, and mouth. Some other people found him and rushed him in critical condition to the Sonora hospital, where he recovered slowly.

Meanwhile, Patricia Schifferle pushed for action in Washington, with help from David Dickson, an ARTA guide who lobbied in Sacramento through the spring. Phillip Burton finally scheduled hearings for August 22. Brad Welton, campaign manager for the entire Stanislaus effort, flew to Washington to be closer to the information, to oversee the campaign, and to prepare for volunteers, who would be called in for the committee and floor fights.

Time was getting short. Congress was scheduled to adjourn on October 3, and the bill had to go through Burton's National Parks and Insular Affairs Subcommittee, Morris Udall's House Interior Committee, the Rules Committee, the full House, and then Senate committees and the full Senate. Subcommittee action was not even taking place because Burton was still getting other rivers together for an omnibus bill that would include designation of the wild Illinois River and the North Fork of the Umpqua in Oregon, the lower American through Sacramento, and the Stanislaus. Fourteen other rivers would be included for national river studies. Burton was pushing Lake Tahoe legislation, Big Sur legislation, and a California wilderness bill setting aside 2.1 million acres. These would all take precedence over the omnibus bill. The Stanislaus was the toughest of the bunch, and politicians do not break the momentum of winning; they save the most difficult battles until last. Schifferle said, "If Burton pulls this off, it will be a miracle." Should the river people trust Burton to move the bill? They had no choice.

Washington was chaotic on the hearing day, Friday, August 22. Schifferle had hastily put together three pages of testimony. Hydrologist Philip Williams arrived at the last minute, and did not have time to prepare adequately. First, Bizz Johnson testified. Then Congressmen Don Edwards, Pete Stark, and Lionel Van Deerlin spoke for the river. The pro-dam heavies, Anthony Coelho and Chip Pashayan of Fresno, attacked. "You're not one of those 'no growth' people are you?" Pashayan asked, intending insult. Pete Stark addressed agricultural subsidies. Coelho called him "Stark," not "Mr. Stark," and the cigar-smoking Pashayan interrupted by asking, "How about your San Francisco airport. It's subsidized, isn't it?"

"Coelho and Pashayan acted like assholes," a congressional aide said later.

Then Schifferle and Williams testified. Brad Welton, trained as an attorney to handle hostile interrogators, did not testify. Schifferle had tried to get non-FOR experts—Phillip La Veen of Berkeley, for example—to testify, but they couldn't come. As to FOR's testimony, Schifferle wanted to handle it alone. Roos-Collins, best able to answer technical questions, did not testify. He was in San Francisco. After all this time, the Stanislaus finally had its day of hearings before a congressional committee, and the river people were not prepared. Coelho and Pashayan barraged Schifferle and Williams. Some important facts were not available. Burton bailed FOR out, saying that resources agency personnel would answer questions on technical aspects of the reservoir operation. As in the California senate agriculture and water committee hearing and radio debates between river people and Milton Kramer, the FOR weakness in verbal confrontation was evident. The other side was fast, hard-hitting, intimidating, and gave the appearance of having stronger convictions. Because of FOR's philosophy, style, and abilities, the heated battles—the tough confrontations—were not won.

Cliff Humphrey gave a good presentation against the wild river designation. Congressman Lagomarsino was at the hearing, and may have been influenced by the testimony. He began probing with questions. Other congressmen are influenced by Lagomarsino. They regard him as careful, but open-minded, a man who reaches decisions painstakingly. "Lago is kind of a good-guy Republican," an Edwards aide said. "We hoped he would come around." But that was not likely.

On Monday the hearings were continued. Ed Roberts of the State Rehabilitation Department gave moving testimony about the river and the disabled. Huey Johnson spoke for twenty minutes, and Guy Phillips for another ten. Phillips reported that the compromise reservoir was larger than the other twelve major Stanislaus reservoirs combined. It would yield 40–50 percent of the energy of a full reservoir and 35–60 percent of the water supply. "Within a generation, twenty-six million people will live within one day's drive of the Stanislaus

—that's more than the combined populations of seventeen states west of the Mississippi," Phillips said. Then Coelho and Pashayan cross-examined him for an hour. At first they gave Phillips an opportunity to respond, which he succinctly did. Then they continuously interrupted him with their interrogation.

Anticipating the committee vote and floor action after the hearing, volunteers flew to Washington to lobby: handicapped people and outfitters and their representatives, including Larry Ormon, Catherine Fox, Gracielle Rossi, and others. The good FOR organizers—Welton, Gaguine, and Linney—were not there, and they were needed. "Sometimes it was bedlam," said Peter Troast of Friends of the Earth, who helped organize and discipline the effort.

They overlobbied. Burton was called late at night when his wife was in the hospital, and he almost dropped the Stanislaus right there. Young Californians saw friendly congressional aides too much. "For Godsake, why are you seeing me again?" they protested. "Go see the opponents."

So they saw the opponents. FOR had tried to get older people to lobby—for example, Republican Jerry Cadagan, a board member and Crown Zellerbach attorney—but for the most part, they were young. And, as an Edwards aide said, "You can't look like you're growing pot in Mendocino County."

On the other side, Cliff Humphrey, John Hertle, Norman Waters, and, of course, Milton Kramer traveled from office to office visiting Interior committee congressmen. Lobbyists from the Westlands district—a giant of agribusiness—were busy, along with representatives of the Metropolitan water district of Southern California and the Calaveras County water district, which was concerned that their proposed North Fork Stanislaus dams would be jeopardized.

Burton said that if California Republicans Don Clausen or Robert Lagomarsino of the House Interior Committee supported the bill, it would move, so in San Francisco, Gaguine and Huntington continued to organize in these two districts. At 10:00 P.M. Huntington hung up the phone and said, "When I was a guide, I saved people from rivers. Now I save rivers from people." He dialed another number from a list of a hundred. Lagomarsino received 2,000 letters, mostly from Santa Barbara. An aide reported that Clausen was looking at the issue really hard, "Anybody who gets 1,600 letters in a month is going to consider his vote carefully."

In Sacramento, Dubois spent hours on the telephone contacting influential friends of Clausen's and Lagomarsino's. "Learning a new language," he said about this game of political leverage. He called Ike Livermore's brother, Putt, who had been Governor Reagan's appointments secretary. Putt said he'd be willing to make "one small call" to Clausen. Others at FOR joked, "One small call for Putt, one giant call for FOR."

Meanwhile, the usual Sacramento things were going on. Ronnie James took a call from somebody offering FOR 5,000 rubber tires for the taking. A real bargain. For what? Maybe they thought FOR was into recycling. Maybe they were old tires with inner tubes to make the greatest rubber navy this side of Phoenix, where 10,000 tubers spin down the Salt River in August. Maybe they were just nuts.

In San Francisco, a dozen people organized out-of-state grassroots. With lists from the American Rivers Conservation Council, Sierra Club, Stanislaus outfitters, Grand Canyon permit applications, and western and eastern river guides associations, files were made for each state. Citizen's names were listed for each congressional district. Telephone banks were run in the evenings, when volunteers would come into the FOR office and monopolize half a dozen phones, calling people all over the country and asking them to contact their congressmen. The FOR telephone bill skyrocketed, but all stops were being pulled out. Money didn't matter. Somehow they would pay. Gaguine said, "The higher the bill, the better. All we do is give out information, so we might as well do a lot of it." Most people who were telephoned agreed to have FOR send a mailgram the day before the vote, billing the charge of $3.50 to the person's home phone. This assured FOR that hundreds of wild river requests would arrive in Washington at precisely the right time. Non-Californians specialized in their own home states. Mike Zischke covered Michigan, Macauley Lord took Kentucky, Briggs called friends in Colorado. David Kay, Jerry Meral's old partner, surfaced to organize grassroots support in Ohio, Indiana, and Illinois. Roos-Collins prepared another round of press packets for newspapers. He said, "We'll either be the hottest group in the country, or we'll be down and need a total revamping of our goals."

Back in Washington, there were thirty-one co-sponsors for the Stanislaus wild river bill, including Representative John Anderson, independent candidate for president. Norman Shumway announced that the battle to fill New Melones was "far from over," and his "number one priority." He said, "Many congressmen are getting enormous amounts of letters from rafters and are not hearing as much from the other side. You should worry. It will provoke a very difficult fight."

Don Clausen had signed a petition to raise the reservoir in the spring, then said that he didn't necessarily support permanent filling.

In discussions with river proponents, he remained uncommitted. FOR continued to aim letters at Clausen.

Everyone waited for Burton's subcommittee to clear the bill for a full committee vote. Burton had said this would not be a problem, but the action was put off. Committee action was expected the week after the hearing. Then the next week. Then the next. "Why won't Burton tell us what's going on, what the problem is?" Roos-Collins asked, and Welton answered, "Because that's the way he operates." Environmentalists on Capitol Hill said the same thing. "The only way you know what Burton is doing is when something comes out the other end of the mill," said David Weiman, who had lobbied for ten years on water issues. FOR was unable to coordinate with its chief political supporter.

Time was running out. It was now almost impossible for the bill to clear the subcommittee, House floor, and Senate. The Senate would have to do it during a lame duck session following the November elections. Lame duck sessions are usually reserved for non-controversial issues. Senator Hayakawa would surely vote against wild river status. Cranston might vote for it or passively let it through. No one knew what he would do. Cranston wrote, "I have not made a final decision on the wild river legislation, H.R. 4223. I am aware that the people of California in 1974 rejected a statewide initiative to add the Stanislaus River to the State Wild River System. But I also know that public use of the Stanislaus has increased dramatically since then, especially by handicapped people."

All anyone could presume was that Burton did not have the support he needed, and so he wasn't moving the bill. Burton never likes to lose. He scheduled a subcommittee mark-up of the bill for September 15, but most Republicans did not attend the meeting. Burton, however, managed to move the bill by a technical maneuver. The subcommittee was adjourning with only three members present. Burton let Representative Keith Sebelius of Kansas introduce an omnibus bill amendment to delete the Stanislaus, which allowed the bill to go to the full committee. On September 17, it would be voted on by the forty-two-member House Interior Committee.

A final volley of support was served to committee members. The mailgrams were wired. And then, on Wednesday morning, the committee voted.

Just the night before, Donald Clausen had told river people that he was undecided, but through another congressman's staff, FOR learned that Clausen had called the Republican members of the committee the same night, urging that they vote for the amendment deleting the Stanislaus. Shumway, appealing to Republican solidarity, told his peers that he needed this vote to get reelected. Bizz Johnson, who had held back until now, strong-armed committee members, including Jim Howard of New Jersey, who had earlier agreed to support the river, and Nick-Joe Rahall of West Virginia, who had been lobbied by his own pro-river constituents and by the West Virginia river outfitters.

The time for educating, communicating, lobbying, soliciting, scheming, pleading, arm-twisting, leveraging, and intimidating was over. It was time to vote.

All the Republicans went against the Stanislaus. Powerfully influenced by Bizz Johnson, Democrats were split, and the final count was 20 to 19 approving the amendment to delete the canyon. The Stanislaus lost.

Chip Pashayan, congressman from Fresno said, "An empty dam is a monument to man's foolishness, not a full one."

Milton Kramer said, "The decision today marks the end of the fight. Obviously, we're delighted."

Phillip Burton said, "I tried my best and didn't make it. At least for the House, I suspect the Stanislaus will not be acted on this year."

Jerry Brown, Huey Johnson, and Guy Phillips called Phillip Burton on the telephone. Brown expressed his thanks and regret. Burton said, "You can't win them all, Governor. See you later, your Holiness."

Burton met with Dubois, Schifferle, and Fox. He said that he had never seen such support mounted for a river, anywhere, and that the Stanislaus effort was stronger than the lobbying had been for Redwood National Park, but that other congressmen didn't see the national impact of this one. They didn't see that it was important to them.

He also said that a deal had been made with organized labor, "but it didn't work out." Schifferle later heard the details: labor lobbyists were to have stayed off the Stanislaus if Burton would not move to protect the Tuolumne in 1980, but they fought the Stanislaus anyway. Burton also reminded the FOR people that they had not delivered the Republican vote of committee members Clausen or Lagomarsino —a vote that Burton had said he needed.

David Weiman, lobbyist for small farmers' and environmental groups trying to reform federal reclamation laws, said, "Unlike elsewhere, the development of water in California delivers wealth, and that wealth is returned to the political machine that delivers the water. The California agribusiness community spent a quarter of a million dollars per month fighting water and reclamation reforms in 1980. They are the same forces who elected Pashayan and Coelho, and they were the ones who fought you on this one. The issue is not the river; the issue is politics."

The Los Angeles *Times* agreed. A September 19 editorial titled "Politics Sinks a Park," observed:

> Congress often moves in such mysterious ways that it is a wonder it performs at all. Its decision this week to let the Interior Department flood out the rapids of the Stanislaus River is a case in point.
>
> Here is Congress scrambling to raise money for a park in one part of California, and there is Congress voting to destroy a park in another part of the state that came as a gift from nature without so much as a budget hearing. . . .
>
> The argument that swung the key votes apparently was made by Rep. Harold T. (Bizz) Johnson (D-Roseville), who said that filling the dam would help him through a close election in November.
>
> We have no particular quarrel with Johnson or his record of service. But a park that the federal government itself has described as "unique" in exchange for a couple of years in office does not seem a fair trade.

Why did the river lose? A congressional staff member said, "The main arguments against the designation were flood control, waste of public money, and that it would ruin the economy of the Central Valley." The state's position, presented at the hearings by Huey Johnson, advocated flood storage above Parrotts Ferry, which should have eliminated that argument. Guy Phillips's work addressed the other questions, but the aide said, "The economic arguments just didn't get through to the committee."

Howard Brown, director of the American Rivers Conservation Council, offered his unemotional analysis: "We depended on the California phenomenon—massive grassroots support—and we relied on Burton to pull a miracle, but it came down to basic politics. We needed Clausen or Lagomarsino. Republicans were solid against us, and some senior members of the California delegation were against us—Johnson and Coelho. We never had open support from Cranston in the Senate, and we didn't have forthright support from Governor Brown. He chose his times and did not openly support the bill. He did not back up Huey Johnson enough."

He continued, "Maybe it was a loser to begin with. Maybe it would have just gone like Tellico even if we had won—the other side would just resurface and beat us next year."

A chief congressional aide said, "It's lost. There's no chance now. The time and amount of energy spent on this was tremendous. You can't spend three or four months on a bill, lose it, and do it again. Too much time is demanded of other things."

Lost. A year and three months after the chaining and after Don Edwards had introduced the Stanislaus wild river bill, it lost. Ever since Proposition 17 in 1974, the fight had been up a steep hill, but now the chances of success seemed to have slipped away. It was hard to imagine that the opportunity of 1980 would ever exist again. This had been the big chance at national river status, and now it was gone. Unless you win, you lose power when you use the vote.

The defeat did not totally shatter the morale of the river people the way Proposition 17 had done. Maybe they had expected defeat all along. Maybe they were used to it by now. Reasonable people recognize a long shot when they see one. At any rate, they did not give up. They immediately started working on the November elections with hopes of keeping Jimmy Carter, and of dumping a few champions of New Melones. Mark Dubois said, "I know so many people care about this river that this issue is far from over."

Stanislaus River one-fourth mile above Parrotts Ferry

Stanislaus River canyon

New Melones Reservoir covering Parrotts Ferry, 1980

New Melones Reservoir covering Chicken Falls, 1980

New Melones Reservoir below Parrotts Ferry

CHAPTER TEN

The Struggle Continues

Before Dubois, Schifferle, Fox and the others left Washington, they knew what they wanted to do.

Dump Clausen.

David Weiman, Washington lobbyist for water development reform, came to a meeting of FOR staff and supporters and said, "For the Stanislaus, the arguments against filling the dam were clear enough. It came down to sticking with the boys—Shumway and the Republicans—and that is what Clausen did. The issue isn't the river. The issue is politics, and politics is the only way you can go. Clausen beat you on that committee. The only thing to do now is to beat Clausen next month."

So Friends of the River joined the campaign for Democrat Norma Bork. Volunteers from the river campaigned with the Bork staff. By helping to beat Clausen, the river movement would gain prestige, and would emerge as a viable political force. They would get revenge, and maybe still save the canyon. With other changes in Congress, and with a reelection of Carter, a Stanislaus wild river bill might pass next session. It all hinged on the election.

Everyone knew that Norma Bork was a small woman running in a big, macho district, but nobody expected a rout. In November, however, Clausen won hands-down on the tide of Republican votes that trounced President Carter and liberal Democrats from coast to coast. Stanislaus co-sponsor Lionel Van Deerlin was defeated. Pennsylvania's Peter Kostmayer, who had successfully fought Tocks Island Dam on the Delaware, and was one of Congress's greatest battlers of pork barrel, was beaten. Gaylord Nelson, the father of Earth Day in 1970, and one of the men who had halted La Farge Dam on Wisconsin's Kickapoo River, was turned out of office, along with a host of Senate Democrats. The election of 1980 utterly dashed the remaining

hopes of the Stanislaus River people. To save the river had demanded
political change, but not this kind. The politics of 1981 would be
magnitudes worse than 1980. Ronald Reagan and his interior secretary,
James Watt, would make Jimmy Carter and Cecil Andrus look like
a dream.

FOR staff was immobilized. "We sat around that table for a month
and listened to Dick Roos-Collins tell jokes," Catherine Fox said. They
were beaten, then beaten again, and now they sat without knowing
where to turn.

Since it looked as though the reservoir would be raised above the
South Fork confluence, Fox and Dubois came out for strong, direct
action. What did they have to lose? Others, especially Roos-Collins,
said no. Dubois and Jennifer Jennings argued. "The credibility of FOR
will be destroyed," Jennings said. "It will hurt us on other rivers. . . .
I don't want to be associated with it."

Eventually a majority view won out. Radical action—a protest of
some kind—would gain nothing right now. Other people felt
differently, and would operate outside the organization.

FOR went to Carter one more time. The Antiquities Act allows
the president, without Congress, to designate national monuments,
affording park-type preservation. This is how the Grand Canyon
was first protected. Because of Dinosaur National Monument, the
proposed Echo Park Dam on the Green and Yampa rivers was killed in
the 1950s. By naming national monuments, Jimmy Carter preserved
Alaskan wilderness in 1978. So he could do the same thing for the
Stanislaus. Or could he?

Interior Secretary Andrus could not be convinced. His assistant,
Guy Martin, said, "I supported the monument proposal but the
secretary rejected it out of hand. He said that Congress had no interest,
that it would be a misuse of presidential power." The way Andrus
looked at it, Congress had decided not to protect the river. A
presidential decree would be more than an extracongressional action,
it would be an affront. It would not be an administrative initiative,
but a contradiction. Why Andrus was worried about an affront or a
contradiction is a good question. Franklin Delano Roosevelt declared
the Grand Tetons a national monument after Congress thwarted a
national park proposal. Wyoming even brought suit, but the courts
upheld FDR, and in 1950, Congress made the Tetons a national park.

On December 1, Congressmen Don Edwards, Lionel Van Deerlin,
and Jim Corman met with Andrus and asked him to push national
monument status. They and Andrus were all Democrats, in this thing
together. The secetary said he would see the president. Meanwhile,
the FOR grassroots organization was mobilized to send letters to
Carter, but Jerry Meral said, "The only way to get the president is for

Jerry Brown to see him personally." Brown would try to do this two days before Carter left office. To make sure that Brown broached the Stanislaus, Mark Dubois would go to see the governor. Not with an appointment—there would be no time to schedule one. Dubois would have to figure out some other way.

The Democratic state convention was held that weekend. Dubois got a pass to the convention floor from river-friend Kevin Wolf, who had somehow, long hair and all, wangled a sergeant-at-arms badge. So Dubois was up close, and followed the governor out the back door after he had given a rousing address. Twenty reporters pursued, but Dubois circled wide and intercepted Brown at his car. One head taller than any newsman, Dubois stood out.

"Hey Mark, how're you doing?" the governor asked.

"We sure appreciate what you've done," Mark answered, "and if there would be anything you'd feel able to say when you go back to Washington . . ." Dubois would not ask exactly what he wanted. He would just let the governor know.

"We've put a whole lot of effort into it . . ." The governor would not say just what he would do, but he knew what Mark wanted.

That afternoon, Doug Linney hustled friendly delegates, who passed a state committee position against filling New Melones. Meanwhile, the second chained protest of the dam was underway.

The reservoir had been rising for weeks when five people chained themselves to rocks on January 5. They were members of the Stanislaus Wilderness Access Committee (SWAC)—a group of handicapped people and supporters. The idea was to get President Carter's attention before he left for good on January 20. The chained people sent the president a key to their lock and asked for national monument designation.

Major networks broadcast the event on coast-to-coast TV, emphasizing the issue of "access for the disabled." Rick Spittler, the main spokesman, had polio, but became more able-bodied than most people without it. He was director of activities for etcetera and a trainer of handicapped river guides. Michael Pachovas was a quadraplegic as a result of injuries while serving in the Peace Corps. Kael Fisher was fifteen years old and not disabled. Two others—Bob Metts and Jeanne Marlow—left after six days, but the first three stayed for ten days in the cold winter rains, waiting out the president, whose spokesman said that alternatives to flooding the canyon were being sought.

With or without the SWAC chaining, Carter knew about the Stanislaus. Gus Speth, director of the Council on Environmental Quality, saw the president three times and talked about the national monument proposal. Jim Copeland of the White House staff saw

Carter. In November, Marion Edey of the League of Conservation Voters was shaking Carter's hand, and when she mentioned the Stanislaus, the president turned and walked away. As the final days of the Carter presidency approached, as Spittler, Pachovas, and Fisher sat chained along the river, the Stanislaus would never surface above the Iranian hostage crisis, which was coming to an end.

The Bureau of Reclamation didn't raise the water. The day that the handicapped people chained themselves, repairs on Woodward Reservoir—an off-river impoundment for irrigation—were completed and the bureau began dumping New Melones water to fill Woodward. According to Jerry King, spokesman for the bureau, this was preplanned and had nothing to do with the chaining. The timing just happened to be perfect for avoiding a confrontation.

Other protests, not sanctioned by FOR, were staged through the winter. On December 17, Lisa Row and Patty McCleary had sat in at the Bureau of Reclamation office and said they would stay until the enlargement of New Melones Reservoir was stopped. Officers of the Federal Protective Service hauled the two women away, and then released them. The next night, Vince Haughey and Alexander Gaguine sat in at the bureau office. Gaguine said, "More than anyplace else, the Stanislaus Canyon is my home. People can't turn away when the places they love are being destroyed." When tree-cutting began in the reservoir area below Parrotts Ferry on February 2, thirty people blocked the road so that workers couldn't drive to the site. Dan Buckley, Tyler Childress, and Kevin Wolf were charged with malicious blocking of a public highway and were arrested. One week later, Vince Haughey and Alexander Gaguine were arrested and put in jail for five days.

Kevin Wolf was behind most of these non-FOR moves. He had been a student at Davis and a river guide for ECHO. One day he had gotten a call from Mark Dubois asking for a volunteer boatman to row on a FOR river trip. Kevin met Mark and heard his gospel of, "You can make a difference. One person can make a difference." Wolf organized a FOR Davis chapter, and rallied the grassroots for the Burton bill in 1980.

When the national river campaign came to its dead-end and the FOR staff, except Dubois, limited their Stanislaus involvement to continuing negotiations over State Water Resources Control Board Decision 1422, Wolf was just getting warmed up. He was not ready to leave the Stanislaus, so he formed the Water Reform Alliance (WRA), a loose-knit group to continue the New Melones fight. The WRA ideology was one of economics: "Full pricing of irrigation water is our goal," Wolf said. "Once we let a free market set a price for agricultural water, Californians can more accurately determine whether we 'need' to dam and divert our few free-flowing rivers and creeks." The WRA style was one of events and protests. Wolf, with wide, dancing eyes and a grin that makes you smile, delighted in showmanship. "We need to bring public attention to what's happening," he said. "If we stay silent over this drowning, we're giving in, calling it legitimate."

The question was, what good were protests going to do? "At this point, it will probably just antagonize people and cause our positions to be shrugged off," said Dick Roos-Collins. Jerry Meral said, "There's got to be a point to it. What's to be accomplished?" Dubois felt that anybody acting out of genuine concern was doing what they ought to do.

FOR researcher Betty Andrews, with help from Jennifer Jennings, prepared more testimony for deliberations over Decision 1422. After months of delay while the water rose, Judge Edward Dean Price in Fresno ruled that the Bureau of Reclamation could fill to elevation 860 (above the South Fork confluence) or higher for power generation. The state appealed, saying that elevation 844 was their limit. A larger reservoir would be allowed for flood control, though in 1981 this point was moot—the Sierra snowpack was light, and there would be no spring deluge.

In April, Dubois and Roos-Collins flew east for the annual conference of the American Rivers Conservation Council, and to see congressmen and administrative officials. Roos-Collins and Dubois stressed hard economics, the Central Valley Project's debt, reclamation law abuses in Westlands, and equitable water pricing. Dubois reported, "Almost everybody agreed that the people using the water should pay the full price of it, but congressmen weren't willing to touch New Melones. It still seemed too much like an environmental issue."

Dubois had clung to a shred of hope that another congressional campaign could be waged, or that somebody in the Reagan administration would be responsive. After all, Decision 1422 had been made when Reagan was governor, he had supported it, and it was a states's-rights issue. But there was no support.

So there Dubois was again. All efforts had failed to save the canyon. It seemed that every path had been traveled. The enthusiasm of friends was gone, but not altogether. Melinda Wright, Kevin Wolf, and Dubois decided to do another state-wide initiative.

Dubois said, "After Washington, I came back realizing again that politicians are seldom leaders—they're almost always followers. We have to take the initiative, to get out in front and let the politicians follow." Dubois remembered how much work Proposition 17 was. He knew that a million dollars was needed, and he resisted. He wanted something else to work. "If two people were half as turned on for legislation as Kevin and Melinda were for an initiative, I might still be there. But given that all it takes is one or two people to make a movement, and we had three, away we go."

At first, the 1982 initiative was a tentative idea. Old time FOR staff members were not enthused; in trying to save the Stanislaus, they had reached a limit. But Dubois, Wright, and Wolf would radiate energy that would attract new, young people who loved the river and were ready to get involved. They were men and women who had not fought and lost, and fought and lost again. Dubois said, "It seems there is always turnover, with new people getting turned on to the river, while others grow in different ways by moving on to new things."

Dozens of volunteers and professionals, including old hands in media, politics, and environmental preservation, would plan the initiative through the fall of 1981. They would decide to tackle the basic problems and not just the New Melones symptom. The initiative would be titled the Water Conservation and Efficiency Act and would call for water conservation, groundwater management, and a limit to New Melones filling until a need for the water is proven. The new initiative drive would be launched in 1982 with another collection of half a million signatures, and then with another state-wide campaign.

"The Stanislaus has been an amazing forum," Dubois says, "teaching people a lot about how we treat our land and water. We still don't have to support the mistakes of the past. Every time we help one more person to better understand land and water issues, we win a small victory. There's nothing to lose and everything to gain by keeping up the fight."

CHAPTER ELEVEN

The People's River

July 1981

It has been quite a journey. Over these last ten years, the Stanislaus has taken us a few places. To hot days at Parrotts Ferry, to the Rayburn Office Building in Washington, to a dairy farm up against the lower river, and to a small stucco house and garage along San Miguel Way, Sacramento. To Peter Behr's Marin headlands, and to Los Angeles with busloads of Proposition 17 volunteers. We have been around.

We have met a few people, beginning at Camp Nine, where we loaded a big raft with a bright-eyed woman, Catherine Fox. She is the same—a charmer—and when she smiles she makes me smile still. Especially when she talks about her favorite place in the Stanislaus Canyon: the wonderful beach above Razorback Rapid, at the mouth of Grapevine Gulch. A beach that is the color of her hair. Why does she like Razorback so much? "Let's talk about it," Catherine says, and we leave the nagging FOR telephones at Fort Mason and walk next door to Greens—the Zen restaurant that faces the marina, the Golden Gate, and the Marin hills. As we wait to be seated, we talk with Huey Johnson, who also happens to be having lunch there. "Razorback beach has come so quiet at the end of wonderful days," Catherine says. "I would sit in the sand and watch fish jump, watch the pool turn gold in the evening, and watch hawks above that straight-up cliff. I'd listen to our river as it roared through the rapid. There were so many good times there! The best river sauna ever was at that beach." It will be one hundred feet under water at the "gross pool" level of New Melones.

"You know, the other place I really like is Chinese Dogleg. That rapid is so beautiful the way it twists," and Catherine twists her flattened, weathered hand in a big bend across the redwood burl table. "You pull on the oars and work to make it through that one. You shave the rock on the right, then the rocks on the left, then go splash into the green pool at the bottom."

Catherine found the Stanislaus while working with blind people; Jerry Meral found it while paddling his C-1 canoe. His favorite place is the bottom of Mother Rapid. Shore-to-shore the river is white, and just behind, the limestone cliffs of Wool Hollow rise almost straight for 800 feet. It is my favorite place too. The canyon's most spectacular view, it could serve to illustrate a Tolkien fantasy.

It was Meral who began the struggle for the Stanislaus, Meral who figured out what to do. Meral who dreamed up the initiative, Proposition 17. John Hertle said, "I've got to give Meral credit. He worked hard; still is. It was pretty apparent to me that he was the brains behind the activities."

After Jerry Brown became governor, the biggest desks in the sixteen-story Resources Building were turned over to a new breed —Huey Johnson as secretary, Rich Hammond, Guy Phillips, Jim Burns, and Larry Moss (formerly chairman of the Planning and Conservation League) as deputies and assistant secretaries. John Bryson, attorney for the Natural Resources Defense Council, became chairman of the State Water Resources Control Board, then of the Public Utilities Commission. Ron Robie became director of the Department of Water Resources, and for deputy director he picked Environmental Defense Fund biologist Gerald Meral.

In 1981, Meral's jobs include the development of policy, planning, data collection, supply-and-demand estimates, water conservation, groundwater programs, and public education. Of Meral, Milton Kramer says, "I have a rather low opinion of his ethical conduct. It seems to me that somebody who was a founder of FOR, who loaned the money to get started, should have disqualified himself from any state considerations with respect to the Stanislaus." About Kramer, Meral says, "I never met the man."

Ron Robie defends Meral to the hilt. "He is a biologist, but he can handle engineering questions, he can meld the two, and that's terribly important. People who objected to Jerry judged too much on symbols. Later they saw that he is very competent. If they're critical of Jerry, they're searching too hard for a scapegoat. They're looking for a conflict, and there is none. I resent Kramer's accusations. The other people with Friends of New Melones are very honorable. Hertle doesn't call us names, and we don't call him names. He has a farm he wants protected, and he has a conventional view of water development. That is an honest view, and we like dealing with it. What Kramer doesn't realize is that FOR has legitimate public interests, and they are as welcome to come into my office as a developer."

Tom Graff, who with Jerry Meral founded the West Coast Environmental Defense Fund office, took a view opposite Kramer's. "Jerry is bright, hard-working, and principled, but I don't see him or

Robie as living up to promise. DWR's main platform is still to expand
the State Water Project and to spend billions on the Peripheral Canal
while they get a few fig leaves of reform. The tough stands on New
Melones have been taken by Huey Johnson and Rich Hammond."
Graff added, "Robie has political pressure totally apart from the chain
of command in government. The State Water Project is one of the
biggest utilities in California. DWR needs to be accepted, if not
beloved, by the water interests."

Meral was the first person to propose designation of California's
north coast rivers in the national wild and scenic rivers system.
Governor Brown requested Interior Secretary Andrus to do this in the
fall of 1980, and Andrus included the rivers a day before he left office,
on January 19, 1981. Meral also debated for the Peripheral Canal,
which he feels is needed for Delta water quality. He strengthened the
water conservation program, in which he and Robie added thirty-five
budgeted positions. Of course, he kept canoeing, slapping his C-1
down Cache Creek, the Sacramento above Shasta Dam, the screaming
North Fork of the Stanislaus below Sourgrass Bridge, and, of course,
the Stanislaus, where he eddied into the pool below Mother Rapid and
looked upstream at the rugged cliffs.

Jennifer Jennings's favorite place in the canyon is the smooth beach
above Razorback—same as Catherine Fox. It was there that seventy
people camped for a Thanksgiving feast of three turkeys after the loss
of Proposition 17—Jenny had organized the trip as one of her first
activities with FOR in 1974.

In 1977 Jennifer entered law school at Berkeley. She passed her bar
exam in 1979, and took a job with the Federal Trade Commission in
Washington, D.C. Washington combines the heat of Sacramento with
the humidity of a riverside sauna, and Jennings didn't like it. She could
kayak the Potomac, but she couldn't drink it. She could ride a bicycle
down to the river the way she did as a kid near Folsom, but only after
crossing a knot of freeways. Washington is not Northern California.
Jennifer came home in September 1980, and the first week back, she
helped FOR researcher Betty Andrews prepare testimony for the
State Water Resources Control Board. Then she took a job with the
governor's Office of Planning and Research.

Brad Welton gave me a clue as to why Razorback is the favorite place
of so many river people: it was the regular camping site of FOR and
etcetera for six years. Dozens of times these people landed on that
shining wet sand and stayed for the night. Brad also loves Rose Creek
in the spring and the South Fork Falls—one mile above the Stanislaus
—in the summer. These are small streams with swimming holes,
waterfalls, and diving rocks. They, too, would be flooded by a full New
Melones Reservoir.

Brad Welton was a mainstay of FOR. He could think up a project and do it, beginning to end. He could get other people working, and could keep them busy and enjoying it. He was the Stanislaus campaign manager, taking lead responsibility for the last few years. Since he first saw the river during his 1973 BLM survey, he was hooked, but after the 1980 elections he left. Too much work burned him out. You have to leave sometime. This was it for Welton.

He traveled in Mexico, then went to Seattle and got a job as a cook on a fishing boat bound for Alaska. "I'll be looking for a job with an environmental litigation group, or with legal aid, or with state government." He pauses, "but I'll always be a Friend of the River and involved. I'll be around to help."

I come to Alexander Gaguine. I think back to Louisiana where our paths first crossed. A national river management conference was being held there. The Sierra Club had money to attend, but no takers, so they asked FOR, and Gaguine said, "Sure, I'll go."

After the conference, where I gave a talk on river planning, there was a field trip through the Atchafalaya Swamp, the country's largest river swamp, which the Army Corps of Engineers proposes to channelize and drain. While most people used Grumman canoes to slalom around cypress knees, mush through lily thickets, and penetrate the habitat of alligators, Gaguine swam much of the way. He backstroked, butterflied, crawled, and sidestroked. Mostly he swam underwater, now and then coming up for air. I wondered who this crazy waterman was, so at lunch we talked. I learned about the Stanislaus, and got invited to Friends of the River's house in Sacramento, where I saw Gaguine again in November 1977, during a year-long trip that I took to photograph threatened rivers nationwide. That is how I first got to the Stanislaus.

Alexander's favorite place in the canyon is Duck Bar, a prairie of gravel and mounded alluvium where the river warps in a wide bend. "That's my favorite, especially at the fig tree in the late summer. Duck Bar is big and open," Gaguine says. The sun beats on the cobbles and makes a furnace of the unshaded bar. Back in the shade it's breezy. Sleeping out in the sand you look up at a big starry sky and the toothy black outline of the canyon cliffs.

Alexander also loved Parrotts Ferry. "But now Parrotts Ferry is gone." He is talking about the reservoir swallowing his place, three times in 1980, the place where he sat chained with seven friends in 1979, stopping the water that year. "And I love Bailey Falls and Rose Creek."

In summer 1979, after the chaining, Gaguine left FOR for three months, then returned. "This is a family, a community, the only one

I've got," he said. Then, in 1980, just before the November elections, he left again; and in 1981 he guided on the Salmon River and in the Grand Canyon. Where will he go next? Who knows? He arrived with a backpack and he left with one, and he has always been a brilliant enigma. He could have had most anything, but he picked the Stanislaus.

"I've been reading Wendell Berry," he says. "Do you read Wendell Berry? The reason I like to read him is that he has strong values and right now I have just about none." But the way he has worked for this river and for his friends, I don't know what he is talking about. He makes no sense to me.

"I left Washington to get away, and all the natural beauty in the Southwest stunned me. I heard myths about California, how people are different here. I said, 'people are about the same anywhere.' Then you're here for awhile, and bam, it hits you. People are rootless. You see it. Lots of movement, but the values are not strong or deep. This is rootless central out here. We're at such a point of individualism I'm completely rootless," he says.

I can appreciate that. I once owned a 150-year-old home and thirty acres of mountain farmland, trout stream and all. I had roots, or at least an anchor in the land. Now I don't. Gaguine had the river. Now he doesn't. And the river is more than thirty acres and a house. It is a whole little universe, and it cannot be replaced at any price. "But isn't this whole place your home?" I ask.

"Northern California is my home," Gaguine admits. "Not San Francisco. Not Angels Camp, but most any of the country from Santa Cruz to Arcata; from the American River down through the Tuolumne. This is my home. But our roots are the river, and we're losing it. There's going to be a big space missing in our lives; it's going to be a lot lonelier. This river has done a lot for people."

Gaguine is quiet, then adds, "We're all alone when we're born, we're all alone when we die, but in between, in between, you may as well be a friend of the river."

Where are the others in 1981? The early dam fighters are scattered. David Kay, who started the New Melones fight with Jerry Meral, is in Ohio, where he organized political support for the Stanislaus wild river proposal in September 1980. Tom Graff of the Environmental Defense Fund is still with EDF in Berkeley, slugging it out for the land and rivers. Ron Coldwell, who introduced Mark Dubois to rafting on the Stanislaus, works for the state, collecting taxes from businesses in Redding. Fred Dennis, initiator of etcetera with Coldwell and Dubois, managed the ARTA headquarters near Vallecito and now guides for

Marty MacDonnell. Bill Center owns the California ARTA franchise and a campground on the South Fork American, where he leads the fight against dams there.

Bruce Simballa guides for Martin Litton in Idaho and for Baja Expeditions in the winter. David Westphal, Dubois's old roommate from Prop 17 days, is studying medicine in Mexico City. Rob Caughlan was a PR man and speech writer for the Environmental Protection Agency in Washington under President Carter, then returned to the same old house, same old telephone at Roanoke. David Oke stayed with Roanoke, which turned out to be a profitable business. John Cassidy has a juggling bag-and-book business called Klutz, is editor of the FOR newsletter, *Headwaters*, and wrote *A Guide to Three Rivers*, an interpretive guide to the Tuolumne, American, and Stanislaus rivers, published by the Friends of the River Foundation.

On the other side, John Hertle dairyfarms with even more cows and less of a flood risk. Milton Kramer was unavailable for comment on his next project. A rift seems to have occurred. On July 24, 1981, the *Modesto Bee* reported that Kramer was suing Friends of New Melones for $87,000. Milton contends that the money is due, based on a verbal agreement to pay him $6,000 a month, plus expenses. Defendants are Friends of New Melones, John Hertle, Nancy Whittle, George Barber, and Jack Broughton, all officers in the fill-it-up group. Hertle said that the group owes money to Kramer, but disagreed on $87,000, and disputed the $6,000 per month figure. Hertle said that Friends of New Melones collected about $130,000 from 1979 to 1981. "It's disturbing to me that volunteers who served Friends of New Melones now have to bear the cost of defending themselves." It seems that Milton Kramer may not be involved in the continuing New Melones debate.

Cliff Humphrey moved from Modesto back to San Francisco, where he works part time as a recycling consultant for the city. Al Sorrenti continues to grow tomatoes, beans, and rice by pumping groundwater, hoping for deliveries from the New Melones or Auburn dams. Thorne Gray continues writing for the Modesto *Bee*; some articles are now pro-New Melones, but others support saving the Tuolumne.

John McFall, father of the dam, got into a heap of trouble. In 1974 it was revealed that he had received $3,000 from Tongsun Park of Korea, deposited it in his congressional office account, and later used it for personal business. In October 1978, the House Ethics Committee recommended that McFall be reprimanded for his part in the Koreagate scandal, and he was. In November 1978, he was defeated by Norman Shumway. McFall moved to surburban Washington, where he works as lobbyist (vice-president) of the American Railroad Association.

Bizz Johnson, the other half of the dam's authorization, had reigned as chairman of the House Public Works Committee and used his leverage to line up the votes of other Democrats against the Stanislaus wild river bill. At the age of seventy-three, he faced a tough election challenge in 1980 from Eugene Chappie, who is far less a conservationist than Bizz. After eighteen years in office, Johnson lost.

Don Clausen, who with Bizz helped to corral votes against the Stanislaus wild river bill, won the 1980 election against Norma Bork. Colonel O'Shei filled a corps assignment in the Middle East. Joe Countryman of the Sacramento corps office is now assistant chief of water resources planning. Billy Martin, regional director of the Bureau of Reclamation, was transferred to Denver.

Back in Sacramento, Huey Johnson talked to water board members in the fall of 1980, trying to garner votes against the filling of the dam. A majority of senators and assemblymen asked for Huey's dismissal after he advocated programs to limit California's population to its carrying capacity. It is an idea whose political time has not come; whose political time will probably never come. Johnson responded, "I'm not in this job for security. This job is a one-time thing for me. When done, I'll be satisfied I paid my dues to society, which has been very good to me." Once he got started against New Melones, Huey battled on and on. The gall. He said, "If the reservoir is filled, the only way to recover the cost is to dump a truckload of lemons in the reservoir, call it New Lemones, and sell it by the glass."

Rich Hammond quit state employ to live a quiet life on the coast north of San Francisco. Guy Phillips left his job to become director of the Sierra Club's John Muir Institute for Environmental Studies. Ron Robie heads the California Department of Water Resources. "We're not pushing blindly in every direction," he says. "Emphasis is on groundwater storage and management and conservation of water."

The fill-it-up politicians—Waters, Garamendi, and others—were reelected by comfortable margins. Mike Gage, leader of the diminutive blow-it-up element in the California assembly, retired, and is guiding raft trips in Idaho, India, and Pakistan.

Don Edwards, author of the Stanislaus wild river bill, is now the dean and leader of the California Democratic congressional delegation, and Phillip Burton still wheels and deals for liberal causes, but does not get so far against Republican resistance in 1981.

Jerry Brown is the all-time river-saving governor, having appealed to Interior Secretary Andrus to designate the state scenic rivers in the national rivers system. For the 1980 election-night victory party in celebration of Proposition 8, which protects the north coast rivers by requiring a two-thirds vote of the legislature to dam them, Brown told Jerry Meral to "bring wild river movies."

Peter Behr enjoys retirement, which he describes as a "repotting" experience. "Getting the tap root down into some new soil." He toured the state collecting signatures for a proposed California constitutional amendment to give people the right to a healthy environment. It failed. Of the Stanislaus and environmental protection, Behr says, "You come to a lifelong protest movement on the basis of understanding the pricelessness of what is left."

Don Briggs, who first encountered the Stanislaus while training to row the Grand Canyon, guides rafts in the Grand Canyon and works on the FOR staff in winter. He is forty, and says something changes: "A couple of years ago, I would have been out there chained to a rock. Now I feel I can do more good here than dead somewhere." Briggs produced an excellent film about the Stanislaus and New Melones, and his photographic exhibit showing endangered Sierra rivers has hung at the Smithsonian and in Jerry Brown's office. For 1982 he will produce a Tuolumne River film.

Gracielle Rossi, who met Mark Dubois when she and her parents took a commercial raft trip in 1970, was involved all through the Stanislaus contest. She was one of the most consistent FOR supporters. During the Proposition 17 struggle, she was Northern California coordinator. The FOR T-shirt factory was in her basement on San Francisco's Taraval Street, near the ocean. Gracielle flew to Washington to lobby for the wild river bill in 1980. She works for etcetera, which over the years took more than 1,000 disabled and special-needs people down the Stanislaus; and she is finishing a master's degree in education.

Tom Burton, FOR's first research specialist, is working toward a master's degree at Santa Cruz. Doris Grimm is out hunting Miwok Indian sites for the Stanislaus National Forest. She hikes through high country, river canyons, big timber, and chaparral, dodging rattlesnakes, catching poison oak, camping along Eagle Creek, hunting and saving—whenever she can—artifacts and archaeological sites where the government proposes timber sales, new roads, or other developments. "This is all a part of my heritage," she says about the saving of what is left.

Tom Huntington organizes grassroots with spirit ("Grass Roots!"). Laurie McCann moved to New Mexico, then returned and may work for the Friends of the River Foundation. Tom Lovering is touring Africa. Debbie Dohm is a Utah river guide in the summer and a part-time nurse in winter. Since she moved from the FOR house, she has variously lived in a tepee, a geodesic dome, a remodeled oil tank, and conventional apartments—shelter is where river guides find it. David Lynch goes to school at Humboldt State and guides hikers in the Grand Canyon.

Dick Roos-Collins hustles publicity. He and his wife, Marget, plan to start law school in 1982. Megan Eymann, who lobbied in Sacramento, then in Washington, finally returned to Portland to finish her college degree after a two-year Stanislaus lapse. Doug Linney moved up from the Los Angeles FOR office to the Sacramento office. Linney likes politics and has a smooth touch, a feel for what is practical. Ronnie James takes care of the membership and miscellaneous pieces of the organization—everything from picking up VIPs at the airport to correcting Mark Dubois's spelling to getting 5,000 north coast rivers action alerts printed and in the mail. Betty Andrews, hired by FOR in November 1979, researches water issues and prepares testimonies and positions. Shortcutt—Patricia Schifferle—returned from Washington and works for the Assembly Office of Research in Sacramento. Kevin Wolf runs full time on the new Stanislaus initiative, organizing volunteers. Melinda Wright, FOR mainstay in the foothills, helped to start a Tuolumne County Environmental Center, began public outreach for a water conservation program, and in 1981 works full time on the new initiative.

Then there are a few other people: half a million who signed the Prop 17 qualification petitions; half a million who floated through the canyon; 2,000 who sent letters and mailgrams to Don Clausen in August and September 1980; 3,000 members of Friends of the River. They are out there going to work, raising children, doing the things that they do, disappointed that the Stanislaus didn't become a national river, and waiting for another phone call from Doug Linney, Tom Huntington, or Tom Hershenow—another grassroots organizer in the Sacramento office. All these people are out there waiting for another caller to tell them what to do next, or which river we try to save next.

There is one other person. "I really didn't do anything different," Dubois says. "Well, it was different in a way, but when you look at what Don Briggs and Dick Roos-Collins did with media for a year, and what Alexander has done with media and organizing for years, and what Jennifer did to get things going with the legislature—it's a lot of people doing lots of things for a long time."

Dubois's favorite place is the middle section of the canyon. "No one spot?" I ask.

"Humm. No. The whole thing. There are places in there that I haven't seen. There are ridgetops and caves. There are the rapids and all the canyon critters. There are cliffs and beaches and gentle places."

Back in Sacramento, Dubois takes a break and "plays" in the weedy garden. He picks chard without a knife. I have never seen him use a garden tool, except for a rubber hose, which connects the American

River to the tomatoes, chard, onions, turnips, and radishes. Even FOR irrigates, carefully. They practice "deficit" irrigation— just enough.

The phone rings, and Dubois talks while he plays, carrying the long-corded telephone from garden to compost pile. Ten minutes later, he is cooking vegetables—just steaming them a little to have them with brown rice and few trimmings. The phone rings again, and he carries it from cutting board to ancient Wedgewood stove. Back and forth. Onions, peppers, carrots, squash. Dubois spends more time on the telephone than on the river, more than with Sharon, his girl friend. More than anywhere. "The telephone's a tool," he says—and it is the only one that he uses unsparingly. While on the phone, he rinses his sprout collection—an FOR institution that is refined as much as composting. There are four sprout jars holding juveniles and adults, beans and alfalfa.

Dubois still bear hugs all his friends. You have to be mighty big to not get lifted off the ground. Now and then, he needs to be reminded about breaking one of his father's ribs with a bear hug ten years ago, and one of David Kay's five years ago. Sounds like someone is due.

Dubois takes a call from somebody who knows where there are three leaky rafts that FOR can have if they want to fix them. Mark wants Ronnie James to track them down, get them fixed, and add the rafts to the FOR Christmas gift lift. They would be in the true Christmas spirit of FOR—recycled—but Ronnie says no. She has the membership to renew this month.

Just what is Mark's position at FOR? "Um, ah, spiritual leader," somebody says. He is not the official leader, not a manager. He involves people, gets them active, but he is not one to limit people, to say "no," or to impose order. He does not plot much long-term strategy. "He does things on his own, and other staff might never find out about them," a FOR person says. He is miserable with money. His management of finances does not exist, so Tom Lovering first served as treasurer. Then, Mark and Laurie McCann became co-directors, with Laurie doing administrative, financial, and management jobs. Late in 1980, FOR hired a director, Walter Arenstein, to tighten the operation up and run it, but things didn't work out. Walter was from New York. He was not a riverman. Normal management doesn't work with these people. Arenstein was unhappy, and so were the staff, so he left. A few months later, the FOR board named Catherine Fox as the new director.

Mark still does everything that he has always done. He testified before the water board: "I guess I feel like we can't afford to keep rushing on as we have been rushing on. Yes, we do have to move, but someone once said when you find yourselves rushing to the edge of a precipice, do you continue going forward and step over, or do you turn around and step forward? It's pretty clear to me that water development in California has taken us over the precipice."

About Dubois, Milton Kramer says, "I think Mark is a very sincere person. I think he believes in what he is doing. I think his values are a little mixed up, but he probably thinks my values are mixed up. I think he has placed recreation and the scenery in which that recreation is pursued above some of the values we've been talking about."

John Hertle says, "Mark is a nice fellow, very believable. I wouldn't mind going on a trip in the mountains with him."

Hertle's son chimes in, "But he would want to walk, and you'd want to ride a horse."

Hertle continues, "He takes a very idealistic approach. In my own view it is not effective with the general public. When you treat that subject abstractly, you may win some converts, but when it gets down to what society really needs, the public sees it differently. They see energy and water."

Tom Graff of EDF says, "Dubois is just an extraordinary human being. He's courageous, obviously, from what he did in the chaining incident. He's also humanistic, tolerant, uncynical. It can even get in his way of being effective, but then there are other people around to do the dirty work."

Peter Behr says, "He keeps growing and learning. It's interesting how sincerity breaks through the language barrier and reaches out to listeners. These days when everybody's motive is suspect, when a lot of us are skeptical, if not cynical, it is difficult to be skeptical about Mark. Mark has the gift of living in the present. Sometimes I think it is a God-given gift, since so few of us have it."

Maybe Dubois lives in the present, but he is always working on the future. What about the future? Dubois says, "There's this idea of healing. It seems that healing the earth is something that will keep me for a long time. The river is the first step."

Win or lose, many people have wondered how Dubois would look beyond the Stanislaus. It seemed to be everything to him. But when Mark heard that I had interviewed Senator Garamendi, his first question was, "Did he say anything about *other* rivers?

"I can't wait to get over this dumb dam fight," Mark says. "There's so much else to do. We're only limited by the time we have available. I'm really excited over what the Kentucky river people are doing— trying to reclaim rivers. That's a new frontier I can't wait to enter. We're pioneers in a way. Maybe FOR is a wagon.

"Much of my life I've spent getting to know the Stanislaus Canyon, and it makes me appreciate other places even more. It's like people. You get to know one person and they help you realize that everybody is special. I find that in my talks now I don't even say much about the Stanislaus. Mostly I talk about people being involved, people being able to do things."

"Will we make it?" I asked.

"The way I see it, the line of destruction is steep and steady, but the line of change is curving upward, and they intersect just off the graph. But there's the chance that the destruction can dip down or the healing can curve up, and maybe we'll make it. That depends on us.

"Each of us has the power to do something. To do what we want to do. We all have that glow inside. Each one of us can make a difference."

All of these people have made the Stanislaus something. It was special to begin with, and now they have made it something more. Through the years of wrangling, it has surpassed itself and become a symbol.

Huey Johnson says, "In fighting for clarity and understanding about this river, we're also fighting for the rest of the wild rivers. The Stanislaus work has been worthwhile. This contest brought out the inequities of water pricing, exposed the crazy business of subsidies, the unnecessary waste. Because of this and other battles, I doubt that there is a Californian who thinks everything will last forever. . . . Future historians will regard our commitment to the preservation of our resources as the most important accomplishment of our era."

Ron Robie says, "It became a symbol of states' rights, of states being challenged, then winning." Robie adds, "There is a value in river recreation and in stream flows that were not recognized until this."

Peter Troast, a lobbyist for Friends of the Earth, felt that the north coast rivers may not have been put into the national rivers system if it hadn't been for the Stanislaus. "Andrus felt there was nothing more he could do on the Stanislaus, yet he wanted to do right by the rivers. Having lost the Stanislaus, he didn't hesitate to use his authority on the north coast."

Billy Martin, regional director of the Bureau of Reclamation says, "Now there is more public involvement in the whole process of resource development."

David Oke says, "Failures have been hallmarks in conservation history. Hetch Hetchy was a fight that started the movement. Glen Canyon was the place no one knew. The Stanislaus brought this battle to everyone."

Tom Graff is tired of hallmarks. "When you lose, you lose. We lost Hetch Hetchy. We lost Tellico. We lost the Stanislaus. So what does that stand for? What does that mean? It means we lost. We need to go after a total change in water policy, and since the destructive boondoggles are so expensive to the taxpayer, we just might succeed."

Joe Nagel says, "To my knowledge, it's the first time the department faced a completed dam, a dam sitting there on a river that was subsequently considered for protection."

Brian O'Neil, who directed the Heritage, Conservation and Recreation Service's wild river study for the Interior Department says, "It's unique in that one committee of Congress [Interior] considered telling another committee [Public Works] that they made a mistake. I can't think of another case where the question would even have been raised. That's testimony to the river and the people trying to save it. With other rivers, people relate on a philosophical, scientific, or economic level, but when people see the Stanislaus they become emotional. There's so much there. People are willing to fight for it."

Mike Gage says, "The water developers feel it has got to be filled because we need to develop more water resources. They feel that if they lose the Stanislaus, it would be an ominous sign for water development."

The Calaveras County Chamber of Commerce agrees, "This could set a precedent that could stop construction of other dams."

Joe Countryman of the corps says, "New Melones is certainly a bellwether case. New reservoir projects are in deep trouble in California and other places."

Milton Kramer says, "If we don't fill this reservoir, we're going to have trouble building anything new in the future because what legislator or what public is going to vote bonds or authorize expenses if there is no assurance that once completed it will be used?"

Guy Phillips says, "The Stanislaus has shown that there are river values that the public sector has helped exploit. It has shown that an agriculture and water industry which considers itself fundamentally independent expects the government to bail them out with a technical fix, and some dumb river better not get in the way."

Vic Fazio, pro-dam congressman from the Davis area, wrote to Mark Dubois in 1980, "I am convinced that the majority of people would not perceive the half-empty reservoir and the power plant operation at a less-than-projected level as a symbol of common sense. The symbolism will cut precisely the other way. The 'moderate' reservoir would not seem moderate. Quite the contrary, the situation would seem absurd, and environmentalists would take the blame for it."

Dubois responded in a handwritten note to Fazio: "Before the Civil War, many considered it absurd to get rid of slavery—it was such a vital part of the American economy. At the turn of the century, San Francisco was able to convince the public it was absurd to save Hetch Hetchy Valley. 'One Yosemite is enough,' they said. I appreciate your pragmatism but I'm glad that Lincoln and Muir were not 'pragmatists.'"

Dubois regards the Stanislaus as a symbol of the change in values.

But he sees it as another symbol, too: "The river brought so many people to realize they had great potential to do something in an age of most people thinking they can't. . . . You can make a difference."

There were some things the river people could not make different. The presumption that dams are good was shaken, but not overturned. And the river people couldn't escape localism—the ability of local politicians to run the show.

Influential representatives and bureaucrats supported the river, but their actions were usually indecisive and ineffectual. They did a lot of "I'll do it if you do it." "No, *I'll* do it if *you* do it." Of all the high-ranking officials, I think that only Huey Johnson and his deputies were willing to lose their jobs. It seems that only they thought the Stanislaus struggle would be won. Dam proponents had more money, media support, and all the conventional means of arm-twisting, backslapping, and good ol' boy politics.

After the river people lost Proposition 17, dam supporters spread the "vote of the people" argument everywhere. The initiative's loss kept high-ranking politicians—Brown, Carter, Andrus, and others—from forthrightly supporting the river. If there is a lesson here, it is this: initiatives tend to be binding and final. Don't do it unless you can win. Polls showed that Proposition 17 would win, but then came Kramer's campaign, the money, the media, the billboards, and the newspaper editorials. Never underestimate an opponent who can get his hands on money. Don't undertake an initiative unless all other routes have been traveled. The Behr bill for state scenic river status and the Burton bill for national designation might have done better if they were tried before the initiative.

There were a lot of reasons why things worked out the way they did. Mainly it was too late. What should the river people have done differently? "Never let New Melones get authorized," Jerry Meral said. But in 1944, when the dam was first authorized, few of these people were alive. In 1962, during the second authorization, nobody was looking. Almost everybody agrees it would not happen today. Even Milton Kramer says, "I'm not so sure that a dam that big should be built again. Not because of lack of need, but because alternative methods would not result in the same political battle." Joe Nagel says that Interior would pursue protection very aggressively on the Stanislaus if the dam weren't there.

"When the river people finally did catch up," Tom Graff says, "John McFall was at his height of power."

"Then," says Mike Gage, "when the national river proposal was up, there was a California political backlash against environmental issues. It started as a reaction against Dow Chemical not being allowed to develop in the Delta's Suisun Marsh in the early seventies, and it continued right through the Waters bill to fill New Melones. It's a crock, but it's there."

When dam construction was underway, then finished, everyone knew it was going to be a tough fight, a long shot. Assistant Secretary of Interior Guy Martin says, "It shows how hard it is to stop a project that has momentum." Yet there was always a chance. It is easy to say that you can't stop a started project, but other examples—the Cross-Florida Barge Canal and the Embarcadero Freeway—show that you can. The Tellico dam fight and New Melones were close enough to shake the notion that it can't be done.

Should all that energy have been put into the Stanislaus instead of into other, more hopeful dam fights? Good question for most people, but hardly a question at all for the Stanislausians. For them, this was not just good river. It was home, and more than home because of the special power of the place and because it offered so much to so many people. More than home because it could not be owned or replaced.

It brought out the most zealous patriotism—a willingness to die for a place. A lot of people think that anyone who chains himself to a riverbank, willing to die for it, is crazy. Yet most of us accept that people die for political systems that may or may not have as much to do with real things in life—real things such as the land on which we live. I'm not knocking conventional patriotism; I would fight to the death for the right to fight the Army Corps of Engineers over a canyon. But without a place, without our earth, rivers, without the wild animals, without our roots, is there true freedom? Is there any pursuit of happiness?

Enough. This is something that nobody can be talked into.

Anyway, there was a remarkable love of place that is rare, especially in the rootlessness of today. For a river, I think this love of place—at least the showing of it—was unprecedented. The river was like a part of the family, and as long as the river lived, its people could no more give up fighting the dam than give up fighting an illness or the kidnappers of a child, lover, brother, sister, or parent.

Without the river and without some of its key people, will there be a FOR? Dubois says, "We're losing some battles, but we're learning a lot along the way. The Stanislaus has taken us to bigger fights—water policy in California and the United States."

At the annual conference that the FOR Foundation puts on, Huey Johnson encouraged the river people: "It's time for you to go out and share your view with the world. You can save the Amazon."

While the Army Corps of Engineers and the Bureau of Reclamation would love to see FOR disappear into the jungles of Brazil, there is plenty to do in California. Dubois says, "We need to keep specific priorities. With the Stanislaus, there were thousands of people who never knew a river; now they're ready to go, to fight the next one. Until more of us pay attention to our own backyards, things won't change. Maybe the most important thing is to get people out to touch the places we're talking about. People from San Francisco should see the Tuolumne, then save the Tuolumne from the dams that San Francisco proposes to build."

Huey Johnson told FOR, "You people are on the cutting edge. You are responsible. You have to succeed. You're dealing with the last remnants of things worth keeping."

The last of the wild rivers. The wildest in California and some of the finest natural rivers of the nation are north of San Francisco. The Klamath, Smith, Trinity, and Eel are in the state and national scenic rivers systems, but they will continue to be challenged. Dos Rios Dam on the Middle Fork of the Eel would bury an outstanding whitewater river. Old state water plans and federal plans identify dam sites on the Klamath, Trinity, and others. Local interests have pushed for a dam on the Mad River above Arcata.

Marine biologists, meteorologists, and ecologists have toppled the "waste to the sea" myth about these untapped rivers. Scientists report that vital nutrients are carried into the sea by the high discharges of the north coast rivers. The plankton of the Japanese current and much of the Pacific fishery is dependent on the flow of these rivers. Not to mention the salmon, steelhead, and shad that need running rivers, high flows, and clear water. Though salmon runs are a fraction of what they used to be, the north coast rivers represent the last chance at maintaining and restoring the anadromous fish.

Logging all over the north results in silt that chokes salmon eggs, in thousands of miles of muddy roads and landslides, and in erratic stormwater runoff—higher during floods, lower during drought because the forest is cut, its spongy floor made hard. "No one needs to stop logging, but improved forest management is essential," says Grant Werschkull of the Smith River Alliance.

Environmental groups lost an important vote on the Peripheral Canal in 1980, when the legislature passed, and Governor Brown signed authorization for, the three-story-deep channel, forty-three miles long and thirty-two freeway lanes wide, that could divert an additional 600,000 to 1 million acre-feet of water from the north around the Delta for pumping south. It would cost $1 billion or more—one of the most expensive single water projects in the history of the nation. If operated as planned, it should improve Delta water quality, but environmentalists fear that the canal will be used to divert more of the northern rivers for San Joaquin and Southern Californian use, that

Delta water quality will suffer, and that the conservation of water will be put off again as more subsidized supply becomes available. Once the hardware is in place, conservationists fear that vested economic interests and Southern Californian politics will rule the roost. A good operating plan can easily be changed. "You can't contain a thirsty beast in a paper cage," said Peter Behr, opposing the canal. Proposition 8 passed in 1980, requiring a two-thirds vote of the legislature to build dams on the state scenic rivers of Northern California, but southern agricultural interests immediately went to work to undermine the initiative.

Auburn Dam, regarded by Jerry Meral and others as the worst dam site of all, remains a threat to the American River and to 700,000 people living downstream. After $200 million was spent, construction was stopped because of earthquake hazards. The Bureau of Reclamation produced a new design in 1980, conforming to seismic standards set by the Secretary of the Interior, but safety remains an issue. The 685-foot-high dam would cost over $1.4 billion, and would flood fifty miles of wild rivers.

On the Tuolumne River, below the Hetch Hetchy site where John Muir waged the first great dam fight, irrigation districts propose more dams and diversions that would eliminate the last Tuolumne rafting. At the same time, the Forest Service has finished a national wild river study finding eighty-five miles of the river eminently eligible. The Tuolumne tug-of-war will be decided over the next few years.

On the North Fork of the Stanislaus, four dams are proposed by the Calaveras County water district. Tuolumne County has proposed a new project on the South Fork of the Stanislaus. Half a dozen dams are proposed on the South Fork of the American, the only accessible and raftable river for many Californians. Other Sierra dam sites are on the Yuba above Marysville and the West Fork of the Carson in Hope Valley, just south of Lake Tahoe.

Pressure for water supply will continue. The Metropolitan Water District of Southern California has an apportionment of 1.2 million acre-feet of Colorado River water, but this will be reduced to 550,000 in the late 1980s, when the Central Arizona Project begins operation and Arizona demands its legal share.

Californians face many questions about their rivers. Should we dam the prodigious Klamath? Clearcut along the Smith? Build Dos Rios and pump water south? Should Los Angeles drain Mono Lake? Should the state regulate the pumping of groundwater by farmers? Should salmon and commercial fishing be restored instead of irrigating more desert? Can water conservation eliminate the need for major new projects? California has over 1,300 major dams; how many more are needed? It seems that FOR will be up against heavy odds even after the Stanislaus struggle is over. It seems that if they are idle, it is because they are broke, or they need a vacation, or they have lost hope. The Friends of the River have a lot to do.

Huey Johnson says, "These young people are full of spirit with high energy. Give me them, and you can have your special interests. They are carrying more than they realize by challenging the system. They are making the system trip over itself. They are linking economics and the environment instead of going after high technology answers."

Back up at Parrotts Ferry, where we have returned again and again since we first arrived in Catherine Fox's raft, there is no river in the spring of 1981. The only sounds are from small waves lapping in the chaparral and in the pines at a bend in the flooded road, not a bend in the Stanislaus. The campers are gone. The kayakers and their bright boats are gone. All those barefoot people in shorts are gone. The field where the June 2 rally was held is murky deep, and the clump of willows where Gaguine, Grimm, Pickup, Lynch, and the others chained themselves is a watery tomb. The trees that Don Edwards, Pete Stark, and Huey Johnson planted in July 1980 are gone. No boatloads of laughing passengers wash up on that sandy shore, and no suntanned river guides gather around to drink a can of beer apiece as they pack up their rafts. The Stanislaus River at Parrotts Ferry is no longer changing anybody's life. Everybody is gone. Who has come? Motorboaters, and their exhaust stinks. The place seems full of ghosts, haunted. But I don't believe in haunted things.

I am looking, thinking about what I don't see, at what is underwater. At what is dead and gone—for what? California author James Houston writes, "Economically, ecologically, the history of the far west has continued to be a saga of exploitation, land abuse, bloody struggle, and enormous thefts." Maybe the loss of this river is like the turn-of-century land grabs from Central Valley wheat farmers by the railroads; like the empires of timber amassed by lumber companies under the Homestead Act; like the water rights bought up from Owens Valley farmers; like the diversion of the Trinity River and the death of the Indians' salmon; like Hetch Hetchy.

Above the sick brown shore, I begin walking upriver through the tangled chaparral. I am retreating higher, as people have done for centuries to get away. Go higher and higher to get away from what is happening. Try to get away, then hope that it doesn't catch up with you.

I crawl through oak, manzanita, pines, toyon. Climbing over rocks I watch for rattlesnakes chased from their dens by rising water. I think of Jennifer Jennings, who knew how hopeless this struggle seemed. Looking out to the river, she was stone-still and silent. "What is it?" I asked, and she said, "Oh, I was just thinking how nice it would be if there was an earthquake." As I scramble, I think of the weight of this reservoir. It is heavy. Ever pick up a five-gallon jug of water? I think of the weight of this reservoir pushing down on the restless California earth. I think of the hanging planters in the Department of Water Resources Sacramento office trembling and swaying during the Oroville quake, seventy miles away, after DWR's Oroville Reservoir was filled.

I come to the place where I used to camp. It was a sandy beach with a big ponderosa pine at its upstream end, a flat rock where I'd pile my gear, a shady oak with a fire circle where I'd cook. It is gone and I keep walking. I hear the drone of a motorboat. I pass the house-sized rocks that rose above Chicken Falls, but the falls is deep under, and I see only the summits of rocks where people used to sunbathe and lie and laugh at rafters as they were clutched, then released by the big hydraulic. At Chinese Dogleg, at what used to be the graceful, dancing bend that Catherine Fox loved so well, I cannot see the river, but the surface of the reservoir is agitated. Now and then it quivers and swirls as a remnant of current boils underneath. I am getting closer to the river again, near the upper edge of the rising reservoir. I walk through a flat that is covered with berry bushes, over ground that is lumpy from the work of old miners. I walk closer and closer to the water. The limestone-cobbled shore is dry and untouched by the silent backwater, and up ahead, very faintly, I can hear a sound.

Rapids. The river again. The Stanislaus not yet touched by the dam. The going is rough, and I scramble over, around, and between boulders. Then I see the wild sight of whitewater. Cliffs climb to pointed tops and the Stanislaus curves smoothly around a bar of colored stones. I've made it back to the river.

What I see—this place—has been the main thing for several hundred pages now. The main thing can be babies and children, a warm lover, a friend who reached out and saved you, your soft-eared dog, a job and a paycheck in the bank, your future, the twisted past, war, evil, crops, or God. But here it is this place. Just a river and a canyon and its life. So what that it's the only one of its kind, so what about that irreplaceable stuff. It's just shapes and forms, a low space for water to run, craggy rocks up high, blue sky, sand, stones, sounds, trees, and animals. Big deal. How can a place do this to people? How can a simple place do what the Stanislaus Canyon has done? I sure don't know. All I know is I feel good sitting here in the sun near the South Fork and listening to the river run by. Why do I feel good? Maybe I was bored and this is different. Maybe I was the opposite of bored, and this is just enough of nothing.

There are powerful places on this earth. Places that uplift people's spirits, as Alexander Gaguine says. He says the Stanislaus Canyon is one of those places. I don't know how this works. There is something here that I cannot hold, but cannot let go of either. Now that this book is almost over, there is something more that needs to be said . . .

Harold Gilliam, a California journalist, writes "To walk by a river or flow with it down rapids and through quiet stretches, to swim in it, to feel on your skin the power of its currents, is to have a direct experience of the flow of time and history and the cycles of the earth that bring the rain and the snow, the winds and the waters that flow down the mountains to the valleys and to the ocean again. This is the mystique of the Stanislaus."

Mary Regan, beautiful crippled Mary, spoke for the disabled who have been to the Stanislaus, "The river and its canyon was our greatest teacher . . . it became for us a wilderness cathedral."

Then there is the other side. When Mark Dubois talked to the Ripon Young Farmers Association and said his spirit belonged to the canyon, they laughed at him.

John Hertle said, "All the talk about a canyon and other things is superfluous. The issue is rafting." Hertle went to China, returned, and said, "They would look at this issue differently. People there don't care about Russia, Taiwan, atomic bombs. The only issue is where their vegetables are coming from. Rafting compared to food to them is utter stupidity."

It was Chief Sealth, from the Pacific Northwest, who in 1854 called the coming of white men, "The end of living and the beginning of survival."

Milton Kramer says this about the canyon: "It provides pleasure. We're so much in pursuit of pleasure that we're losing values that have built the country. It's the sign of a decadent society."

I wonder, is the pursuit of pleasure the same as the pursuit of happiness? You know—life, liberty, and the pursuit of happiness?

This is decadent? I'm looking upriver as the Stanislaus rips around a sunlit bend and picks up the South Fork. A raft drifts into the bend, and the people in the raft paddle and have the gall to laugh while others are working.

I have nothing against a good time, but an important question has been posed: what, if anything, does this canyon provide besides fun?

"It's really hard to find words," Mark Dubois says. "It's not kilowatt hours or recreation days. It cannot be counted, but it is still a value that is important and real to many people. On trips I usually ask people to try to go and sit alone. They return with a glow on their face. They've touched something that they haven't touched anywhere else. This canyon feeds people's spirits."

This is so vague. No matter how you say it, it sounds like thin air. I'd rather just sit on my boulder and not bother, but nobody is going to call me a rafter for wanting to save this canyon. Rafting gets you to some nice places, I'll say that for it, but I'm not a rafter. I'm a canoeist.

Some people believe in nature. That is part of what's going on here. Water cycles, the chain of life, all that. The fact that we're made from earthy elements and when we die, these things go back to the warm ground and feed some other life. It is a belief in life, a reverence for it.

A wild river shows life like no other place. Simple truths of the earth—as Gilliam said—are seen more easily here. That helps to make this place powerful.

Then there is this thing about flowing water. People love it. Maybe some of it stems from being 75 percent water ourselves. Maybe it stems from a heritage of gills and webbed feet. Loren Eiseley said, "If there is magic on this planet, it is contained in water." Whatever magic is.

Alexander Gaguine says, "There is so much beauty and perfection. To realize that it exists adds a huge new dimension to what I thought the world was." Gaguine is coming close. Keep talking, Alexander . . .

"Trying to keep up with the demand for more water or more power does not uplift people, but spending a day in the Stanislaus River Canyon often does. The experience can raise people's spirits or bring out feelings of wonder and joy. The Stanislaus becomes a very real part of their home, whether people are there for three days or three months.

"I feel that two of the most important things are home and community, and we have both in the Stanislaus River Canyon. It has been the home of people for thousands of years. We can see that heritage more clearly than in any museum, and now the canyon is our home.

"On the river, people work as a community and even strangers find themselves helping each other, getting to know each other because of the special demands, the special opportunities that are faced in the canyon. You don't find that in other places today.

"Europe has its great cathedrals, but in America it is our own great natural landscape which uplifts our spirits and souls as individuals and as a whole nation."

Deep in our past is the ideal of a perfect place. A paradise, an island, Shangri-la. The original garden. It is what many people work toward, whether we think it can be right here or someplace else. To get there is the reason that a lot of people do good. People devote their lives to getting there. Though I have never done that much good, I look at this river and I think I have made it.

The story goes that way back, an apple was eaten. Poor Eve has taken all the blame. What can be so wrong with eating one shiny apple? Even an apple a day. She may have turned around and tenderly planted the seeds, for all we know. It is easy to blame Eve, since she is long gone, but it seems to me we are missing the point. What we are doing now is not eating an apple, but smashing barrels of them into cider that will sour in no time. Eden is being lost today. "What will inspire us when the holy places are gone?" Gaguine asks.

I feel a spirit of the earth. These river people dream that others will feel it too; but here, in this canyon, it is a dream that has not yet come true.

February 1981, Parrotts Ferry covered by New Melones.
March 1981, Chicken Falls covered.
April 1981, Chinese Dogleg covered.
Because of low runoff, the level of the reservoir receded through the summer of 1981, uncovering Parrotts Ferry once again. For now, the Stanislaus remains. The other rivers remain, and a very special friend says that you can make a difference.

Sources

The following list includes works from which the data in this book were drawn
and works containing further information. Sources are also mentioned at
various places in the text. Many individuals were also interviewed in the course
of my research. Most quotations in the text which are not given specific sources
are derived from those interviews.

CHAPTER ONE : THE CANYON

American Rivers Conservation Council and Friends of the River
　Foundation. *Stanislaus Wild and Scenic River Study*. Washington, D.C.:
　The Council, 1979.
Cassidy, John. *A Guide to Three Rivers: The Stanislaus, the Tuolomne, and
　the South Fork of the American*. San Francisco: Friends of the River
　Foundation, 1981.
McEachern, J. Michael, and Grady, Mark A. *An Inventory and
　Evaluation of the Cave Resources to Be Impacted by the New Melones
　Reservoir Project, Calaveras and Tuolomne Counties, Ca*. Albuquerque,
　New Mexico: Adobe Press, January 1978.
Moratto, Michael J. *New Melones Archaeological Project, Stanislaus River*.
　San Francisco: Archaeological Research Lab, San Francisco State
　University, 1976. (a study for the U.S. National Park Service)
U.S. Army Corps of Engineers. *New Melones Lake Environmental Impact
　Statement*. Sacramento: The Corps, May 1972.
Wright, William H. III. "The Stanislaus River—A Study in Sierra
　Nevada Geology." *California Geology* 28 (January 1975), 3–10.

CHAPTER TWO : THE VALLEY

Berkman, Richard L., and Viscusi, W. Kip. *Damming the West*. New

York: Grossman Publishers, 1973. (costs of Bureau of Reclamation projects, effects on farms and crops elsewhere)

California. Department of Water Resources. *The California State Water Project*. Bulletin No. 132. Sacramento: Department of Water Resources, 1974, 1977, 1978.

California. Department of Fish and Game. Planning Branch. *California Riparian Study Program: Background Information and Proposed Study Design*, by Richard E. Warner. Sacramento: 1979.

Dasmann, Raymond F. *The Destruction of California*. New York: Macmillan, 1965. (environmental history)

Hartman, David N. *California and Man*. Santa Ana, Calif.: Pierce Publishing Co., 1977. (general and agricultural information)

"The Homestead Act Hits Home." *Time*, October 17, 1977, p. 20 sidebar. (160 acre provision)

Jones, Robert A. "Equity of Water Projects Costs Debated." Los Angeles *Times*, June 9, 1980, pt. 1, p. 1.

Kahrl, William L., ed. *California Water Atlas*. Los Altos, Calif.: William Kaufmann, Inc. [dist.]; Sacramento: Governor's Office of Planning and Research, 1979. (history, State Water Project, groundwater; prepared by the Governor's Office of Planning and Research in cooperation with the California Department of Water Resources)

Knickerbocker, Brad. "Salt Where Crops Should Be." *Christian Science Monitor*, June 21, 1979, pp. 12–13. (salinization of soil)

Moritz, M. "California's Golden Touch." *Time*, June 9, 1980, p. 57. (California economy and agricultural production)

Natural Resources Defense Council Newsletter. New York: The Council, December 1977.

Richard, R. L., and Tsao, K. *Energy and Water Use in Irrigated Agriculture During Drought Conditions*. Report No. LBL-7866. Berkeley, Calif.: Lawrence Berkeley Laboratory, University of California, June 1978.

Rand Corporation. *Efficient Water Use in California*. 7 vols. Santa Monica, Calif.: The Corporation, 1978.

Salisbury, David F. "Water Fights: The West Goes to Court." *Christian Science Monitor*, March 1, 1979, pp. 12–13.

San Joaquin Valley Interagency Drainage Program. *Agricultural and Salt Management in the San Joaquin Valley: Final Report Including Recommended Plan and First-Stage Environmental Impact Report*. [Fresno, Calif.]: The Program, 1979.

Seckler, David, ed. *California Water: A Study in Resource Management*. Berkeley: University of California Press, 1971.

Security Pacific National Bank. *Central Valley Counties of California Newsletter*. Fresno: November 1979. (Central Valley water supply)

U.S. Department of the Interior. Bureau of Reclamation. *Central Valley Project Data as of September 30, 1979*. Sacramento: Bureau of Reclamation, 1979. (costs and revenues of the Central Valley Project)

_____. Office of Audit and Investigation. *Review of the Central Valley Project, Bureau of Reclamation.* [n. p.]: The Department, January 1978.

_____. Office of the Inspector General. *Review of Municipal and Industrial Water Activities, Central Valley Project, Bureau of Reclamation.* Washington, D.C.: The Department, September 1979.

CHAPTER THREE : THE DAM

Drew, Elizabeth B. "Dam Outrage: The Story of the Army Engineers." *The Atlantic,* April 1970, pp. 51–62.

Gordon, Roy. "Engineering for the People, 200 Years of Army Public Works." *Military Engineer,* May/June 1976, pp. 180–85.

Jackson, W. Turrentine, and Mikesell, Stephen D. *Stanislaus River Drainage Basin and the New Melones Dam: Historical Evolution of Water Use Priorities.* Davis, Calif.: Calif. Water Resources Center, University of Calif., 1979.

U.S. Army Corps of Engineers. *Environmental Impact Statement: New Melones Lake, Stanislaus River, California.* Sacramento: The Corps, 1972.

_____. *Water Resources Development, California.* Sacramento: The Corps, 1979.

U.S. Bureau of Reclamation. *What Is Reclamation?* Washington, D.C.: The Bureau, 1976. Pamphlet.

U.S. Statutes at Large. Public Law no. 874, 87th Cong., 2d sess. (October 23, 1962).

Warne, William E. *The Bureau of Reclamation.* New York: Praeger, 1973.

CHAPTER FOUR : FOR THE RIVER

"Central Sierra District Says Melones Visitors Will Cost County." *Calaveras Californian,* September 16, 1979. (impacts of reservoir recreation)

California. Water Resources Control Board. *New Melones Project, Water Rights Decision.* (Decision 1422). [n. p.]: 1973.

_____. *State Constraints on Allocation of Water from Federal Projects— the New Melones Dam Example,* by Steven Macaulay. Sacramento: September 1979. (6 pages, on file at State Water Resources Control Board)

Jackson, W. Turrentine, and Mikesell, Stephen D. *Stanislaus River Drainage Basin and the New Melones Dam: Historical Evolution of Water Use Priorities.* Davis, Calif.: Calif. Water Resources Center, University of California, 1979.

Parry, B. Thomas, and Norgaard, Richard B. "Wasting a River." *Environment,* Jan./Feb. 1975, pp. 17–27. (arguments against the Army Corps of Engineers' benefit-cost ratio)

Reagan, Governor Ronald. Letter to Army Corps of Engineers Lt. Gen. W. C. Gribble, Jr., June 28, 1974. (Governor Reagan's position regarding the filling of New Melones Reservoir)

Train, Russell E., Chairman of the Council on Environmental Quality. Letter to Kenneth E. Belieu, Army Corps of Engineers, April 17, 1973. (position of Council on Environmental Quality on Decision 1422 and the need for an Environmental Impact Statement)

White, Bob. "Lode Counties Dread Influx of Tourists to Melones." Modesto *Bee*, July 15, 1979, sect. C, p. 1.

CHAPTER FIVE : PROMISE AND DESPAIR

Californians Against Proposition 17. *Californians Against Proposition 17 Information Packet*. 1974. (dam supporter's statements opposing the initiative, on file at Friends of the River, Sacramento)

Friends of the River. *Proposition 17, A Fact Sheet*. September 1, 1974. (Friends of the River's statements supporting the initiative, on file at FOR in Sacramento)

"It's a Hoax, All Right." Editorial. Los Angeles *Times*, October 25, 1974, pt. 2, p. 6. (anti-Proposition 17 billboards)

Jackson, W. Turrentine, and Mikesell, Stephen D. *Stanislaus River Drainage Basin and the New Melones Dam: Historical Evolution of Water Use Priorities*. Davis, Calif.: Calif. Water Resources Center, University of California, 1979.

"No on Proposition 17." Editorial. San Francisco *Chronicle*, October 13, 1974.

"Saving a River: No on Proposition 17." Editorial. Los Angeles *Times*, October 21, 1974, pt. 2, p. 6.

Scott, Jim. "Is This Any Way to Run Part of the U.S. Army?" *The Times Magazine*, June 18, 1975, p. 9. (*The Times Magazine* is published by Army Times Publishing Co., Washington, D.C.)

CHAPTER SIX : THE CASE FOR COMPROMISE

California. Department of Water Resources. *Water Conservation in California*, by Glenn B. Sawyer, et al. Bulletin No. 198. Sacramento: California Department of Water Resources, 1976.

California. Resources Agency. *The New Melones Project: A Review of Current Economic and Environmental Issues*, by Guy D. Phillips. [Sacramento]: The Agency, September 1979.

_____. *Response to Comments Received on "The New Melones Project: A Review of Current Economic and Environmental Issues."* [Sacramento: The Agency], November 1979.

California. Energy Resources Conservation and Development Commission. *Conservation as an Energy Resource: Policy Implications for California*. Sacramento: The Commission, 1978.

Friends of the River. *Operation of New Melones Dam to Generate Electricity.* Sacramento: Friends of the River, July, 1980. 22 pages. (FOR's case for a moderate reservoir)

Hall, Richard D. "Farmers Can Pay More for Crops, Study Says." Sacramento *Bee,* March 18, 1981, sect. A, p. 4.

Jones, Robert A. "Equity of Water Projects Costs Debated." Los Angeles *Times,* June 9, 1980, pt. 1, p. 1.

Lovins, Amory. *Soft Energy Paths: Toward a Durable Peace.* Cambridge, Mass.: Ballinger Publishing [distributors]; San Francisco: Friends of the Earth International, 1977. (energy conservation)

Natural Resources Defense Council Newsletter. New York: The Council, December 1977. (use and waste of irrigation water; costs and benefits of Bureau of Reclamation projects)

Salisbury, David F. "Coming to the Bottom of the Water Barrel." *Christian Science Monitor,* February 28, 1979, pp. 12–13.

San Joaquin Valley Basin Study: A Type IV River Basin Study Conducted Under Sect. 6 of the Watershed Protection and Flood Protection Act (*Public Law 566, 83rd Congress,* as amended). Prepared by the U.S. Department of Agriculture, River Basin Planning Staff [et al.] in cooperation with the California Department of Water Resources. [Davis, Calif.: Soil Conservation Service], 1977.

U.S. Comptroller General. *Better Federal Coordination Needed to Promote More Efficient Farm Irrigation: Department of the Interior, Department of Agriculture, Environmental Protection Agency: Report to the Congress.* [Washington]: U.S. General Accounting Office, 1976.

———. *Federal Charges for Irrigation Projects Reviewed Do Not Cover Costs: Report to the Congress, March 13, 1981.* Washington, D.C.: U.S. General Accounting Office, 1981. (repayment of irrigation costs)

U.S. Department of Energy, Western Area Power Administration. News release, Oct. 5, 1979. (response to *The New Melones Project,* published by the California Resources Agency and cited above; on file at the WAPA in Sacramento)

U.S. Federal Energy Administration. *National Energy Outlook.* Washington, D.C.: The Administration, 1976.

U.S. Fish and Wildlife Service. Division of Ecological Services. "Request for Technical Assistance Concerning CVP Reauthorization and Alternative Operations of New Melones Dam and Reservoir." Memorandum to U.S. Bureau of Reclamation, Sacramento. June 5, 1979. [Washington: Dept. of the Interior, Fish and Wildlife Service, 1979.]

U.S. Water Resources Council. *The Nation's Water Resources, 1975–2000: Second National Water Assessment.* [Washington]: Water Resources Council, 1978. (obtainable through the U.S. G.P.O.)

Walker, Richard, and Storper, Michael. "The California Water System: Another Round of Expansion?" *Public Affairs Report,* April 1979.

Berkeley, Calif.: Institute of Governmental Studies, University of California, 1979.

Wiegner, Kathleen K. "The Water Crisis: It's Almost Here." *Forbes,* August 20, 1979, pp. 56–63.

Williams, Phil, and Friends of the River Foundation. *New Melones Project Operating Plan, Submittal of Friends of the River before the State Water Resources Control Board.* San Francisco: Friends of the River Foundation, September 1979. (paper stating FOR's case for a moderate reservoir)

CHAPTER SEVEN : A NATIONAL RIVER

American Rivers Conservation Council. *Flowing Free.* Washington, D.C.: The Council, 1980. Pamphlet. (national wild and scenic rivers system)

American Rivers Conservation Council and Friends of the River Foundation. *Stanislaus Wild and Scenic River Study.* Washington, D.C.: The Council, 1979. (eligibility of the Stanislaus for the national wild and scenic rivers system)

Barone, Michael; Ujifusa, Grant; and Matthews, Douglas. *The Almanac of American Politics, 1980.* New York: E. P. Dutton, 1979. (profiles of congressmen)

Johnson, Huey D. Statement to the National Parks and Insular Affairs Subcommittee of the House Interior and Insular Affairs Committee. Presented to the Subcommittee on August 25, 1980, in Washington. (statement distributed to the press in mimeograph form; also on file at the California Water Resources Control Board, Sacramento)

League of Conservation Voters. *Presidential Candidates Report.* [Washington, D.C.: The League, 1979.]

"Mr. Small-Is-Beautiful." *Newsweek,* December 15, 1975. (Jerry Brown)

"Procrastination Is Bad, But . . ." Los Angeles *Times,* November 6, 1979, pt. 2, p. 6. (postponement of the filling of New Melones Dam)

U.S. Bureau of Land Management. Folsom District Office. *Report on the Instream and Recreation Value of the Stanislaus River.* Folsom: The Bureau, 1979.

U.S. Congress. House. Committee on Interior and Insular Affairs. *Amendment to the Wild and Scenic Rivers Act by Designating Certain Segments of the Stanislaus River in California as a Component of the National Wild and Scenic River System.* 96th Cong., 1st sess., H. R. 4223. Washington, D.C.: G.P.O., 1979.

U.S. Department of the Interior. Bureau of Outdoor Recreation. *Guidelines for Evaluating Wild, Scenic and Recreation River Areas.* Washington, D.C.: The Department, February 1970.

———. Heritage Conservation and Recreation Service. *Stanislaus Wild and Scenic River Assessment.* Washington, D.C.: The Department, February 1980.

Index

Designer: Marilyn Perry
Compositor: Innovative Media Inc.
Text: VIP Palatino
Display: Phototypositor Palatino
Text Printer: Vail-Ballou Press
Binder: Vail-Ballou Press
Jacket/Insert Printer: New England Book Components
Color Separations: Color-Tech Corporation